Criminal Artefacts

Law and Society Series
W. Wesley Pue, General Editor

The Law and Society Series explores law as a socially embedded phenomenon. It is premised on the understanding that the conventional division
of law from society creates false dichotomies in thinking, scholarship,
educational practice, and social life. Books in the series treat law and
society as mutually constitutive and seek to bridge scholarship emerging
from interdisciplinary engagement of law with disciplines such as politics,
social theory, history, political economy, and gender studies.

A list of the titles in this series appears at the end of this book.

Dawn Moore

Criminal Artefacts:
Governing Drugs and Users

UBCPress · Vancouver · Toronto

16 15 14 13 12 11 10 09 08 07   5 4 3 2 1

Printed in Canada on ancient-forest-free paper (100% post-consumer recycled) that is processed chlorine- and acid-free, with vegetable-based inks.

Library and Archives Canada Cataloguing in Publication

Moore, Dawn, 1974-
  Criminal artefacts: governing drugs and users / Dawn Moore.

(Law and society, ISSN 1496-4953)
Includes bibliographical references and index.
ISBN 978-0-7748-1386-0

  1. Drug abuse and crime. 2. Drug addicts – Legal status, laws, etc. 3. Drug addiction – Treatment. 4. Sociological jurisprudence. I. Title. II. Series: Law and society series (Vancouver, B.C.)

HV5801.M664 2007   364.1'77   ·   C2007-905383-1

Canadä

UBC Press gratefully acknowledges the financial support for our publishing program of the Government of Canada through the Book Publishing Industry Development Program (BPIDP), and of the Canada Council for the Arts, and the British Columbia Arts Council.

This book has been published with the help of a grant from the Canadian Federation for the Humanities and Social Sciences, through the Aid to Scholarly Publications Programme, using funds provided by the Social Sciences and Humanities Research Council of Canada.

UBC Press
The University of British Columbia
2029 West Mall
Vancouver, BC V6T 1Z2
604-822-5959 / Fax: 604-822-6083
www.ubcpress.ca

This book is for Karl.

I worked with Karl for about six months while he was incarcerated in a treatment prison. He was awaiting deportation. Karl grew up in Canada, spoke only English, and never, for lots of reasons that don't really matter, became a Canadian citizen. He lived on the edge his whole life, grew up poor, dropped out of school, got busted (many times), and had an enduring heroin habit. He loved dogs and had bad headaches. Karl was terrified of his impending deportation. He feared going to a country where he couldn't speak the language, didn't know the street culture, had no one to trust and no one to cover his back. We fought Karl's deportation and lost. He was taken out of the country in the middle of the night and put on a plane to somewhere he hadn't been since he was an infant. One week after his plane landed, Karl was killed, beaten to death in a drug deal gone wrong. There was no one to tell about Karl's death except those of us at the prison. I guess we were the closest to family he had. That was the winter of 2001, the year I started researching this project. Karl has stayed with me ever since.

Karl's problem was never the smack, it was all the rules.

Contents

Acknowledgments

There are many people and organizations without whose support and labour this book would not have been possible. The research was funded in part by a doctoral fellowship from the Social Science and Humanities Research Council. Staff at the Archives of Ontario were exceedingly helpful in locating documents and securing access to files. Financial support from the Centre of Criminology at the University of Toronto and the Faculty of Public Affairs and Management at Carleton University assisted with travel and other research expenses. I owe a huge debt of gratitude to staff at the probation offices and treatment courts and the probationers and treatment court clients who participated in the project.

Krista Lazette, Tara Lyons, Jenny Rodopolous, Akwasi Owusu-Bempeh and Jackie Shoemaker-Holmes all provided superior and talented research assistance.

Many friends and colleagues have contributed to this work, talking through sticky points, reading drafts, and offering encouragement. Connie Backhouse, Doris Buss, Xiaobei Chen, Simon Cole, Aaron Doyle, Pat Erickson, Kevin Haggerty, Kelly Hannah-Moffat, Jennifer Henderson, Ron Levi, Cheryl Lousley, Sunny Marriner, Mike Mopas, Pat O'Malley, Paula Maurutto, George Rigakos, David Sealey, Neora Snitz, Carolyn Strange, Peter Swan, Sarah Todd, Smita vir Tyagi, Kimberley White, Diana Young, the Ottawa CRAT group, the Ottawa basement security group, the Ottawa feminist legal theory group, and the Toronto History of the Present group have all left their marks on this piece. Likewise, I am indebted to staff at UBC Press for their ongoing support of this work and, especially, to my editor Randy Schmidt for all the help along the way. A special and profound appreciation is reserved for Mariana Valverde, a trusted friend and mentor.

My family, in their own way, have given me the foundation on which to build. I am particularly grateful to Joyce and Tedd Wood, Terry Moore, and Katie Wood for just about everything you've ever done. My mother and brother also deserve thanks for helping me to discover my own capabilities.

And finally, I give thanks to two people who bring their own lights into my imagination: my partner Carrie Leavoy and my son Kier Sider. Kier, although he may not realize it, is the reason behind all of this. He has always been my motivation, my ground wire, and my constant. As this project grew, so did he become one of my very favourite people. Carrie, who entered into my world as I was closing off this project, is my delightful reminder of the creative promise of beginnings. I treasure her clear intellect, boundless talent, and brave tenacity and am so very grateful for the many ways she believes in me. Together we have a friendship and love I never dreamed possible. Every day I am astonished by my great fortune.

Acronyms

AGB	Alex G. Brown
AA	Alcoholics Anonymous
ANT	actor-network theory
CBT	Cognitive Behavioural Therapy
CDSA	Controlled Drugs and Substances Act
CSC	Correctional Services Canada
CSO	Community Service Orders
CJS	criminal justice system
DOJ	Department of Justice
DTC	drug treatment court
MLA	Members of the Legislative Assembly
MPP	Member of Provincial Parliament
NDP	New Democratic Party
OCI	Ontario Correctional Institute
OMCS	Ontario Ministry of Correctional Services
OMPSS	Ontario Ministry of Public Safety and Security (the Ministry)
OPSEU	Ontario Public Sector Employees Union
OSAPP	Offender Substance Abuse Pre-Release Program
PCC	psychology of criminal conduct
PO	probation officer
PPSDM	Probation and Parole Service Delivery Model
RCMP	Royal Canadian Mounted Police
SCNMUD	Special Committee on Non-Medical Use of Drugs
SOC	Stages of Change
SSCID	Senate Special Committee on Illegal Drugs
TDTC	Toronto Drug Treatment Court
THC	Tetrahydrocannabinol
TJ	therapeutic jurisprudence
WOD	War on Drugs
VDTC	Vancouver Drug Treatment Court
YCJA	Youth Criminal Justice Act

Criminal Artefacts

1

Introduction

There is something about crime and drugs, something to which we ought to pay attention. Eighty percent of people incarcerated in Canadian federal penitentiaries are said to have some sort of substance abuse problem that correlates with their criminality.[1] The federal and many of the provincial penal authorities offer in-house addiction treatment programs to those serving both custodial and community sentences. Addiction treatment orders are the most popular requirements placed on offenders given conditional sentences. Six drug treatment courts are currently in operation, and more are scheduled to open. The federal prison service has an entire research institute dedicated to studying and devising cures for addiction. The drug user turned criminal addict is a fulcrum of criminal justice, sitting at the centre of both the cause of and cure for crime.

This book is about the criminalized drug user. Depending on the questions you ask, this person proves tricky to know. In mainstream criminology, where the bulk of research on the intersection of drugs and crime lies, researchers tend to ask questions concerning either the descriptive correlations between differing variables (i.e., is there a link between crack use and crime) or the effectiveness of varying treatments of the drug-using criminal (regenerations of the what-works debate) (c.f. Harrison et al. 2001; Incardi 1981; Leukefeld 2002). This administrative epistemology largely drives contemporary thinking about the "crime problem" and shapes criminal justice responses, many of which are based on the assumption of an assured drug/crime nexus in which the link is etiological, with drugs as the cause and crime as the effect.

Moving beyond questions like "does drug use cause crime?" and "how can we cure criminal drug addicts?" critical criminologists have taken us a long way down the road to questioning the inevitability and truth of the drug/crime nexus and ensuing claims that "rehabilitating" the drug-using criminal is necessary, right, and humane. Even as addiction is presented as the heart of crime, there is good reason to believe that drugs and their use are no more readily linked to criminality than are socio-structural issues, histories of trauma, learning disabilities, the shape of one's head, and/or the amount of serotonin in one's brain (Keane 2002; Marez 2004; Mitchell 1990; Peele 1989). It is clear that the link between drugs and crime is spurious and that the war on drugs has racist, sexist, colonialist, and class-based effects (Boyd 2004; Carstairs 2005; Courtwright 2001; Giffen, Endicott, and Lambert 1991; Musto 1973, 2002; Sheptycki 2000). It is also clear that the wedding of medical/therapeutic and legal powers that comes with attempts to cure people in conflict with the law of an array of pathologies or criminogenic tendencies tends to obscure structural factors implicated in criminality and also lays open the possibility for the heavy hand of social control to come down on the offender, functioning to criminalize, pathologize, and further oppress those who are already marginal (cf. Kendall 2000; Proctor and Rosen 1994; Sim 1990). What is not clear is how the criminal addict emerges as the prime cause of crime and why drugs and their use continue to appear as such appealing actors in bids to eradicate criminal behaviours. My project is to address these issues.

While there is a sizeable body of literature condemning the War on Drugs (WOD) (Acker 2002; Boyd 1984; Campbell 2000; Comack 1991; Courtwright 2001; Erickson and Smart 1988; Jensen and Gerber 1993; Mosher 1998; Marez 2004; Reeves and Campbell 1994; Sheptycki 2000; Sloman 1979), some of it concerning attempts to cure the criminalized addict (Boyd 2004; Carstairs 2005; Fisher, Roberts, and Kirst 2002; Nolan 2001; Peele 1989), to date, little of this literature locates drug control within the broader context of governing.[2] The criminal addict is of interest not only because the WOD is unjust and there is good reason to be concerned with attempts to coerce people into treatment, but also because she is a many-headed personage playing multiple roles simultaneously through a number of different, even unrelated, strategies. She is a threat to dominant morality (Carstairs 2005), the vehicle on which to fix enduring beliefs in the curative promise of therapy (Nolan 2001), the dark other who serves as a foil for white, middle-class existence (Reeves and Campbell 1994) and the icon of human loss and deviance (Boyd 2004). The criminal addict is one of the touchstones of criminal justice whose existence is so wholly unremarkable, so completely taken for granted, that questions are rarely raised about why she is a feature on the landscape at all. But in paying attention to this, in seeing the criminal addict as a contingent creation, a strange feature of criminal justice, it is not only possible to begin to develop an alternate critique of drug control, one that gets at the very foundations of drug policy and drug laws, but also to gain important insights into a system whose functioning depends in part on constituting such figures as problems of order in need of solutions.

Using a blend of methodologies, I chart the rise of criminal justice addiction treatment from the 1950s to the present day and offer close analysis of two contemporary sites: the drug treatment courts and a probation program. My study shows that the lurking spectre of the criminal addict in iterations of criminal justice is not inevitable, true, or natural. Instead, I reveal the criminal addict as a social artefact whose existence depends on particular arrangements of structural factors, clinical knowledges, cultural understandings, and legal practices. Birthed through these constellations and other factors, this figure is the target of governing strategies that work to make her up in particular ways and then try to remake her into a new, healthy, non-criminal, normalized person. The criminal addict identity is a strategy of governing whose "discovery" marshals an array of intervention techniques and knowledges that, located in the criminal justice system (CJS), have a good deal to tell us about the ways in which practices of justice are themselves made and remade.

Even as I describe this character as a governable identity, the criminal addict is also revealed here as a being capable of action. That is, people who find themselves constituted as criminal addicts in conflict with the law take their own actions in negotiating the governing strategies introduced through that identity. Acquiescence, compliance, and resistance are all strategies used by these people to manage or care for themselves in a system that would see them changed.

This text starts with an interest in the criminal addict as a particular problem of, and solution to, crime through the latter half of the twentieth century and into the twenty-first. The foregrounding of criminal addiction and the ensuing rise of drug abuse treatment programs is understood as a constellation of rationalities, actors, culture, knowledges, power, and selves. Or, in simpler terms, there are connections between drugs, drug users, the state, and official agents (both legal and therapeutic) that escort the criminal addict into the criminal justice spotlight and help to keep her there. Treating the criminal addict is one way for criminal justice actors to maintain their intentionally benevolent project of changing offenders even as the political landscape shifts. Cultural and clinical actions attributed to the drugs themselves also play a notable role in fixing the criminal addict as a feature of change-oriented criminal justice initiatives. Personalities are attributed to drugs (both as a general category and as specific entities) through both cultural and clinical factors. These personalities help to shape the ways in which drugs are responded to in the CJS. Thus, part of understanding the criminal addict as an artefact of governing involves developing an understanding of how drugs themselves are artefacts that contribute to governing strategies.

The notion that we can find particular individual pathologies attached to crime guides much of Canadian penal practice and ensures that crime in this country is squarely understood as a product of particular individual pathologies, of which substance abuse is arguably the most salient. This fetishization of the psychology of criminal conduct (Andrews and Bonta 1998) is worthy of critical investigation as part of the process of crafting a broader understanding of the criminal addict as a social artefact. I argue that the particular brand of psychological intervention that has come to epitomize Canadian punishment is well understood as a socio-political and cultural enterprise that quests after scientific truths that can only be found in certain historical and political moments. I am interested in unveiling the conditions under which these particular truths are made possible.

This orientation sets the project apart from other critical work done in the area. In Canada, there is an important movement comprised of critical criminologists who work to challenge the assumptions of mainstream criminology by revealing criminal justice practices as oppressive, discriminatory, abusive, and myopic. A good deal of this work is interested in the criminal addict. Giffen, Endicott, and Lambert's (1991) venerable history of Canadian drug law is perhaps the most fundamental and important text in this regard. Through careful historical study of the birth and evolution of Canadian drug laws, Giffen et al. weave a tale of "panic and indifference" in which a system of control is devised that uses drugs as a means of dominating varying undesirable populations (the Chinese, blacks, women) and a wide range of behaviours and relationships (i.e., sex, parenting, employment). Giffen's work, although theoretically barren, leaves the clear impression that the drugs/addiction/crime link is very much a political, and largely repressive, project.

These same views are echoed by contemporary critical criminologists concerned with drugs. Boyd's (2004) work on women and drugs reveals class, gender, and race bias and points to patriarchy, colonialism, and amplified social control as driving forces behind all manner of developments around drug control. In other work, the so-called "war on drugs" is revealed as a tool of disenfranchisement, and attempts to cure addiction through the CJS are considered vengeful and hyper-punitive (Boyd 1984; Fisher et al. 2002; Jensen et al. 1999; Mitchell 1990). Anderson (2001) and Fisher et al. (2002) flag specific concerns about mandating people in conflict with the law to treatment through the advent of treatment courts.

Critical criminologists have also done a good deal of work to challenge assumptions that any criminal justice initiative coupled with therapeutic goals is, by definition, benevolent, right, and good. Much of the important critical analysis in this regard comes out of work done on mental health and women. Building on the anti-psychiatry movement, scholars argue that the wedding of law and therapy results in the amplification of control, works to responsibilize and pathologize individual (women) instead of vying for broader structural understandings of particular behaviours, and reinvents age-old gendered stereotypes (Burstow 2005; Chunn and Menzies 1990;

Dobash, Dobash, and Gutteridge 1986; Kendall 2001). For these scholars, contemporary moves readily apparent in Canada to "reaffirm rehabilitation" (Cullen and Gilbert 1982) mean an explicit rejection of social explanations for criminal behaviour in favour of individualized narratives of the causes of crime. Responding to drug control, the intersection of law and therapy, or a wider range of other, important concerns with contemporary criminal justice practices, the critical criminology project calls for a reorientation of the criminal justice enterprise around issues of structural and social inequality as a means of alleviating the deep flaws of the current system.

Although I am sympathetic to the claims of critical criminologists that structural issues and determinates ought to be foregrounded in considering explanations and remedies for crime, I think it is worthwhile to step outside these claims about justice and to look curiously at these moments in which drugs and crime intersect to place the criminal addict at centre stage. I want to see the criminal addict as a social artefact, a relic of our time whose existence and treatment is not only remarkable in its own right but also has broader things to tell us about the ways in which we iterate and attempt to solve social problems. I want to respond to my above description about the current and repeated entrenchment of the criminal addict in criminal justice by asking: "how did this come to be?" and "how does it manage to flourish?"

These are important questions, given that we live in a time many would characterize as "post-rehabilitative," where the penal branch of the criminal justice enterprise is depicted as having reached a state of ennui vis-à-vis the welfarist project of changing people and is now capable of little more than basic warehousing and crude practices of control (Bauman 2000; Garland 1996, 2001; Garland and Sparks 2000). In the face of claims that penal welfarism died alongside social welfarism (Rose 1996b), it is pertinent to ask how it is that, in Canada (and virtually every other Western penal jurisdiction), criminal justice systems still try to cure people and why the criminal addict plays such a formidable role in this. To do this means to complement extant critical accounts of intersections between criminal justice, therapy, and drug addiction by revealing how our current practices became possible.

My inquiry starts not with an eye to revealing systems of structural oppression but, rather, with an eye to particular problematizations. Foucault (2001, 171) describes problematization as a methodology by which one explores "how and why certain things (behaviours, phenomena, processes) became a *problem*" (emphasis in original). The intent of such a method, he explains, is not to negate or deny the experiential reality of a certain phenomenon (i.e., madness or addiction) but, rather, to understand its genealogy: how did a certain constellation of things, behaviours, and ideologies come to be known as "mental illness?" In understanding how something comes to be seen and maintained as a specific kind of problem, it is also possible to understand how certain practices emerge as solutions to that problem, as governing strategies.

Following Foucault, my goal here is not to erase the lived reality of addiction or to challenge claims that there are, in fact, people who struggle with dependency on certain substances; rather, it is to look at how and why the problem of crime came to be framed through a causal narrative carefully bound to drugs and addiction. In other words, how did the trouble with crime become the trouble with addiction? This particular problematization results in calls for therapeutic responses. In querying how and why this came to be, it is possible to understand the criminal addict as a condensation of mentalities of governing, expert knowledges, individual actions, and cultural factors.

To explore the governance and knowledge aspects of this problematization, I use the governmentality framework set out by Foucault (1991a; Dean 1999; Gordon 1991). O'Malley, Valverde, and Rose (forthcoming) define governmentality as a perspective

> that sees [political power] not as universal, but as always operating in terms of specific rationalizations, directed towards certain ends, with certain styles of refection on its bases and its limits. An analysis of "governmentalities" then, seeks to identify these different styles of thought, their conditions of formation, the principles and knowledges that they borrow from and generate, the practices that they consist in, the ways in which they are carried out, their contestations and alliances with other arts of governing.

As a method of analysis, governmentality guides the researcher to study rationalities and practices of the "conduct of conduct." In so doing, it is possible to unveil the ways in which governance works as a means of shaping the conduct of selves and the conduct of others. The point here is to view political power as a broad spectrum, stemming from and flowing through a wide range of relationships and actions. Such a viewing, according to Foucault (1991a, 91), reveals

> that practices of government are, on the one hand, multifarious and concern many kinds of people: the head of a family, the superior of a convent, the teacher or tutor of a child or pupil; so that there are several forms of government among which the prince's relations to his state is only one particular mode; while, on the other hand, all these other kinds of government are internal to the state or society. It is within the state that the father will rule the family, the superior the convent etc.

The kind of state power described through the governmentality framework does not only reflect state-centric sovereignty; that is, it is not only about the Machiavellian power of the state to rule. Studying governmentalities is meant to break open the notion of rule, thus enabling us to see that a range of actors and practices are recruited into broader governance projects.

Through studying mentalities, it is possible to see how particular technologies of governing are constituted. Ewald's (1991) study of insurance and risk mentalities is instructive here. Ewald shows how the rise of actuarialism through the nineteenth-century insurance industry lays open the possibility of governing through the notion of risk. The ability to calculate the chance of misfortune leads, according to Ewald, to a new way of thinking about governing people. The rise of actuarial assessments and notions of risk and certainty meant that people could be governed in relation to their risk levels rather than in relation to more definite codes of what they ought or ought not do. More important, actuarialism also meant that people could be encouraged to govern themselves through managing the levels of risk around them. By the end of the nineteenth century, the governing practices of insurance are invested much more broadly, becoming, according Ewald (210),

> the principle of a new political and social economy. Insurance becomes social, not just in the sense that new kinds of risk become insurable, but also because European societies come to analyze themselves and their problems in terms of the generalized technology of risk. Insurance at the end of the nineteenth century signifies at once an ensemble of institutions and the diagram with which industrial societies conceive their principle of organization, functioning and regulation.

The impact of the mentality of actuarialism on projects of rule does not stop in the nineteenth century. Risk technologies and discourses are familiar features of contemporary criminal justice (Ericson and Haggerty 1997; Feeley and Simon 1992; Hannah-Moffat 2001) as well as broader projects of governing through individual responsibility (O'Malley 1996). In revealing the relationship between technologies and governmentalities, it is possible to see the relations of power that would otherwise remain hidden. Ewald's study on the rise of actuarialism depicts actuarial technology as a particular governing strategy that is able to effect subtle but complete governing on an everyday level. Taking Ewald's work into the contemporary realm, Hannah-Moffat (2001) interrogates the use of actuarial risk assessments on women prisoners. She shows how these technologies work to create an amoral affect within the system, suggesting that the work of securing, controlling, and treating prisoners is the product of cool mathematical calculation rather than moralized, subjective, biased valuation. The effect is that prison governance is constituted not as the oppressive hand of the state, which comes in and places a woman in maximum security, but, rather, as an actuarial risk assessment that reveals her as high risk – a revelation that sets off an entire governing regime that is presented as "risk management" rather than as "punishment." Thus, the woman prisoner, in Hannah-Moffat's estimation, is governed through the language, technologies, and rationalities of risk and actuarialism.

The governmentality framework assists in understanding, then, how and why particular practices and mentalities of rule emerge within certain contexts. Jonathan Simon's (1993) study on parole in California is another case in point. Simon charts the rise of parole from the nineteenth century onwards. He aptly describes how changing political and social climates ushered in shifts in practices and mentalities. For Simon, parole shifts from being a means of keeping people occupied through assigning them work to, in the post-Second World War era, a rehabilitative model designed to make them better people. Contemporary practices of parole are managerial rather than rehabilitative. According to Simon, all these changes are to be understood against their respective economic and social backdrops.

A similar approach is helpful in my project. The criminal addict first emerges on the penal landscape in the decidedly welfarist post-Second World War era. This era, marked generally by a turn towards "cradle-to-grave" mentalities of governing that took up social service delivery and citizen-building projects, saw the rise of a particular rehabilitative ideal in Canadian punishment. Bolstered by the concomitant rise of the medical model in Canadian penal systems (Ekstedt and Griffiths 1988), criminal justice officials were deeply concerned with addressing the causes of crime through largely "psy"-based interventions,[3] which were carried out on people in conflict with the law. Alongside electro-shock therapies, yoga classes, and individual psychotherapies, prisoners were treated for addictions through the advent of "therapeutic-community" prisons. Reflecting the mentality of the times, these institutions offered holistic treatment for prisoners with addictions, attempting to make them both drug/crime free and good citizens. While criminality was understood as driven largely by individual factors like addiction, social factors were also considered. The political terrain shifted in the 1980s as welfarist ideals fell away, making space for decidedly neoliberal regimes. Somehow, as my introductory observations reveal,[4] the ethic of changing people survived this shift in mentalities. The project of curing the criminal addict is still a feature of Canadian punishment. While the goal stays, however, the technologies by which it is to be achieved change to match shifting mentalities. Attempts to work on the criminal addict today are notably different from those utilized in the 1970s. Social explanations are erased, leaving individual pathology to stand as the sole cause of crime. Holistic responses are replaced by initiatives shaped by a mantra of efficiency and effectiveness.

The criminal addict's ability to endure these shifting governmentalities is understood in light of shifting expert epistemologies. Foucault links power and knowledge, seeing them as two sides of the same coin. The role of expertise in governing strategies is a good example of this. Foucault charts the rise of expertise in particular realms (psychiatry, medicine, punishment) and shows how, in exercising and acting through these knowledges, the exertion of power is made possible. Pasquino (1991) takes this notion as a means of understanding the rise of criminology as a discipline. Studying the work of Enrico Ferri, the acclaimed "father of criminology," Pasquino shows how criminological knowledge reimagines the target of criminological intervention. Before the "science" of criminology emerges, the person who commits a crime is "homo penalis" – a person who is worthy of punishment as a result of engaging in criminal behaviour. Developing criminological expertise (hugely facilitated by the birth of the prison and the ensuing ability to study its captives) meant that homo penalis became "homo criminalis" – the delinquent. The shift from being someone who commits an act to being someone whom the act commits (i.e., to being defined by the act) is made possible by criminological expertise that takes as its starting point the notion that "criminals" exist. And if criminals exist as a type and can be known, then they can also be worked on and changed (i.e., normalized). Acting through knowledge of the criminal and the nature of criminality lays open the possibility of a whole range of power relations. If there are criminals, and if these people are criminals because they are somehow sick, then other people can work to cure them. There must, then, be relations, programs, interventions in which some people (experts, practitioners) work on other people (offenders) in order to make them different people. Without criminological expertise, these new relations of power would not be possible.

Attempts to cure the criminal addict are driven by psy epistemologies. The addict's endurance is attributable, in part, to the ability of these knowledges to shift with the political landscape, allowing the nature of his character and, thus, the prescription for his cure to change with the times. The criminal addict of the 1970s is a very different, much more social creature than is the criminal addict of the 1990s. Both characters are in need of clinical treatment as a means of alleviating their criminal tendencies, but, in the 1970s, reflecting broader welfarist sensibilities, this treatment is far more socially oriented than are the responses that emerge in the 1990s, when the advent of cognitive behavioural therapy allows all troubling human behaviour to be whittled down to a handful of problems solved through quick and standardized interventions.

Governing sites are a meeting point for different kinds of knowledges that amalgamate to work on the individual. The strategies deployed through these regimes are articulations of a certain kind of power exerted over the individual. For Foucault, this power is productive rather than repressive. Foucault (1977) notes the rise of disciplinary power, a governing strategy that is meant to incite conduct just as much or more than it is meant to stop it. If some power is productive, then certain mentalities of rule work to build people up and encourage them to behave in certain ways. The woman rendered "high risk" through actuarial assessment may find herself held in repressive conditions in a prison, but, at the same time, governing practices in the form of prison programs, disciplinary regimes, surveillance, and psychological interventions all work to encourage her to do certain things, behave in certain ways, and become a certain kind of person. The power of the prison lies in its ability to make people.

The initiatives I describe do not deploy strategies of brute force or repression nearly as much as they offer "opportunities" for people in conflict with the law to "choose to change." The process of curing the criminal addict is meant, by and large, to be generated in the mind of the individual herself. The clinical and legal actors around her are merely guides on her own, individual path to self-realization, improvement, and change. The system, in this sense, works to build her up much more than it attempts to break her down.

In studying power, Foucault (1980, 97) rejects the idea that we ought to claim that this institution or that person has power and that others do not; instead, he counsels a relational view of power:

> Analysis should not concern itself with power at the level of conscious intention or decision; ... it should not attempt to consider power from its internal point of view and ... should refrain from posing the labyrinthine and unanswerable question: "Who then has power and what has he in mind? What is the aim of someone who possesses power?" Instead, it is a case of studying power at the point where its intention, if it has one, is completely invested in its real and effective practices. What is needed is a study of power in its external visage, at the point where it is in direct and immediate relationship with that which we can provisionally call its object, its target, its field of application, there – that is to say – where it installs itself and produces its real effects.

Seeing governing through this lens not only means that we are able to chart practices of governing carried out by one person, group, or institution in relation to another but also that we can see the ways in which we are encouraged to govern ourselves. Foucault (1978) understands practices of the self, the ways in which we care for ourselves, as features of broader governmental rationalities. Viewed this way, simple practices like getting a flu shot, going to therapy, or engaging in an exercise regimen are all part of what many would characterize as neoliberal practices of self (Rose 1998). The ways we take care of ourselves are derivations of the governing structures within which we live. The healthy, fit, and well-adjusted self of 2006, for example, is as much political obligation as personal choice (Cruickshanks 1996). After all, what are the fat, sick, and neurotic in contemporary parlance if not irresponsible, bad citizens?

What Foucault calls "practices of the self" are fundamental to attempts to cure the criminal addict, who is worked on to become self-sufficient and self-regulating. The people caught up in the programs I study are not locked away in dry-out cells for weeks on end; rather, they are encouraged to develop their own practices of self, such as developing "internal incentives" to increase their personal motivations to change their substance-use habits.

If power is constituted in relationships, then the people who are targets of the exertion of power can resist it. Even though neither he nor many of those who use his work develop the point (with the notable exceptions of Bosworth [1999] and Sawicki [1991]), Foucault is clear that, in every relation of power, there is also the possibility for resistance. Power is not a zero-sum game. In *Discipline and Punish* (1977), he uses the example of the scaffold, suggesting that, even as the execution is a profound moment of the exertion of state power, the potential for resistance still exists. The people could tear down the scaffold and call for the liberation of the condemned. In my research, acts of resistance are revealed to be closely tied with notions of self-care. The probationers and drug treatment court (DTC) clients who are part of this study engage in varying actions as ways of managing themselves. In some cases, these actions are subversive, taking the form of rejecting the governable identity of addict; in others, refusals of micro-governing strategies (such as being directed to live in a particular shelter) emerge as ways of maintaining a sense of individual selfhood within a broader normalizing project. In all instances, these negotiations of power are mediated by pre-existing desires and dispositions and are articulated as practices of self-care. Ultimately, the bodies and minds of the people subjected to these initiatives are the busiest sites of power.

While many of the relations in these sites are well understood through the lenses of governmentality and the care of the self, Foucault's method does not allow for careful attention to the day-to-day interactions in which these strategies of rule are carried out. I turn to ethnomethodology to complement my analysis. Following the urban tradition of the Chicago School, ethnography of drug use tends to focus on street-level interactions. Becker's ground-breaking *The Outsiders* (1966) is the most notable, but there are others, including Lindesmith (1965), Waldorf and Reinarman (1975), and, more recently, Bourgeois (2003), Denton and O'Malley (2001), and Acker (2002). From these scholars I adopt an ethic that involves sympathetically studying marginalized and maligned populations such as drug users. This body of scholarship argues for the need to see communities and people through the actualities of their day-to-day lives rather than through a prejudging lens that imbues their actions with normalized assumptions (e.g., drug use is bad, all drug users are functioning at diminished capacity, and so on). These scholars approach drug users with a research ethic that assumes a clear respect for all people. The result is research that reveals the intimate ties in drug-using communities (Becker 1966; Waldorf and Reinarman 1975), the sharp intellect required to participate in the drug trade (Bourgeois 2003), and the deleterious effects of drug control and medical intervention on the lived experience of the user (Lindesmith 1965).

The discovery of, and work done on, the criminal addict occurs by in large through the daily goings on of the courts and probation offices. To help explore these interactions, I draw most extensively on the ethnomethodology of Erving Goffman. In his study of the inner workings of an insane asylum, Goffman (1961) attributes the power of the mental hospital to take near total control over an individual's life to the micro-interactions of its daily routine. Through the strategic harvesting of case histories, the management of relatives, and careful interactions with the soon-to-be patient, Goffman shows how the hospital works to make people up as mental patients not in accordance with any real "need" guided by an illness but, rather, in accordance with the institution's ability to constitute and then govern an individual:

> The psychiatric view of a person becomes significant only in so far as their [psychiatrists'] view itself alters his social fate – an alteration which seems to become fundamental in our society when, and only when, the person is put through the process of hospitalization (128).

Goffman reveals the mental patient as a sociological phenomenon rather than as a scientific truth. For Goffman, this phenomenon can only be viewed in observing the minutiae of everyday life. In looking at a site from the bottom up, it is also possible to see how, for example, patients try to negotiate and resist the governing authority of the hospital officials and the disciplinary effects of the hospital itself. The routine happenings of the hospital are sites of near constant power negotiation, all of which are mediated by the mental patient role.

If Foucault's method flags the importance of noting relations between projects of rule and projects of self from the top down, Goffman gives us a means by which to invert this gaze, studying the same relationships but from the bottom up (see Hacking 2004). The benefit for this work is a much richer account of the small negotiations and interactions that inform the broader practices of working on the criminal addict. It is possible to see not only how, for example, the rise of cognitive behavioural therapy serves to revive the project of change vis-à-vis the criminal addict (by responsibilizing this character in her own recovery) but also how she uses the same language used to govern her as a means of offering a counter-narrative of herself and her criminal justice status.

Crafting this analysis troubles assumptions about the criminal addict by showing this individual as a condensation of particular factors rather than as a medical/legal condition. The map of governing in this site so far appears as a vertical stripe. Governmentalities and psy expertise are at the top and criminalized drug users at the bottom. A good part of my project interrogates this line, searching out its composition and charting the ways in which actors move along it. But the rise of the criminal addict does not depend only on the relationships between drug users and governing/expert authorities. There is a third group of actors in this site whose contributions bear consideration: the drugs themselves. There is something particular and important about drugs that drives these developments. Drugs (both specific substances as well as the general term) are prominent actors in our society. Our relationships with our children are shaped in part by fears about what drugs will do; entire neighbourhoods are characterized by the presence or absence of particular substances; social ills, individual pathologies, and, of course, crime are all caused by drugs. Drugs have particular personalities shaped by both culture and scientific knowledges. These personalities (crack is evil and volatile, marijuana is disinhibiting but relatively benign) participate in establishing criminal justice responses to particular substances and their use. Some drugs are thought to be more dangerous than others. Users are infected with a sense of danger because of what the drugs "do" to them. In popular, clinical, and criminal justice parlance, crack use and crack users are more criminogenic than are marijuana users and pot heads. These distinctions are reflected in the Controlled Drugs and Substances Act, which sets higher penalties for any infraction associated with crack.

I take up actor-network theory (ANT) as a means of accounting for the actions of the drugs themselves. ANT scholars (Callon 1999; Latour 1987, 1993; Law 1999) set out a post-humanist methodology that places all actors involved in a particular scientific action within a network. Latour, for example, states clearly that his area of study is the relations between *collectives*, not humans. By using this notion of collective, Latour is able to include in his analysis objects that may be "soulless" but that nonetheless act within the network. In deprivileging humanity in the constitution of truth, Latour shows how objects themselves have character and influence within a given setting. Latour (1993) uses several examples to illustrate this point, but perhaps the most salient, given my particular concerns in *Criminal Artefacts*, is his example of how expanding knowledge about the effects of brain chemicals influences conceptions about mental illness. As he suggests, "as for the unconscious subjects stretched out on the analyst's couch, we picture them differently depending on whether their dry brain is discharging neurotransmitters or their moist brain is secreting hormones" (4). Likewise, in *Criminal Artefacts*, the drugs themselves as well as the individuals who use them are all considered part of a collective. This approach allows the researcher to work to destabilize the assumed hierarchies of power within a site. Rather than observing how projects of rule are designed and carried out on subjects of rule, Latour's approach blurs the channels of power, recognizing how each person and thing involved in the network is active and influential and is influenced by every other thing. Returning to Latour's example of the person on the analyst's couch, the utility of this approach is clear. All of the "things" involved in this site – the analyst, the brain and its chemicals, and the individual subject – are acting, and each action influences the other actors and the network as a whole. The network does not distinguish between humans and non-humans, and it unhinges assumed notions about fixed divisions. Using this approach, it is possible to see how things, machines, microbes, and drugs have generative capabilities that affect the other actors in the network, playing an active role in whether or not the goals of the network (e.g., to invent a machine, to cure a disease) are realized.

My project is not identical to the science studies projects taken up by ANT scholars. I am not studying laboratories and quests for scientific innovation per se. This being the case, I do not use a strict ANT methodology; rather, I borrow from ANT the notion of inanimate action in order to show how and why understanding the personalities of drugs is important in understanding the rise of the criminal addict. The ANT lens, which allows for the contributing actions of inanimate objects, enables me to consider how these clinical and cultural properties shape criminal justice responses.

The actions attributed to drugs are not shaped only by clinical epistemology. Drugs have a distinctive cultural existence that serves to fix their links to crime as well as to inform the ways in which we understand and respond to the criminal addict. For example, the elevation of opiates such as heroin on the drug schedule is, I argue, as much a reflection of the substances' cultural resonance as it is of their clinical properties.[5] In fact, in most instances, it is through cultural, not clinical, means that we "know" drugs. The effects of these cultural notions are easily viewed in the sites I examine in *Criminal Artefacts*. The cultural impact of notions of drugs and the ways in which cultural products mould different drug personalities are fundamentally important to the ways in which the CJS responds to drug users. To show this, I borrow tools from cultural studies, particularly from Klein (1993) and Szasz (1985). Both these scholars place drugs at the forefront of attempts to understand social relations. For Szasz, the effects of drugs shape their "ceremonial chemistry," or the cultural rituals that surround their use or avoidance. The drugs drive people's reactions to them. In his study of cigarettes, Klein submits that the nature of these substances has a cultural importance that has resulted in a global response to their use. The point is not to set up a deterministic chain but, rather, to say that the ways in which substances are understood culturally shape the ways in which they are clinically understood and responded to. In Canada, much of the push behind the early forming of drug laws came not from governing mentalities or clinical observance but, rather, from the popularized writings of Emily Murphy. Her work vocally and unwaveringly demonized specific substances, situating them as the causes of racial degeneration and threats to the Canadian moral order (Carstairs 1999, 2005; Giffen et al. 1991; Murphy 1922). Today, drugs are everywhere in contemporary culture, from news reports to popular songs. Given their cultural importance, a study that attempts to understand the elevation of the criminal addict ought to pay attention to the "personalities" of drugs. These cultural understandings are all that much more important in light of the fact that the people who design and implement interventions and policies aimed at the criminal addict are not outside of culture. Cultural influences are evident in the ways in which judges, lawyers, therapists, and probation officers understand the drug use of people in conflict with the law. In beginning to reveal these influences, I hope to broaden our understandings of the networks of influence that shape governing initiatives.

I also find the notion of the network helpful in understanding the knowledge relations that a governmentality analysis would view through a hierarchic lens. Where Foucault's primary interest lies in power, Latour starts from the question of truth – a starting point that, when followed through the network approach, also serves as a useful guide to understanding microrelations of power. Truth is a feature of knowledge; and knowledge and power, as Foucault points out, are one and the same. While Foucault is a strong advocate of watching the minutiae of everyday life, he spends considerably less time thinking about humans interacting with humans on the same level than he does thinking about humans interacting with the state or with experts. In using Latour's method, it is possible to see how different human interactions function within a governing strategy. I find this approach particularly useful in Chapter 4, where I map out the knowledge relations of experts. Seeing expert actors and knowledges uncoupled and circulating within a governing network (in this case, the drug treatment courts) is a useful exercise in understanding the kinetics of power and the ways in which law and psy work in concert to exert power over the addict.

This image of the network serves as a broad theme throughout *Criminal Artefacts*. Latour advocates the network approach because it functions to remove imaginative barriers from the research site. In Latour's world, if you see an engine, for example, as existing only in the realm of science, then you miss the opportunity to see all the other factors that affect that engine's invention: the social "need," the economic viability, and the ability of the investors to change their interests. Latour argues that we cannot view things, scientific or otherwise, within boxes that assume that there are divides between the natural and the social. Latour's (1993) claim that "we have never been modern" suggests that the boxes are historically specific artefacts, that nature and science do not "naturally" stand outside each other. As such, an attempt to understand any phenomenon is well served by opening an inquiry into all spheres of influence, by viewing action within a network that can have multiple, indeed, potentially countless, influences.

Criminal Artefacts is about the networks that exist between three phenomena: drugs, the user, and the state. I show that governing initiatives are messy, that they draw upon and are driven by a variety of sources and forces. Governing the criminal addict is not solely a result of governing mentalities articulated through legal authority and expert knowledge; rather, it is a result partly of these factors and partly of others, including culture, science, and individual selves.

The mixed methodology I deploy here belies the scholarly compulsion to carefully align one's self with a particular theoretical tradition to which one must stay "true" in one's research. Following scholars like Valverde (2005) and Cole (2001), I am not interested in orienting my work as "Foucauldian," "Latourian," "Goffmanesque," or otherwise. These scholars offer methods, not theories, of understanding the social world. As such, it should be possible (and this is Valverde's argument) to borrow from an array of methods in order to do research. My approach is to use these perspectives in so far as they complement each other. Foucault's strengths in noting power relations and understanding the ways in which broader projects of rule filter down to the individual is complemented by Goffman's method of ethnographically mapping human relations as a means of understanding those broader projects. The relations observed through these methods are more richly understood when placed within a network of relations à la Latour. Within the network, other factors and actors (such as the generative capabilities of drugs) come into focus through their cultural and scientific resonances. However, the Latourian approach, because it tends to ignore hierarchies, is not particularly well suited to seeing power relations. And it is for this reason that I return to a Foucauldian methodology.

Ultimately, this is a book about practices of governing. I seek to contribute to bodies of criminological scholarship that challenge the "necessary rightness of the status quo" (Garland 2001). I build on work of scholars like

Bosworth (1999), Cruickshanks (1996), Doyle (2003), Hacking (1999), Hudson (1987), O'Malley (1996), Rose (1998, 1999), and Valverde (2003a). All of these scholars use the careful research of particular social phenomena as a means of destabilizing systems of order. The points of disruption vary. Doyle (2003) uses communications technology as his entry point for rupturing contemporary thinking about how we view crime. Hacking (1999) is interested in revealing assumedly natural identities, like the abused child, as social products whose discovery has the remarkable effect of reorganizing the past. What draws these scholars together is not their substantive areas but, rather, their common interest in systems of rule and how they come to be – their interest in the conduct of conduct. Locating my project in relation to this work means that I am interested in participating in the disruptive project. Looking at the criminal addict offers another avenue for challenging the seeming inevitability of what is. Thus, this text is not only about the criminal addict but also about strategies of governing. The criminal addict presents an opportunity to explore the roles played by therapists, judges, and lawyers in their attempts to make people better. She lays open for study governing mentalities and disciplinary epistemologies, and she is a handy site in which to see how these interact. Further, her strong cultural presence lays bare the often obscured and/or ignored connections between governing and culture (Garland 2001). *Criminal Artefacts* is about multiple sites and strategies of governing; it is about the different ways criminal justice systems attempt to maintain order without exerting extreme, obvious, or austere force.

Part of the messy actualities (O'Malley 2001) of everyday life are the difficulties of crafting genealogical research of the kind I describe in relation to the CJS. Criminal justice institutions are closed institutions, difficult to gain access to at any level. To study regimes for curing the criminal addict, following the method I set out above, I need to be able to study history, culture, and science as well as the actual practices of cure. The first iteration of *Criminal Artefacts* was a tight genealogy of the treatment programs offered by Correctional Services Canada (CSC). I imagined doing a history of the programs offered by the CSC and then spending time in the prisons watching their implementation and interviewing the prison officials involved in their make-up and delivery as well as the prisoners who were subject to them. After several months of negotiations with the CSC, it became clear that they were not comfortable with granting me the kind of access I required. In fact, they eventually refused to grant me any access at all.

Luckily, the Ontario Ministry of Public Safety and Security (OMPSS, as it was then known; throughout, I refer to it as "the Ministry") was just getting its probation treatment program under way, and officials were happy to grant me access to the probationers involved in the program, although I could not sit in on program sessions. The second iteration of this project, then, was organized around compiling a genealogy of the Ontario system and then observing, at least in part, the mechanics of power through interviews with probationers in the treatment program. This approach worked well in so far as I was able to piece together the important historical narrative of the rise of addiction treatment in Ontario (which, as it turns out, ended up being the main generative location for these initiatives), and I was able to talk to people who had experienced the kinds of interventions I was interested in studying. At the same time, there were two problems with this approach. First, because the Ministry did not grant me access to the actual program or to any of the probation officers delivering the program, I felt that an important piece of interaction – the actual practices of governing – was not captured. At the same time, the interview portion of the study coincided with a major labour dispute in the Ontario Public Service, the results of which were less than felicitous for this project (below, I discuss these events in greater detail). All was not lost, however! When approached, the Toronto and Vancouver DTCs were happy to grant me limited access. Through the courts I could watch governing interactions and also interview practitioners, although I was not granted access to court clients.

A pessimistic read of this folly of events is that the project ends up looking like a patchwork quilt of research, a little from here and a little from there, cobbled together in a vain attempt to form a coherent whole. To be sure, the lack of obvious continuity between the sites is a weak point, but this is not a fatal flaw to the project and, in some ways, constitutes a strength. This is a study of "slices" of criminal justice interventions with the criminal addict. The genealogical analysis describes the broader socio-political and cultural context within which both the treatment courts and the probation program emerge. The sites themselves give perspective on different aspects of these interventions. The treatment courts are instructive with regard to the use and circulation of expert knowledges and expertise, and the interviews with probationers provide insights into practices of the self. At the same time, the two sites are also responding to the same problem: criminal addiction. The courts and the probation program both work through the notion of the drug/crime nexus, focus on the individual, and rely heavily on the incorporation of psy into their intervention practices. Far from a patch-work quilt result, what I produce here is a triangulated account of interventions on the criminal addict that looks at these initiatives from a number of different perspectives. *Criminal Artefact* is not a deep chronicle of a particular initiative but, rather, a broad survey offering rich analysis of particular moments of intervention.

Methods and Sources
I begin my research post-Second World War for several reasons. Most important, the post-Second World War era in Ontario, as in other jurisdictions

in the Western world, witnessed the high-water mark of the welfare state. The economic boom, coupled with increasing faith in medicine and the psy disciplines, all contributed to the rise and maintenance of state practices concerned with the social welfare of citizens. Punishment was not the only system that underwent notable changes during this time. Moves towards decarceration and increased psy programming characterized the mental health sector as well as the criminal sector (Simmons 1982). Likewise, concerns about crime spurred the creation of a variety of social intervention programs aimed at directing individuals into socially desirable behaviours (Valverde 1995). The fact, then, that the 1950s mark the success of welfarist mentalities makes this time period a logical point to begin this inquiry.

I choose Ontario because it is comprised of the largest English-speaking population in the country. Ontario has the biggest penal system and, thus, the most resources to develop new initiatives. It is also the province in which, since the Second World War, some of the most significant developments in penal drug policy have emerged. Ontario had its own research and treatment centres, and it ran experimental treatment programs linked with the penal system. The high level of activity around penal drug treatment that characterized the province in the 1950s continues today. Ontario was the first province to host a DTC, and it continues to run and develop penal treatment programs. My focus on Ontario does not preclude the extension of my observations to other jurisdictions. I show in Chapter 2 that, while it serves as a case study, the trends and developments found in Ontario are mirrored elsewhere.

The historical aspects of *Criminal Artefacts* are based on archival sources from the post-Second World War period in Ontario, an archive that is not particularly rich. While the holdings at the Archives of Ontario include several files related to punishment in the province dating from this period, for the most part, these files deal with administrative issues such as obtaining funding sources or training support staff. There are, however, some files that do speak directly to issues of treatment within the provincial penal system, or indirectly, through discussions about best practices, law reform, and resource allocation. I began the archival research process by requesting a list and description of all files located at the Ministry of Correctional Services and Attorney General, beginning in the 1950s. The Archives of Ontario is interdicted, through the Freedom of Information Act, from releasing any files that either identify individual offenders by name or that are fewer than twenty years old. As such, all files I requested were first screened by archival officers and dated no later than 1980.

Based on the descriptions of file content provided by the archives, I requested access to twenty-four different files, including minister's correspondence, minutes and files of subcommittees, pamphlets and training materials relating to specific institutions, and minister's and deputy minister's speeches and reports. I went through every file provided by the archives, making notes on archival material and photocopying pieces of particular interest.

In order to supplement the patchiness of the archival data, I also relied heavily on the Hansard transcripts of provincial legislative debates covering the fifty-year time period. Using the Hansard index, I checked every reference made about punishment, corrections, and drugs from 1950 to the present within the legislative debates. In addition, I read the Ministerial Estimates for every year available. Estimates are a ministry's report of activities. They appear before the Legislature (and, later, before the Justice Sub-Committee) typically every one-and-a-half to two years. From the mid-1990s onward, it is possible to conduct archival research from the Ministry's website. Press releases, yearly business plans and ministers' speeches are all posted on the website as well as news updates and general information about the different branches of ministerial services.

To further supplement the archival data from Ontario, I also conducted interviews with seven key informants. These interviews focused on the informants' experiences of working as government or non-governmental employees. I identified individuals of interest based on their past involvement with the Ministry, current accessibility, and recommendations from other informants. I then contacted them, provided a brief account of the research project and the potential for publications coming out of it and asked whether they would be interested in becoming involved. Names of all participants are withheld in the interests of protecting anonymity. However, I do this recognizing that, given the high-profile positions held by some participants, no one who took part in the study could be offered full confidentiality. All participants signed consent forms, in which they acknowledged they were fully informed of the nature and purpose of the research as well as of their rights as research participants. They were also given information sheets detailing this information. In general, the interviews focused on the individuals' perceptions of general trends within the field as well as of specific experiences around various initiatives and programs.

For another part of the research, I conducted interviews with ten individuals who had completed Ontario's Substance Misuse Orientation Program for probationers. These interviews were qualitative and were guided by an open-ended questionnaire. Interviewees were solicited from the program through a presentation made by me (typically in the last program session) regarding the research. Interested participants were asked to complete a form, giving their first names and the means by which they preferred to be contacted (i.e., directly, via phone, or through their probation officers). I followed up with phone calls to those who agreed in order to set up interviews in the probation office. At the outset, I anticipated interviewing upwards of forty men; the 2002 labour disruption meant that most of the programs were cancelled soon after the study started. Many offices opted not to re-offer the program after this labour disruption. In the end, I completed interviews with ten probationers. When participants arrived for interviews, they were given consent forms and briefed regarding their rights as research participants as well as regarding the purpose of the study. They were also given an information sheet that detailed the same. If the participants consented, interviews were tape-recorded using a micro-cassette system and later transcribed by a research assistant. All identifying information has been erased from the transcripts, and the tapes are kept in a locked cabinet. I attended a training session for probation officers that was focused on how to deliver this program. I also studied the training manual and interviewed the program developer.

Criminal Artefacts also draws on research from the drug treatment courts in Toronto and Vancouver. As of December 2005 (when I completed this research), these were the only two treatment courts in operation, although funding has now been secured for four additional courts across the country (Ottawa, Edmonton, Winnipeg, and Regina). I conducted courtroom observations over a six-month period, from July 2002 through January 2003, in the Toronto court. A research assistant observed the Vancouver court from March through July 2005. Court is in session in both jurisdictions twice a week. In both courts, all the members of the court (including the court "clients") were made aware of the research. Before I began my work, I met with the presiding judge in each court to explain the purpose of my research. The judges circulated my proposal to the other members of the treatment court team. I circulated an information flyer, which included a brief synopsis of myself and this project, among the clients. My research assistant and I kept research journals of court observations, and these were updated after every court visit.

In researching the courts, I also conducted interviews with key informants, including the judges, duty and Crown counsels, treatment court liaisons, treatment coordinators, parent-child advocates, and several of the therapists. Like the interviews conducted with key historical actors, these interviews were semi-structured and were tailored to the individual's role in the court. There are only a limited number of individuals who might be identified as "key players" within the court. Thus, the sample here was non-random and exhaustive (with the exception of the therapists). I interviewed every key player and solicited all of the therapists in the Toronto court.[6] Four of the eight therapists responded to my solicitation and agreed to participate in the research project. Again, as with the historical interviews, anonymity was not guaranteed. Because some of them (i.e., the therapists and lawyers) are low profile, I have refrained from using their names and identify them only numerically. I was denied access to the court clients and was, therefore, unable to interview them.

All aspects of this project involving research with human beings were presented to and approved by the Ethical Research Review Board of the University of Toronto.

Chapter Summaries

I start with a genealogy of addiction treatment in the CJS. Chapter 2 gives an overview of therapeutic initiatives through the second half of the twentieth century, locating the addict as a central and re-emerging figure therein. I argue that the criminal addict is a useful character in current criminal justice initiatives. This entity is able to shift from the pathological welfarist subject in need of holistic interventions to the ultimate neoliberal criminal who suffers from poor individual choice making based on a curable individual pathology that is directly and etiologically linked to crime. My evidence suggests that it is largely through the work of mid-level practitioners (a mix of psychologists, bureaucrats, and program designers) that the criminal addict manages to endure considerable shifts in political sensibilities. By adopting liberal psy technologies like cognitive behaviouralism, these actors are able to maintain the overall goal of curing the offender.

Chapter 3 uses actor-network analysis to study the generative action of drugs, which emerges in attempts to work on the criminal addict. I argue that both cultural and clinical notions of drugs shape particular understandings that support the notion that drugs are criminogenic. I show that both the personalities of the overarching term "drugs" and the specific substances marijuana, crack/cocaine, and heroin shape the ways in which criminal justice officials respond to their use.

Chapters 4 and 5 focus on the day-to-day attempts to cure the drug addicted criminal. Chapter 4 takes the drug treatment courts as a case study of the ways in which addicts are worked upon. I show that, in the treatment courts, law and psy actors and knowledges circulate within a formalized network. The liberated flow of knowledges and actors in this site serves to exacerbate the rationalities and practices of care and control carried out on the court "clients." Through this network, typically legal actions, such as placing someone in prison, are directed by therapists for therapeutic purposes and vice versa. The power of these knowledge exchanges raise concerns about the protection of the criminal addict both as an accused person and as a therapeutic client.

The final chapter concerns the practices of self performed by the criminal addict. I draw on data from the DTCs as well as interviews with probationers to reveal the constitution of the addict identity as a strategy of governing. Having people in conflict with the law accept this identity mobilizes an entire strategy of intervention that centres on practices of self-care as a means of achieving addiction recovery. The addict identity traps people in this strategy. People caught deploy a range of self-care practices, some of which reflect those directed by governing authorities and others of which serve to maintain counter-selfhoods or to subvert the governing strategy.

2
Mentalities of Treatment: The Criminal Addict and the Project of Change

The goal of curing the offender of his addiction, like the broader project of change, endures through changing political climates because the practices of achieving it are able to change to fit with broader political and social sensibilities. Moving from the welfarism of the post-Second World War period to contemporary neoliberalism, the criminal addict is not always a popular figure, but he is always present. He is also a shifty type, an artefact whose significance changes depending on the context. The criminal addict of the 1960s and 1970s is a very different character from the addict of the 1990s. Thus, even while the etiological link between drugs and crime holds fast, the particulars of the criminal addict change to fit the wider landscape. By charting the rise and endurance of this character, it is possible to see how discourses and practices reroute, laying open the opportunity to invoke this personage in different political climates.

The Project of Change
The claim that those who break the law can be rehabilitated is not new. Lawbreakers have been "worked on" in the hope of effecting real and lasting reforms in the individual for the last two hundred years. But, while the objective of rehabilitating and reforming individual "offenders" has remained constant, the techniques by which this objective is brought about have differed. The practice of changing people has included physical torture; carceral regimes that rely heavily on religion; psychological interventions like psychoanalysis, group therapy, and individual counselling; and physical interventions like lobotomies and pharmacological administrations, including a range of psychoactive substances (Foucault 1977; Garland 1985; Proctor and Rosen 1994; Rothman 1980; Simon 1993). The choice of a particular technology by which to change lawbreakers is influenced by political economy, culture, and science (Garland 1996; Simon 1993). Thus, underlying each different practice of "criminal" intervention, there is a

specific idea that stems from the way in which, during the time in question, people regarded the etiology of criminal behaviour. Different problematizations of crime give rise to different technical solutions, which resonate with particular ideologies. Bentham's (1791 [1962]) panopticon, for example, strove to work on the errant and perverse soul of the prisoner and was born of a time when crime was very much understood as a product of waywardness. In contrast, 1960s encounter groups attempted to address the individual's self-esteem and ability to relate to others, understanding crime and its resolution as being very much a social issue.[1]

The "what-works/nothing-works" debates of the 1970s heralded, in the eyes of many theorists and historians, the demise of the rehabilitative age in contemporary penality (Cullen and Gilbert 1982; Garland 2001; Martinson 1974; O'Malley 1999b; Feeley and Simon 1992). In the shadow of rehabilitation's shallow grave, there have been several attempts among theorists to characterize the "new" age of punishment. Feeley and Simon (1992) argue that we have entered into an age of *new penology*, in which the concept of punishment shifts. They reason that, where the *old penology* was concerned with "responsibility, fault, moral sensibility, diagnosis, or intervention and treatment of the individual offender," the new penology "is concerned with techniques to identity, classify and manage groupings sorted by dangerousness. The task is managerial not transformative" (452). Feeley and Simon define three distinguishing characteristics of the new penology: first, a language of actuarialism and managerialism replaces languages of therapy and morality; second, in criminological discourse, the individual is displaced in favour of the aggregate; and third, effectiveness and efficiency are the guiding principles for the development of new techniques of punishment, ranging from "de-frilling" the system to implementing actuarial assessment tools.

Reacting to Feeley and Simon's claims that we entered a postmodern era of punishment, Garland (2001) accepts that the practices of punishment used today are significantly different from those used in the modern era. He argues, however, that denoting our current times as "postmodern" sets too strong a demarcation between the recent past and present. Garland is more inclined to place changes in penal practice and rhetoric on a continuum of modernity that has yet to reach its conclusion. The decline of rehabilitation, according to Garland, must be understood as arising out of much more than technological and rhetorical transfigurations in the administration of punishment. We ought to see the influence of cultural shifts as well as the "limits of the sovereign state" on the ways in which we imagine and carry out punishing (Garland 1996).

O'Malley (1999b) offers perhaps the most thoughtful account of changes, suggesting that we cannot create a tidy narrative of contemporary penality; rather, we must understand current regimes as "volatile and contradictory," offering little in terms of an overarching rationality or generalized agenda. Instead of having one grand narrative of punishing, what we have is a meshing of neoliberal[2] and neoconservative[3] concepts of punishing, and this has created a penal scheme that is both efficient and punitive. This is an approach that O'Malley refers to as a product of the "new right."

Most recent is the "new punitiveness" thesis. Here, attention is paid mainly to practices of warehousing and mass incarceration. Pratt et al. (2005, xiii) introduce their edited collection on the subject, noting that, "from a social laboratory designed with the purpose of improvement, the prison has been reborn as a container for human goods now endlessly recycled through what has become a transcarceral system of control." This thinking is echoed by a number of notable authors whose work is featured in the collection (e.g., Loïc Wacquant, Mona Lynch, and John Pratt) and also reflects broader theoretical debates (cf. Bauman 2000; Beiras 2005). The punitive turn is marked by a number of socio-political shifts, including what Wacquant (2005) labels, "the great leap backward" in American political sensibilities – a regression into carceral favouritism after a promising period of decarceration. Wacquant identifies a number of "engines" of this initiative, including, echoing Feeley and Simon (1992), the demise of rehabilitation and the decentring of the correctional professional, the rise of hyper-punitive popular sentiments, and the need to invent new forms of control for the dangerous classes. Bauman (2000) also points to populism in his account of the same phenomenon as well as to a certain tyranny of liberalism, which injects notions of individual freedom and security with practices of fortification. Pratt (2005) locates the new punitiveness in the context of Elias' (1984) notion of civilization, arguing, like Wacquant, that current trends indicate a certain "reversal" into decivilizing practices.

While there is little agreement about how to characterize our current age of punishment, leading penal theorists all appear to agree on one crucial point: rehabilitation is dead, nearly dead, or somehow shunted off to the side within a correctional paradigm that is increasingly interested in efficiency and (now) austerity and punitiveness (Garland 1996, 2001; O'Malley 1999b; Feeley and Simon 1992).

Another body of literature, coming out of American socio-legal realism, offers a totally inverted theory of contemporary justice. Nolan (1998, 2001) argues that we are witnessing the rise of the therapeutic state, as evidenced by the investment of feelings and "the new psychologism" in legal and governing discourses. Families are awarded sizable damages for the distress caused by the loss of a pet, and Bill Clinton gushes about how much he understands the emotions of the American public. In criminal justice, Nolan sees the therapeutic state iterated through the drug treatment courts, a burgeoning movement whose centrifugal nature will eventually revolutionize justice, bringing all legal proceedings squarely into the realm of therapy.

Many jurisdictions (including some in Canada) have born witness to a surge of retributive, hyper-punitive modes of punishment that favour austerity over therapy – trends that are reflected in theorizing the new penology and the punitive turn. There is also, however, compelling evidence indicating that ideas and practices familiar to rehabilitation are by no means extinct. While it is apparent that the medical model of rehabilitation was abandoned as an accepted purpose of imprisonment, "that does not mean that rehabilitation either as a concept or a practice that may benefit individual offenders has been removed from the correctional enterprise" (Ekstedt and Griffiths 1988).[4] The focus on "what works" in offender interventions continues to dominate many practitioner and academic debates in Canada, Britain, and some areas of the United States, giving evidence of the ongoing commitment to the essence of rehabilitation. For the most part, penal theories do not account for this "reaffirmation of rehabilitation" (Andrews and Bonta 1998; Andrews et al. 1990; Cullen and Gilbert 1982; McGuire and Priestley 1985; McGuire 1995), which persists alongside the more punitive tendencies evident in many regimes throughout the late 1980s. The "what-works" movement, or "new rehabilitationism," rejects the nihilistic claim that "nothing works" (Cullen 2005; Hudson 1987); instead, it clings to the idea that treatment programs are effective correctional strategies, which, if used properly, can reduce the likelihood of recidivism and thus contribute to the wider goal of public safety. This new rehabilitationism also resonates with broader trends in governing. Penal theorists who tend to focus on managerialism and risk-based trends have not adequately captured how the institutionalization of "what-works" claims have transformed the contemporary penal landscape.

The tendency of metatheoretical analyses of penal change to focus on the rise and proverbial fall of rehabilitation overlooks more subtle shifts in penal practice. There is now a deeply embedded organizational and professional investment in the claim that lawbreakers can be changed and their behaviour altered to improve their chances of becoming law-abiding citizens. And, perhaps most important, this project remains, at least in Canada, a primary justification of punishment (Ekstedt and Griffiths 1988). At the same time, there is good reason to resist allowing the pendulum to swing in the other direction, suggesting an alternate grand theory of the state as defined through therapy (as does Nolan). The state is both therapeutic and punitive as well as a whole host of other ontologies. This is O'Malley, Valverde, and Rose's (forthcoming) point regarding more general attempts to theorize governance. They reject projects that theorize governance through sweeping periodization, claiming that these initiatives are totalizing and "replete with the overtones of grand theorization that explains the transformation of 'society' into something substantially novel."

A more satisfactory method of theorizing penal trends, then, eschews the epochal project for a more subtle and nuanced approach. For *Criminal Artefacts*, this means moving away from terms like "rehabilitation." When such terms are used to denote specific moments in penality, a false linear temporality is delivered, which suggests that we can draw clear distinctions between one age and another. Anyone who has taught or taken a traditional penology course is familiar with this episodic project. The history of punishment is divided up into specific temporal units that are often demarcated by specific years. Students in penology classes are typically taught that the age of retribution gave way to the age of reform, the age of reform to the age of rehabilitation, the age of rehabilitation to the age of incapacitation, and so on. This way of thinking about punishment gives the impression that, when we mark the end of a particular era, all of its technologies, practices, and rationalities fall out of favour. Following this logic, for example, the end of the reform era would have seen a secularization of punishment and the removal of the brutal sanctioning of prisoners. Anyone who has walked into a prison in Canada knows that brutal punishments are still practised (even if not legally sanctioned) and that prisons are far from secular. Every prison employs a chaplain, has a chapel, and runs many of its programs through the voluntary work of faith-based groups.

Why, then, should we not talk about an "age of rehabilitation," an "era" when rehabilitation was privileged as a justification of punishment? Why use the term "project of change" instead? Doesn't this just overgeneralize historical transitions? The notion of project of change proves satisfactory as an analytic tool because it allows us to see the commonality in *goals* of punishment while appreciating the differences in the *practices* of punishment. Punishment is about many different projects, all of which coexist: the project of change, the project of safety, the project of vengeance. No penal scheme is ever without these projects or their underlying assumptions: that people can be made "uncriminal," that we can protect society through punishing offenders, and that punishment can satisfy a societal bloodlust directed at those who break the law. These assumptions are resolute; however, their implementation within a specific penal scheme varies over time and across jurisdiction. The evangelical reform movement and the rehabilitation movement both took as their basis the same assumptions about the capacity of the prison experience to transform the offender. Of course, the implementation of the project of change in each of these instances differed vastly. The reformers sought to work on the prisoner's soul, advocating prayer, isolation, hard labour, and austerity (Carrigan 1991). The rehabilitationists sought to work on the prisoner's psyche through psychoanalysis, pharmacology, and electroshock therapy (Caron 1978; Ekstedt and Griffith 1988). Thus, while various movements share the assumption that those in conflict with the law can change (or be changed), each movement has a different set of policies and practices.

Thinking about these broader projects, rather than about eras, also makes it possible to extract *Criminal Artefacts* from the implicit normative debates in the existing literature. The claims of the punitive turn are also political claims, meant to reveal rising conservativism, inflated societal intolerance, fear, and a desperate need to mark and act out on the other (Bauman 2000; Garland 2001; Wacquant 2005). If punitiveness is about punishment, cruelty, austerity, and conservativism, and it is also patently distinct from rehabilitation, this would seem to imply that rehabilitative tactics are somehow not punitive, cruel, austere, and conservative. Those critical of rehabilitation would clearly contest such claims (Proctor and Rosen 1994; Kendall 2001). In talking about eras, we obfuscate practices to the point where the "rehabilitative era" can only be marked by attempts to treat – initiatives that are necessarily more liberal and less harsh than are the bids to punish that accompany an era of incapacitation (Moore and Hannah-Moffat 2005). In shedding "eras" in favour of "projects," it is also possible to extract the analysis from these bifurcations and thus to reveal the punitive nature of all sanctioning, including that which claims to be therapeutic.

The obvious criticism of adopting "project of change" over "rehabilitation" is that the term itself is over-broad and fails to capture the specifics of the rehabilitative project. I am not suggesting that terms like "rehabilitation," "reform," and the broader terms used to located these ("neoliberalism," "welfarism") be erased from the lexicon of penal analytics. On the contrary, I think these terms provide useful ways of describing the technologies through which a particular project of change is brought about as well as specific genres of thinking about governing more generally. I don't dispute that there is a set of practices we could name as rehabilitative, or that there is utility in marking a way of arranging knowledge as neoliberal. What I want to caution against is taking up these terms as though they are totalizing markers of a time period – markers whose existence means the absence of others. While practices and rationalities certainly do change over time and across jurisdictions, there are no tidy ways to delineate one genre of changing people from another. Typically, there is a messy constellation of practices and rationalities that may privilege a certain mentality but that still mobilizes assumptions and pursuits from other times and places (O'Malley, Valverde, and Rose, forthcoming). Thus, in contemporary prisons, psychologists, psychotropic drugs, religious programming, and cognitive behavioural therapy are all employed in the same overall project of trying to change a prisoner.

Setting up a framework that allows for distinctions between goals and practices also lends itself to understanding the project of curing the criminal addict. Like the broader project of change, this more specific project endures over time as its practices change. As I note in the introduction, the criminal addict is still a target of considerable interest (and resources) in criminal justice, but the contemporary addict – a neoliberal, responsible, and choice-making subject (O'Malley and Valverde 2004) – is notably different from her pathological, socially troubled, and possibly crazed counterpart from the 1970s. Not only is today's criminal addict thought about differently but she is also the target of dissimilar interventions. The criminal addict of the welfarist period was subject to therapeutic communities, encounter groups, and didactic therapies, whereas the contemporary criminal addict undergoes motivation-based programs and standardized cognitive behavioural therapies.

The Reality Check

Part of the problem with trying to understand changing trends in punishment is methodological. A genealogical analysis is a study that wants to understand the connection between broader governing trends and particular practices and epistemologies of rule (Gordon 1991; O'Malley, Valverde, and Rose forthcoming). I have already spent some time detailing the genealogical project and want here to revisit one of its finer points. In setting out his method, Foucault (1991a) underscores the importance of studying the conduct of conduct – the particular acts of governing in their most everyday, pedestrian sense – because it is in those acts that power is most importantly revealed. The troubled spot in the grander theories of punishment, which take genealogy as their method, is that the actualities on which they are based occur only on a particular level, that of rationality; thus, they pay little attention to the question of practice.

Rose (1999) makes a plea for governmentality research to pay close attention to the minutiae of projects of rule. In *Powers of Freedom*, he articulates his interest in relations of rule at the "molecular level" and lays out his concern with "practices, arenas and spaces where programs for the administration of others intersect with techniques for the administration of ourselves" (5). He evokes Latourian methodology in arguing that we need to understand micro and macro not as inherently different but, rather, as mobilizing different technologies in their relations of power. He argues that, in analyzing any sort of governmental practice, we need to

> pay particular attention to the ways in which, in practice, distinctions and associations are established between practices and apparatuses deemed political and aimed at the management of large-scale characteristics of territories or populations, and micro-technologies for the management of human conduct in specific individuals in particular locales and practices (5).

O'Malley (2001), taking direct aim at Garland's work, echoes this, reminding us that good genealogical research is concerned with the "messy actualities" of everyday life.

It is the lack of attention to these messy actualities that trips up penal theorists. The major problem with grand narrative is that it looks closely at punishment only at the level of mentalities and not in actualized practice. When not enough attention is paid to material realities, the result is a rather lopsided view, in which commentaries on trends in punishment are really only commentaries on trends in governmentalities of punishment (or what Garland would call penalities) and not practices. This is Matthews' (2005) point in his careful and cogent critique of the punitive-turn thesis. Matthews distills the literature on punitive trends down to a set of interesting ideas that use, in his estimation, poor social science to inflate the importance of a rather narrow range of phenomena. The result is what Matthews refers to as a "zero-sum" game of theorizing, in which practices are bifurcated into categories such as "punitive" and "rehabilitative." The messy actualities of penal addiction treatment and the project of change show not only that they both endure as features of contemporary punishment but also that they do so through shifting practices.

The Medical Model and Penal Welfarism

Typically, the post-Second World War period is cast as the halcyon days of welfarist practice, with the techniques of penal intervention having switched from reforming individuals by working on their souls and giving them vocational skills (as at the turn of the twentieth century) to working on their minds and making them normal, productive, moral citizens. According to theorists and historians (Ekstedt and Griffiths 1988; Morris 1995; Sim 1990), the purpose of punishing during this period was to effect real and lasting changes in the individual, taking the sick criminal and transforming him into a well-adjusted, normalized citizen (the prison as social laboratory). In practice, reinvigoration of positivist notions of criminality in the post-Second World War period hastened the widespread adoption of the medical model of punishment. Enrico Ferri (1967, 18), a key figure in the early biological-positivist school of criminology, describes the medical model:

> And as medicine teaches us that to discover the remedies for a disease we must first seek and discover the causes, so criminal science in the new form which it is beginning to assume, seeks the natural causes of the phenomenon of social pathology which we call crime: it thus puts itself in the way to discover effective remedies.

Through the medical model, interventions with lawbreakers evolved, and criminal justice systems became increasingly interested in psychological and psychiatric assessments, interventions with prisoners (and, to a lesser extent, probationers and parolees), and pharmacotherapies and electroshock treatments (Kendall 2000; Sim 1990). Not surprisingly, many of these earliest forms of psychological and psychiatric interventions were retrospectively revealed to be cruel, degrading, and often barbaric. Both Ken Kesey's (1969) *One Flew Over the Cuckoo's Nest* and Anthony Burgess' (1967) *A Clockwork Orange* offer critical, popular social commentary on practices of psychiatric intervention used during the post-Second World War period, and both became iconic critiques of modern psychiatry. There are plenty of examples in penological literature of the abuse of prisoners via psychiatric interventions (Caron 1978; Culhane 1991; Hornblum 1998).

Medicalizing Criminal Justice in Ontario

While there is a dearth of comprehensive chronicles of punishment in both the federal and provincial systems in Canada during this time, the extant accounts indicate that the medical model was desired and adopted in both political and administrative rhetorics. In the 1950s, the commissioner of penitentiaries advocated increased vocational training, education, and therapeutic programming. In his *Annual Report* for 1957, the commissioner (cited in Ekstedt and Griffiths 1988, 52) states:

> The asocial and antisocial type of individuals who are sentenced by the courts to the penal system have failed through unfortunate circumstances and the vicissitudes of their past life to develop mentally as the average person does ... Reformation, which is the ultimate aim of incarceration, stands to succeed best when the deficiencies and needs of the inmate are known.

These sentiments are also present in the *Report of the Fauteaux Committee of Inquiry*, released in 1956. The committee, struck in 1953 to study remission of federal prisoners, strongly recommended the penal system take up a decidedly more change-oriented agenda at both the federal and provincial levels. Fauteaux called for the expansion of probation and parole systems, the establishment of treatment prisons and treatment programs within mainstream prisons, the increased use of minimum security institutions, and the professionalization of staff (Fauteaux 1956). The adoption of the medical model also factored heavily into Fauteaux's report (Hannah-Moffat 2001).

The adoption of the medical model more generally in criminology, and as advocated for in federal commissions, facilitated the establishment of a disease model of drugs and crime (Carstairs 2005). Giffen et al. (1991) document the emergence of this particular type of thinking, whereby drug use (specifically heroin use) is considered a disease that could spread in its own right, along with the criminal behaviour that is its constant companion. Emerging out of these assemblies of the drug/crime nexus are the country's first treatment prisons and in-house treatment programs, which initiated a multi-purpose vision of penal systems. Penal systems could now cure one individual pathology (addiction) and, thus, individual criminality. The criminal addict quickly became one of the central personalities in this project.

Treating Ontario's Addicts

In 1951, the Government of Ontario opened the treatment-oriented Alex G. Brown (AGB) Memorial Clinic in the Mimico Reformatory. Originally mandated to treat alcoholics, AGB expanded in 1956 to treat drug addiction and then again in 1965 to treat paedophilia. The function and design of AGB conformed almost perfectly to the description of penal-welfarist practices set out by Garland (2001). Garland assigns a number of axioms to the welfarist project, reflecting an initiative designed to effect social reform through the appreciation of state responsibility to care for and cure the criminal. In this project, social work and psy expertise are pre-eminent. An early statement of purpose sets out specific goals for those imprisoned there. The clinic aimed to provide prisoners with:

1 opportunities to replace their illegal behaviour with a legally acceptable way of life
2 opportunities for growth towards better psychological and social adaptation
3 assistance towards their integration into the community (Archives of Ontario 1968).

Alongside these prisoner-based goals, the clinic also mandated itself to "accumulate and disseminate knowledge with regard to the identification and treatment of sexual deviation, drug abuse and alcohol abuse" (ibid.). AGB was the Ontario government's only attempt to develop a comprehensive, intensive treatment program, either carceral or community-based, anywhere in the penal system during the post-Second World War period up until the 1970s.[5] AGB did not employ any full-time psychiatrists or psychologists, although it did work in consultation with experts on certain programs.

AGB imagined the criminal addict most clearly as a welfarist penal subject (Garland 2001). In the three- to six-month treatment program, prisoners were immersed in a treatment milieu, where everything they did was meant to facilitate their recovery. The grammar of treatment does not simply address stopping an individual from using drugs but, rather, the much bigger project of teaching her good citizenship (Miller 1993). The starting point for this regime is the assumption that the criminal addict is a sick individual who, in order to be rehabilitated, is in need of total intervention. For example, in the AGB resident information booklet, new residents are encouraged to engage in all aspects of the treatment program (including arts and crafts and "industrial therapy"). Full engagement means following the strict prison schedule, meeting dress codes and codes of cleanliness, and seeking help for feeling "uptight." Residents are told when they might drink coffee or lie on their beds, and they were required to watch films that deal with "people and their feelings" (Archives of Ontario n.d.).

The treatment ethic of AGB reflects the penal welfarist ideal of personal transformation through the application of the medical model (Garland 2001; Hannah-Moffat 2001). The prison's handbook outlines a program of reality orientation that is designed to facilitate rehabilitation and reintegration by fostering close relationships between staff and inmates to the end of creating a community (Archives of Ontario 1968). The handbook counsels prison staff to teach inmates about personal responsibility by confronting them whenever they exhibit problematic behaviour. The therapeutic aspects of the prison are meant to be widely variant and, at least in these earlier stages, not necessarily based on expertise. Thus, individual and group psychotherapy were coupled with a wide range of other therapeutic practices, including didactic therapies oriented around teaching prisoners about sexual hygiene and the proper use of medication; recreational and relationship therapy, meant to initiate prisoners into norms of "non-criminal" leisure time; and interpersonal communications and aversion therapies, meant to provide behavioural disincentives for "inappropriate" responses.

AGB was unique to the penal scheme in Ontario during the 1960s. Outside of AGB, no in-house interventions were offered to either addicts or alcoholics incarcerated in the province's jails and reformatories (McMahon 1992). Probationers and parolees, at that point governed by the Ministry of the Attorney General, did receive addictions-related programming as well as other vocational and psychological interventions. These interventions, along with probation and parole supervision, were regularly provided by not-for-profit organizations (like the John Howard Society) or benevolent religious organizations. Self-help groups like Narcotics Anonymous (newly introduced to Canada) also offered interventions for those with addiction problems. AGB, however, remained the lone treatment institution in the province until the 1970s.

Speaking at the conference entitled Classification and Treatment: New Concepts in Correctional Custody and held at the AGB clinic in 1970, G.R. Thompson, then the minister's chief administrator for female institutions and later provincial deputy minister, states, "we might best meet community needs and those of the offender group through application of a new concept in prison custody."[6] Thompson understands the need for these changes as a response to the calls for increased emphasis on rehabilitation outlined in the Fauteaux report and, later, in the Ouimet report.[7] He, however, challenges the Ontario correctional enterprise to think beyond the sorts of static, traditional forms of rehabilitation relied upon in these reports and mobilized in the past. Instead, Thompson advocates the use of a dynamic model of punishment that is relationship- and community-based.

Thompson was not alone in his sentiments. In the 1960s, members of the Legislative Assembly (MLAs) became concerned with penal issues. Ministerial reports that previously met with little interest began sparking debate within the Legislature. Key to placing correctional issues centrally on the political landscape was the appointment, in 1963, of Alan Grossman as the minister of Correctional Services. Grossman, dubbed the "unlikely Tory" (Oliver 1985), was determined to move the Ministry away from the "bad old days" of punishment in Ontario. He consistently pushed for a therapeutic agenda in Ontario, exercising his decidedly modernist belief in the promise of psy science to cure criminality. To this end, he was pivotal in introducing psy discourses and practices into the day-to-day operations of the Ministry and, in turn, redefining the purposes of punishment in Ontario from punitive incapacitation and deterrence to self-change.

Grossman began to introduce psy-based therapies into the province's correctional centres in the mid-1960s, although, compared to the relatively coherent reform agenda under way in British Columbia, these initiatives were piecemeal and lacked coherence (Oliver 1985). In 1968, Grossman's Ministry introduced the Correctional Services Act. Partly a housekeeping initiative to merge several pieces of legislation, this act also introduced significant legislative changes to correctional methods in the province, creating the legal framework necessary to usher treatment initiatives and other change-oriented enterprises into the daily practices of the province's jails and correctional centres. Reflecting back on the importance of the legislation, one piece of Ministry correspondence states that the new act "reactivated and added dimensions to rehabilitation of the offender programs in Ontario."[8]

While Grossman's revisioning of Ontario's penality embraced an array of treatment modalities and goals, with a considerable emphasis on training and education, treating the criminal addict remained a primary political and practical concern.[9] The question of addiction is almost never mentioned in the Legislature through the 1960s. It does, however, emerge as a legislative topic in 1970, when, in a regular question period, Grossman is encouraged to adopt a methadone maintenance program at Toronto's Don Jail.[10] In his estimates speech later that year, Grossman discloses his plans to build a new treatment prison for drug addicts, a plan that is reasonably well received by other MLAs, many of whom are unsettled by growing unrest in some of the province's worst prisons (most notably the infamous Guelph Reformatory).[11]

Placing these developments in context, Giffen et al. (1991) show that public awareness and concern about the evils of drug use started to rise at the end of the 1960s. Given the time period, this isn't particularly surprising. Giffen et al. describe a rising sense of panic about drugs, illuminating age-old concerns about the pernicious effects of any kind of substance use. It is in response to these growing fears that the federal government assembles the LeDain Commission of Inquiry into the Non-Medical Use of Drugs, the mandate of which was to explore claims about the deleterious effects of illicit substances on health and society (Erickson and Smart 1988). This growing concern is also evident in the archival material. Showing how quickly these anxieties slip into the penal realm, records from a 1970 conference on drug abuse reveal a proposal for an educational program for prisons aimed at reducing drug use. The need here is justified by the claim that at least 40 percent of prisoners are drug addicts (Archives of Ontario 1970a). Probation and parole guidelines from 1972 show similar concerns. In *An Outline for Group Work within the Framework of the Ontario Probation Service*, probation and parole officers are instructed that, "five years ago drug use was about hippies smoking pot ... now the attitude to drugs is total abuse" (Archives of Ontario 1972).

Responding to these concerns as well as a general need to restructure the system, in 1970, Grossman slated AGB for closure; the facility was thought to be too small to accommodate the growing need for treatment spaces within the penal system. The Ontario Correctional Institute (OCI) opened in 1973 to replace AGB and offer the province's first psychological-assessment unit.[12] Inheriting AGB's mandate to treat alcoholics, addicts, and paedophiles, OCI was also slated to become a major research centre for correctional treatment. OCI modelled itself after therapeutic communities like Daytop and Synanon,[13] which had gained popularity in the United States, and had also built on the existing treatment model at AGB. This meant that, despite changing locations, the welfarist mentalities about the criminal addict endured. Group and individual therapy, art and music therapy, as well as vocational and educational programming were all part of the technologies of change initially exercised at OCI. In "encounter sessions" prisoners confronted each other about their addictions and criminal behaviours and took responsibility for their actions. On the ten-year anniversary of OCI, Alf Gregerson, past assistant superintendent, reflected on the decidedly welfarist treatment philosophy popular during that time:

> My idea of treatment is to dig down until you find something good in a person, that I could not find something good in. It is true that in some persons the good you might find will provide only a pitiful small lot to build on, but such is the game we are in. Winston Churchill once said, "there is a seam of good in every man," I believe that to be true.[14]

To a lesser extent, the Vanier Institute for Women, the only prison in the provincial system to incarcerate women exclusively, also followed OCI's treatment mandate. The prison, built adjacent to OCI and sharing staff and resources, housed the women in "family" grouped cottages intended to facilitate their treatment.

Therapeutic treatment milieus developed less intentionally in other prisons in the province. One correctional centre placed a great deal of emphasis on the treatment of alcoholism and later included drug addiction. One of the key psychologists from this centre (also one of the key figures in developing contemporary modes of treatment) explained that, when he was designing the programs there, he felt very strongly that there was no need to see a drug addict as different from an alcoholic, claiming that substance-specific programs are "stupid."[15] He argued that people do not specialize in their drug of choice, that addiction is the problem, not particular substances. This thinking was most unorthodox for the 1960s and 1970s, when the trend was to view alcoholism and drug addiction separately (hence the distinctions made between the two at AGB and, later, at OCI). These same distinctions are made at other treatment prisons across the country (see below) as well as in broader rhetorics about addictions and crime (Simon 1993; White 1998). This person's comments foreshadow coming changes in the system. The move towards thinking about and treating addiction as a general category rather than embracing the divide between alcoholism and drug addiction is a familiar practice of the project of change as it currently exists. The kinds of programming offered at this correctional centre are also indicative of immanent changes. It adopted a significantly different approach to treatment based in the behaviourist school of intervention (see below, section on psychology). The program combined behavioural modification and electroshock therapy. By the late 1970s, the centre offered programming on "Anger Management" and "Lifeskills."[16] Many of the standardized, actuarial assessment tools still in use today were first developed at this correctional centre.

The Bleak 1980s
The 1980s is the period that, for penal theorists, marks the start of shifting mentalities of punishment (Feeley and Simon 1992; Garland 2001; Wacquant 2005). The main contributing factors include the economic recession and the rise of conservative politics. In the United States (and, to a lesser extent, in Canada, see Chapter 3) the war on drugs was declared, an event that continues to have a massive impact on incarceration rates (Mauer 1999). In Ontario, the economic downturn of the 1980s marked a deceleration of the project of change. Even as there is evidence that the province managed to

maintain many of its change-oriented practices during this time, in both the archival materials and the Legislative debates, little attention is paid to therapeutic issues (see also McMahon 1992). This silence suggests the relative flatness of the project of change. Those working in the system at the time paint the decade as one that they all needed to "get through." One key informant, who worked at the executive level in the Department of Corrections before going to work for the Ministry in the late 1980s, offered a shopping list of losses in the treatment movement throughout this time. Program cuts meant that many of the psychologists who had been working for the Ministry left to work in the federal system. The Ministry also adopted a contract model of operations during this time, the effect of which was the contracting out of a wide range of services, including addiction treatment, to private not-for-profit organizations. Much of this contracting out was done in the realm of community corrections, leaving the institutional side with very few resources.

Still, the project of change does not disappear; instead, building on the developments at the Rideau treatment centre, change-oriented practices adopt a new grammar and new strategies. Throughout the 1980s, "new" psychological interventions (Hudson 1987; Kemshall 2003) that focus on criminogenic factors are lauded as the promise of success for the project of change, and there is widespread affirmation that this is a desirable direction for the Ministry. In 1987, for example, Minister of Correctional Services Kenneth Keyes made an impassioned speech to the Legislature, in which he outlined his Ministry's commitment to "developing correctional programs that will motivate offenders toward positive personal change."[17] One year later, David Ramsay, the new minister of Correctional Services, clearly outlined the Ministry's perspective on changing lawbreakers, highlighting the move towards more specific, directed programming:

> the Ministry's corporate plan recognizes that positive rehabilitative intervention is both feasible and desirable for a great many offenders and most particularly for those with psychiatric and psychological problems, substance addictions, educational deficiencies, underdeveloped social skills and life skills and lack of work experience.[18]

Comments by MPP Sam Cureatz exemplify the acceptance and desirability of the Ministry's project of change during this period. The Conservative critic comments:

> The Ontario government has, to its credit, maintained some belief in the rehabilitation approach when other jurisdictions have abandoned it. The rehabilitation model certainly presents many dangers which must be watched very carefully but there is research now, some of which has been

conducted by the staff within the provincial government, which has identified certain types of programs which appear to actually reduce recidivism.[19]

This new strategy differs from the technologies of change deployed in the 1970s in that it rejects the notion that offenders ought to be cared for holistically and understood through their criminal pathologies. Rather, the emergent initiative wants only to address those pieces of the criminal that are empirically proven to be directly linked to crime (Hannah-Moffat 2001). Such targeting streamlines the criminal justice project, maximizing its effectiveness while minimizing its cost. Contrary to claims about the rise of managerialism and its concomitant disavowal of attempting to rid societies of crime (Garland 2001; Feeley and Simon 1992), this approach continues to maintain that crime can be eradicated through therapeutic measures. The difference now is that these measures are finely tuned to ensure precision. While these initiatives start to take hold through the 1980s, it is in the 1990s that they exert a firm grip on the system.

The 1990s: The Return of the Project of Change
The 1990s saw two major changes in the Ontario government. In 1990, the New Democratic Party (NDP) was elected under Bob Rae. Rae's "third way" (Giddens 2000), quasi-left government overhauled most of the social systems in Ontario, introducing many of the cuts to social programming that came to characterize the decade. In 1995, the Conservative government came to power under Mike Harris, who ushered in drastic changes. Harris introduced considerable spending cuts as well as neoconservative social policies like "workfare" and the Safe Streets Act,[20] all targeting marginalized populations.

During its four-year tenure as the party in power, the NDP government effected very few alterations in the practice of punishment in Ontario. From 1990 to 1995, penal issues were virtually never addressed in the Legislature. Those changes introduced did not appear to affect the ways in which punishment was actually carried out in the province. The Ministry of Correctional Services was absorbed into the larger Ministry of the Solicitor General, accounting, at least to some degree, for the decentring of penal issues in favour of policing and drug policy, which were foregrounded in political rhetoric. A past regional director with the Ministry, reflecting back on the "Rae Days," sees the only major changes as labour related. This person argues that the guard's union (Ontario Public Sector Employees Union [OPSEU]) had a great deal of influence within the largely labour-supported NDP government. OPSEU was integral, according to this individual, in the Ministry's adoption of an affirmative-action hiring policy, increased staff training, and other labour-related issues. Another key informant echoes this individual's views of the Rae government's impact on the penal system: "They came in with no policies and they left with no policies." According to this person, the government only paid attention to the correctional system when OPSEU was "causing problems."

Shortly after coming to power in 1995, the Harris government introduced its plan for correctional restructuring. The agenda consisted of a complete overhaul of every aspect of the system under a mantra of "get-tough efficiency" (Moore and Hannah-Moffat 2002). The orientation adopted by the Conservative government reflected penal trends in other jurisdictions at that time. Harris and his first minister of Correctional Services, Bob Runciman, ushered in a new age of punishment that O'Malley (1999a) accurately describes as "volatile and contradictory." Private prisons; the elimination of parole; the creation of austerity in the prisons; the concomitant rise of "megajails"; the loss of programming in detention centres; and the increased use of incarceration, conditional sentences, public shaming, and work crews are all characteristics of the new face of punishment in Ontario.[21]

While these measures moved Ontario into a far more conservative space, they did not signal the end of a commitment to the project of change. On the contrary, part of the government's mandate in correctional renewal was to develop "effective" correctional treatment programs that were economical and empirically proven (Moore and Hannah-Moffat 2002). While the government planned the closure of the treatment prisons and the loss of half-way houses and other community-based services, it also opened a research branch dedicated to the development of correctional programming. The plan for "correctional renewal" forwarded by the Harris government also included an explicit mandate to develop "effective" and evidence-based correctional programs.

In debating Bill 144, legislation intended to increase "accountability" by forcing prisoners to undergo drug tests, then minister Rob Sampson initially took a hard line, explaining that the purpose of the legislation was to

> combat the scourge of drugs that plagues our institutions and our communities ... This Bill will establish a program of random and regular drug testing for offenders. If an offender fails to demonstrate that he or she is drug free, then the response will be swift and sure. That offender would find himself losing his earned remission or he would be back in jail if he was serving his sentence in the community.[22]

Later, in response to a question regarding the need for treatment programs to combat drug use, Sampson tempered his stand:

> Mr. Speaker, you know yourself, as everyone does here, you have to get to the root cause, the psychological disorder in their life, the lack of economic

resources, the lack of training. We're saying here we provide those resources in our institutions and we would like the people to take advantage of them. I want to repeat that the fundamental thing in Bill 144 is they shouldn't be on drugs. It's very difficult to learn when you're on drugs. You've seen the commercial, "your brain's fried on drugs." I agree with that.

This legislation was adopted in 2000. In 2006, backing away from Sampson's original hard line, the Ministry, now under a Liberal government, promoted this legislation as offering assurance that prisoners would actually participate in the now considerable range of treatment programs available in the province's prisons.[23] On this website, the Ministry lists fifteen different prison-based treatment programs, including anger management, parenting skills, vocational and education training, and, of course, substance abuse. It is worth cautioning that the extent to which these programs are actually operating in the province's institutions is unclear. For example, when I was conducting this research in 2002, only one prison was offering a correctional program (for substance abuse). When I checked back with the province in 2005, Ministry officials could not give me a definitive answer on the number or type of programs operating and advised me to direct my inquiries to individual institutions, which, in turn, directed me back to the Ministry website.

In September of 2000, the Ministry adopted a new service delivery model for probation and parole. The model is also reflective of the Ministry's continued emphasis on transformative programming. The introduction to the model states:

> The model incorporates core rehabilitative programs. These programs are designed to address the criminogenic factors that have been empirically determined to be most common within the offender population. They include, but are not limited to, anger management, substance abuse and criminal thinking. Offenders with needs in non-criminogenic areas such as housing, finances or emotional problems with no clear criminogenic potential will generally be referred to their agencies or clinicians in the community.

Again, while the language here concerning the ways in which lawbreakers are meant to change and the factors around which a change-based initiative should be organized has been modified, the Ministry is still manifestly maintaining its commitment to the project of changing those facing criminal sanction. Of the core programs offered by the Ministry, substance abuse is the most readily available. The Ministry developed its own intervention program for drug use in 2000 (see Chapter 5).

The addict who emerges as a target of this programming is a very different person from the one treated at AGB and OCI. The program, called Change Is a Choice, imagines the addict as a rational subject whose "substance misuse" is born of troubled thinking patterns rather than a deep pathology (Hannah-Moffat 2001; Kemshall 2003). This criminal addict can *choose* to change. This criminal addict is also not a whole person; rather, he is fractured by actuarial assessments that reduce him to a set of criminogenic factors, which includes his addiction. It follows that this person needs interventions not to make him a better person but only to address that in him which is defined as criminogenic. Thus, this type of programming meets not only the goal of effecting change in the individual but also the goal of shaping correctional practices to meet the mantra of efficiency and effectiveness.

Contrary to the claims made by Bauman (2000), Feeley and Simon (1992), Garland (2001), and Wacquant (2005), professionals continue to have a central and generative role in penal schemes. The ability of the general project of change, along with the specific project of curing the criminal addict, to endure through political changes comes largely out of the work of a core group of psychologists at Rideau who introduced cognitive behavioural therapy (CBT) into the system. The practices of CBT blend seamlessly with the emerging political climate. The new nature of the criminal addict as a rational subject readily fits into this modality, making the addict a handy target for these interventions.

CBT and the Politics of Therapy
Almost all the historical actors whom we interviewed described the penal system in Ontario, up until the 1990s, as disparate and heterogeneous. The province continued to be divided into geographic regions, each headed by a regional director. Up until 1996, when the Harris government introduced its correctional renewal plan, the regional directors had a great deal of leeway with regard to interpreting legislation and issuing policy directives (McMahon 1992). The shape of programming and therapeutic initiatives was left to the discretion of these regional directors, who often relied heavily on the direction of the professionals around them.

Thus, the treatment programs offered in the southern Ontario region (including the Greater Toronto Area) focused on classic psychiatric interventions. The western and northern regions offered little in terms of programming, suffering from the eternal predicament of Canadian rural and remote areas – lack of access to adequate resources.

The Ottawa region was particularly active, especially in the late 1970s and early 1980s, in developing programming and therapeutic initiatives. One individual described the "fair bit of freedom" they had throughout their tenure as correctional psychologists, which gave them the ability to develop a singular identity for the Ottawa region. This person made a conscious decision to adopt a change-oriented programming model and relied on a core group of supportive staff to develop the vision for the penal system in their realm. She attributes much of the success of the programming model adopted in the Ottawa region to the work and "charisma" of one particular psychologist.

One of the first full-time psychologists hired by the Ministry brought early forms of CBT into the Ottawa region. Through treatment programs for alcoholism and then drug addiction, as well as anger management interventions, she initiated what was to become the core of penal programming across the country.[24] The support of one particular individual not only allowed for direct funding of the psychologist's programs but also enabled her to hire other, like-minded practitioners, all of whom became widely known correctional psychologists. Together, they were central in solidifying the role of CBT in the change project.

Of course, none of this would have been possible without the availability of the CBT paradigm. CBT is rooted in many psychological and psychiatric traditions, including the structuralist and cognition-based Adlerian and Freudian schools and Skinner's behaviourism. It was shaped in the 1970s, primarily by Aaron Beck,[25] who first used it to address depression. CBT quickly became the therapy of choice for dealing with everything from anxiety to body-image issues to schizophrenia (cf. Dobson 2001). In clinical initiatives, the draw of CBT is that it can be designed to meet very specific needs, targeting identified problematic behaviours instead of having to engage in more holistic, long-term interventions (like those offered in Ontario in the 1970s). CBT focuses on cognition and begins with the assumption that a problematic behaviour (violent outbursts, depression, drug use) is directly linked to errors and distortions in thinking. The therapeutic process is designed to give the client tools through which she can correct her flawed thought processes. Often, therapy sessions with a psychologist are combined with "homework" so that the client can practise her new thought skills. In Beck's (Beck and Rush 1989, 1541) words:

> The techniques [of CBT] are designed to help the patient to identify, to test the reality of, and to correct distorted conceptualizations and dysfunctional beliefs underlying these cognitions. By thinking and acting more realistically and adaptively with regard to here-and-now psychological situations and problems, the patient is expected to experience improvement in symptoms and behaviour.

CBT, as a means of conducting all manner of therapeutic interventions, is set up as a progression from the widespread popularity of psychoanalysis in the 1950s and 1960s. When CBT arose in the 1970s, it promised scientifically provable interventions that were rooted in observable behaviours rather than in what the early CBT champions dismissed as somatic and psychic vagaries (Hoffman 1984). CBT is further distanced from psychoanalysis in that it destabilizes the notions of client centredness and client direction. Where the psychoanalytic paradigm relied heavily on the client to direct the discussion and to raise pertinent issues, CBT centres on the therapist. The therapist has more agency to set the therapeutic agenda and to decide which of the client's thoughts are appropriate and which are indicative of distorted thinking.

There is no evidence to suggest that CBT itself developed as a primarily economic or political initiative. The writings of each of the "fathers" of CBT – Beck (cf. 1970), Ellis (cf. 1962), and Frankl (cf. 1973) – all display an earnest desire to improve the range of therapeutic initiatives available to individuals suffering from specific psychological "disorders." This therapeutic spirit carries through to contemporary uses of CBT; however, it would be naive to assume, particularly in the case of the CJS, that CBT gained popularity in a political and economic vacuum. Rather, CBT's emergence coincided with significant political and economic changes. These changes arguably influenced the use of CBT interventions in the penal system and helped shape the nature and technologies of CBT as practised in the early twenty-first century.

In the face of a nation-wide recession, CBT developed through the 1980s and 1990s and emerged as an avenue for intervention under a rubric of efficiency and effectiveness. The CBT model is held up as offering short-term but effective care. When compared with more traditional interventions, such as psychoanalysis, CBT is said to show marked results in individuals within months as opposed to years. CBT was born out of a strong positivist and empiricist tradition, and it offers an air of scientific provability that is rarely present in therapeutic initiatives.

CBT's appeal also held for the penal system. While the early 1970s celebrated and generously funded therapeutic initiatives in the penal system, those involved in the system in Ontario, particularly from a policy and programming standpoint, feared the onset of spending cuts. In the words of a past president of John Howard Ontario, spending cuts inevitably mean cuts to therapeutic programs:

> There's the big C, small T equation. When the economy is good then there's lots of money for treatment, but programs are the first things to go when the economy starts to take a nose dive. What you get instead is the big C – corrections. And it becomes law and order, security, not treatment. And so when the recession hit in the 1980s we all knew what was coming.

While the recession of the 1980s did not usher in a new mentality epitomized by "get-tough" punishment in Ontario (that came a decade later), all services in the province certainly underwent significant spending cuts. During this time, the fee-for-service contracts were eliminated, as were many "questionable" interventions like art therapy and yoga. Still, largely due to the continued commitment of the deputy ministers and their advisors, change initiatives managed to maintain a central role in the practice of punishment in Ontario. However, the Ministry felt increasing pressure to provide accountability and efficiency in the system.

One individual made the link between economics and the rise of CBT quite apparent. In reflecting on policies initiated during the late 1970s in the Ministry, this person noted the rise of CBT and attributed its introduction into the penal system to two of the psychologists originally stationed at Rideau.[26] When asked why it was that the Ministry was keen on CBT, she replied: "Underlying all this is the recession, so we were looking for programs that could be run by volunteers and it seemed this one [CBT programs] could be." On the heels of the cost-cutting campaign introduced by the Ministry (as part of a wider government initiative) in 1980, the face of intervention began to change considerably.

In studying political rhetoric and policy documents, one sees a marked shift in language from the 1970s to the 1980s. "Treatment" becomes "education," and "therapy" is traded for "programming." This shift in penal argot signals a significant modification in the technologies of the project of change (Hannah-Moffat 2000; Moore and Hannah-Moffat 2005). Therapy and treatment are part of the "old" lexicon of immersion therapy, encounter groups, and therapeutic communities. The "new" jargon of education and programming reflects the move towards CBT-based initiatives, which de-emphasize the emotional in favour of the rational. Penal interventions intended to bring about change in the individual are no longer "touchy-feely"; instead, they are detached, clinical, and hyper-rational. State agents retain their roles as caregivers who want to make people better, but the nature and essence of that care changes considerably.

The empirical provability of CBT programming was the central justification for the continued orientation towards a project of change. During one debate, the Conservative corrections critic questioned Keyes about using "cost-saving short cuts" in lieu of the more "costly and drawn-out" system. Keyes responded by saying that the Ministry was maintaining its emphasis on change-based initiatives but was in the process of adopting new models of intervention that had been proven, through psychological research, to be effective.[27] One year later, the new minister, Ramsay, reiterated Keyes' point, citing the "growing body of professional opinion supporting the rehabilitative potential of ... programs" as one of the key justifications for continuing on with the project of change.[28] Ramsay went on to explain that

> the Ministry's corporate plan recognizes that positive rehabilitative inter-
> vention is both feasible and desirable for a great many offenders and most
> particularly for those with psychiatric and psychological problems, substance
> addictions, educational deficiencies, underdeveloped social and life skills
> and lack of work experience.

In the face of funding cuts in the 1980s, many celebrated psychologists left the Ministry. Some went to work with federal corrections while others took academic postings, continuing on with the Ministry as consultants. While the exodus of these psychologists slowed the progress of CBT programming within the Ministry, it by no means put a stop to the initiatives.

The absorption of CBT into the rhetoric of punishment is nowhere more apparent than in *The Psychology of Criminal Conduct*, written by Don Andrews and James Bonta, both of whom came from the Ottawa network of correctional psychologists. This book, published in 1994, is representative of a growing body of research by this network of Ottawa-based psychologists. All of these individuals challenged the "nothing-works" debates, and they have been writing for almost thirty years on the viability of empirically proven correctional treatment (c.f. Gendreau and Ross 1978, 1980). Andrews and Bonta (1998, 2) define the psychology of criminal conduct (PCC) as an orientation to correctional psychology that is rooted in "rational empiricism" and borrows from a wide variety of psychological, psychiatric, and sociological traditions in order to "strategize an efficient, effective and ethical approach to lawbreaker interventions." While Andrews and Bonta claim that their approach is multidisciplinary, they intentionally draw on a limited body of knowledge and explicitly reject critical criminological and sociological analyses of criminal activity.[29] The PCC acknowledges social factors such as socio-economic status, gender, and race only in so far as they contribute to individual pathology and account for variance between individuals. In other words, social, political, economic, and cultural factors are only implicated in criminal activity as ancillary factors that might amplify an already flawed psychological makeup. Poverty, racism, marginalization, and the like cannot, under this model, be understood as direct, etiological links to criminal behaviour. Social factors, under the PCC rubric, while implicated in criminal activity, are neither problematized nor targeted as locations for changing offenders or reducing criminal activity; instead, what lies at the root of the problem is individual cognition and behaviour.[30]

The effect here is to create what Latour (1987) would call a black box around the etiology of crime and its solutions. Black boxing erases processes of production so that a certain practice appears to exist a priori, becoming a natural fact free of contingencies. The black box moves an object or practice from its position as "a carefully elaborated, innovative network whose components had to be explained and justified by the inventor" to the status of "taken for granted tool" (Valverde, Levi, and Moore 2005). PCC, in this sense, develops its own inevitability, becoming the only possible, progressive response to crime, existing as a truth rather than as a product of the kinds of contingent assemblies I describe here.

The work of the core Ottawa group of psychologists is widely published and has been taken up by penal jurisdictions through the Western world. Ontario is the Canadian jurisdiction that has most readily adopted this orientation. When the Harris government came to power in 1996, it introduced, under Bob Runciman, a mantra of "safety, security, efficiency and effectiveness." Runciman's foremost challenge was to strike a balance between the "get-tough" approach championed by conservatives and the therapeutic, change-based approach already established in the penal system (Moore and Hannah-Moffat 2002). The programming offered in the provincial system could not appear to be coddling prisoners in any way. The need to achieve this balance is reflected in comments made in the debates by John O'Toole, a Conservative MPP. In discussing the restructuring under way within the Ministry, O'Toole commented:

> Inmates not only have to behave themselves when in jail but they should also have to actively participate in programs – now this is good – which address their criminal attitudes and behaviour. I'm all for this, the psychological warfare issue here, that they should have to participate in programs like corrective behaviour, positive attitude, all this stuff.[31]

This "psychological warfare" is now uniformly carried out in both carceral and community settings. Anger management, substance abuse, anti-criminal thinking, sex offender, and spousal abuse programs, each similar to its corresponding federal cousin, are now all offered to those under provincial sanction. In keeping with the need to maintain efficiency in the system, however, these programs are not unilaterally offered to all sentenced people; rather, those mandated to supervision (either community or custodial) undergo an actuarial risk-assessment process intended to reveal their level of need with regard to programming. Only those individuals deemed at a high risk to re-offend and in high need of interventions are offered programming. These programs are intended to meet their targeted needs (Hannah-Moffat 1999; Kemshall 2003). Thus, if a risk assessment concludes that an individual has a high level of risk and a substance-abuse or anger management problem, he will be mandated either by his probation or correctional officer to enrol in programming specifically designed to address those issues.

A Ministry program designer explained the allure of this model in economic terms:

> The thing about this programming is it is evidence-based. It's coming right out of all that good research done by people like Gendreau, Andrews and Motiuk, and it appeals to those of us coming from a psych background. It helps to justify the way we spend money. In this Ministry you have to have a rationale for everything you do and having that scientific evidence behind us, that's a good justification for these programs.

To this individual, the use of CBT programming was the way to "take a political agenda and have it make good correctional sense." She went on to explain that many civil servants within the Ministry, especially those like herself, who made their careers with the Ministry, never gave up on the notion of change. Instead, they spent their energies constantly trying to adapt what they were doing to the political climate of the day, holding firm to their common belief that, despite what Martinson claimed, some interventions do work and some people can be changed. One of the criminogenic factors consistently cited by this individual and others as a viable target for intervention is substance abuse. The importance of intervening with substance use rests on the notion that drugs and crime occupy a close-knit nexus.

Targeting the Addict

Addiction is one of the core criminogenic factors targeted under CBT. In the growing body of research on treatment initiatives, substance abuse is always identified as a core criminogenic factor and as a salient explanation for criminal activity (Gendreau and Goggin 1996; McGuire 1995). Treatment for drug addiction is a useful entry point for penal authorities to push change-based initiatives. Out of all of the "need" areas identified by Andrews and Bonta, drug use is easiest to measure in terms of efficiency and effectiveness of interventions. For example, degrees of anger are not easily gauged. If a person has six angry outbursts a week before he receives programming but only four afterwards, is that success? What constitutes an angry outburst? Similar questions can be raised about education and employment. Is a high school diploma a measure of success even if the person does not get a job afterwards? Is a minimum-wage job a success even if it entrenches the individual as one of the working poor? Substance use, on the other hand, is much more scientifically accessible. A simple drug test proves whether or not and which substances a person has been using. Because the question of whether or not a person has been using is so easily answered, it is quite easy to prove effectiveness: a decrease or cessation of use indicates the program is working.

Substance use is also appealing because it can be read as a behaviour that is independent of outside factors. An individual may lack opportunities to obtain an education, may have a troubled or traumatic family life or poor social skills. In each of these cases, it is difficult to attribute the criminogenic factor directly to the individual; rather, these factors are best understood as arising out of a blend of social, environmental, and individual considerations. Substance use, on the other hand, can be understood as an exclusively individual behaviour that only arises out of its immediate context. In keeping with the wish of Andrews and Bonta to extract social factors from the enterprise of explaining criminal behaviour, this logic lends itself directly to a neoliberal agenda that sees individual responsibility as paramount and social responsibility as subordinate or non-existent. Penal systems maintain their commitments to the project of change, although the technologies have altered. Emerging as important factors in contemporary practices of change is the use of targeted, neoliberal therapies like CBT and the focus on drug use as a core criminogenic factor. The addict is an addict because she chose to use drugs, not because she was sexually abused as a child, grew up poor, or has a learning disability. Her choice to become an addict is also, based on the assumptions of the drug/crime nexus, a choice to become a criminal. Responding to criminality, then, is a matter of teaching this person how to choose differently.

The linguistic shift here is important. The argot of the 1970s, including words like "addiction" and "drugs" is erased from the discourse. In its place are much more vague and general words like "substance" and "misuse." The purpose here is to erase the distinctions between alcoholism and drug addiction as well as to remove the moralizing sentiments embedded in words like "addict." Part of the shift to managerial criminology more generally is meant to reflect a demoralization of penal therapeutic interventions. Treatment programs are no longer meant to be normalizing, as they were in the 1970s; instead, these new initiatives are designed to take on an air of non-judgment. The idea here (developed in Chapter 5) is to responsibilize the criminal subject and so enable her to reach her own conclusions about her addictive status. Disavowing the totalizing interventions found in places like OCI, under this rubric, vague and open language is meant to be used to facilitate a process of self-discovery.

At the same time, one of the hallmarks of efficiency is the ability to reach as many people as possible with the same, standard strategy. This standardization is familiar in managerial penal strategies (Hannah-Moffat 2001; Moore and Hannah-Moffat 2002). The term "substance misuse" is vague enough to achieve the neoliberal goals of appearing non-judgmental while also locking in the ability to marshal anyone at all into the program. A substance misuser could be anyone, whereas a drug addict is someone quite specific.

The longevity of the project of change is attributable to the work of mid-level bureaucrats as well as innovative psychologists like Paul Gendreau and Don Andrews. In this sense, the cure of the criminal addict is the product of the vision of a small group of people who were able to mobilize the practices of CBT so that, recalling a key informant's comments, political agendas could make good correctional sense. Viewed this way, current practices of intervening with the drug addict are as much about political manoeuvrings designed to maintain particular visions and goals in the face of changing political sentiments as they are about best practices or particular innovations in effective treatment. CBT has been adopted because it conforms with prevailing neoliberal mentalities.

Current Context

In Ontario, very little has changed over the last few years with regard to punishment. Harris stepped down in 2002 and was replaced by Ernie Eves, who, throughout his short term as premier, maintained the trajectory established by Harris. In 2003, the Conservatives were replaced by a Liberal government headed by Dalton McGuinty. Aside from changing the name of the Ministry yet again (it is now known as the Ministry of Community Safety and Correctional Services), the McGuinty government maintains much the same plan as was set out by the Harris government. Treatment programs are being extended into the realm of youth in custody as a result of the newly implemented Youth Criminal Justice Act, and the Ministry continues to expand its adult treatment programs across the province. (The probation and parole program targeting addictions is discussed in Chapter 5.)

Broader Context

Thus far, I have focused on Ontario as the jurisdictional loci in which penal welfarism has endured and indeed flourished under changing political circumstances. My point is that the practice of changing people – a practice that typically characterizes welfarism – has endured over the last fifty years even as its languages and technologies have changed. The criminal addict surfaces as one of the main targets of intervention throughout this period, first as the pathological welfare subject and then as the rational, choice-making, neoliberal subject. The endurance of the project of change is not unique to Ontario. A cursory glance at penal jurisdictions elsewhere in Canada and across the Western world suggests that this phenomenon is not unusual.

The overlaps between Ontario and the Canadian federal penal system are apparent in the above analysis. These overlaps are also apparent when we consider the history of treatment within Correctional Services Canada.

Shaping their own response to the Fauteaux Commission, CSC opened the medium-security Matsqui prison just outside of Vancouver exclusively for the treatment of addicts. The program at Matsqui was famously chastised by the LeDain Commission for succeeding only in producing "well educated, well adjusted dope fiends" (Murphy, cited in LeDain 1972, 12). More recently, CSC has been very active in developing and implementing penal substance abuse treatment programs. Despite the implicit rivalry between them,[32] CSC and the Ontario Ministry share much the same orientation towards the project of change and currently deploy many of the same technologies and discourses in their bid to effect change in prisoners. In the early 1990s, CSC underwent its own process of renewal: the organization, on the vision of the (then) new commissioner, Ole Ingstrup, fully embraced a therapeutic and change-oriented position regarding punishment. In *Our Story*, CSC's own reflection on its "rebirth," Vantour (1991, 7) describes the purpose of federal punishment in Canada:

> We have part of the responsibility to deal with one of society's most fundamental values – its collective security. But we must do much more. Corrections is not just confinement – keeping people in cells until they have reached the end of their sentences. We must also deal with the freedom of individual members of our society, including the offenders under our jurisdiction. As the name of the organization implies, we are an agency devoted to bringing about a change for the better in those legally committed to our care so that they may eventually return to their communities as law-abiding citizens.

In practice, these changes meant the adoption of the same standardized, "core" programs across the country (Hannah-Moffat 2000). Living skills, substance abuse, and anti-violence are all mainstays of penal treatment initiatives. The substance abuse program sees the most activity as CSC suggests that close to 80 percent of its prisoners have addiction problems.[33] CSC's commitment to the project of change also boasts an extensive research branch intended to broaden criminological knowledge, primarily with regard to the psychology of the prisoners themselves, in order to further the "best practices" agenda of offering the most "effective" and empirically proven penal programming (see Comack 2000; Hannah-Moffat 2000; Kendall 2000).

The similarities between punishment in Ontario and punishment in the federal system may also be found in the penal system of British Columbia. Much of this history is chronicled by Doherty and Ekstedt (1991). British Columbia had a comprehensive plan for penal reform earlier than did Ontario and was quick to create treatment initiatives aimed at drug addiction.

In the early 1950s, British Columbia established a heroin addiction treatment wing in Burnaby's Oakalla Prison Farm. This initiative expanded in the 1960s to a series of organized "narcotics research units" for both male and female prisoners. Treatment in these centres followed the same kind of therapeutic community treatment modality, targeting the same kind of criminal addict, found at AGB and OCI. The notable difference between the two institutions comes from the populations they serve.

The City of Vancouver has a unique history which I explore more carefully in Chapter 4. Here, I want only to note that, through another constellation of influences, Vancouver's Downtown Eastside has suffered almost a century of being arguably the most concentrated drug-using centre in Canada. The Hastings and Main corridor is the birthplace of Canada's drug laws and continues to be the nation's poster neighbourhood for the ravages of addiction. It is to the perennially troubled Hastings and Main corridor that Labour Minister William Lyon MacKenzie King is called in 1907 to investigate damage to an opium den caused in the race and labour riots (Carstairs 2005; Giffen et al. 1991). Following further investigation, King is persuaded by local church groups and non- (or anti-) Chinese business owners and community leaders of the necessity of opium prohibition, an argument he lays out in his report on the riots, which he presented to Parliament. King submitted a second report in 1908 entitled *The Need for the Suppression of the Opium Traffic in Canada*. Three weeks after this report was tendered to Parliament, Canada had its first anti-drug law, the Opium Act.[34] Of course, this piece of legislation and its descendants do little to solve the growing and increasingly visible levels of drug use in the area. In keeping with global trends in drug control, the events that precipitated Canada's first drug laws as well as the consequent century of drug law enforcement are all now generally understood to be heavily informed by racist agendas. The first drug laws clearly targeted the Chinese on the west coast. Black and Aboriginal populations quickly also became the prey of anti-drug legislation.

Giffen, Endicott, and Lambert (1991) note the emergence of a "drug scare" in Vancouver in 1951, where the xenophobic and youth-saving concerns that fuelled the inauguration of Canada's drug laws resurfaced in the face of widespread worry that Vancouver was facing an epidemic of addiction. The public, in a now familiar trope of drug regulation (see Moore and Haggerty 2001), acted out fears that white, middle-class youth would fall prey to the heavy-handed law enforcement by calling for an increase in treatment options for addicts in conflict with the law. The addiction treatment programs offered at Oakalla represent some of the earliest extensions of treatment into criminal justice. The perceived severity of the drug problem in Vancouver, the ensuing pressure placed on governments to respond with a more curative approach, and the fact that Oakalla already had segregated addicts made it the ideal location at which to usher a therapeutic ethos into the penal system.

Facing the same socio-economic concerns as Ontario (and the rest of the country), British Columbia continued to offer behavioural programming in its prisons throughout the 1980s, even as social programs were drastically cut elsewhere in the province. Doherty and Ekstedt (1991) note lifeskills programs, psychological assessments and interventions, and specific programs for young offenders alongside a victim's rights discourse and the implementation of reparative initiatives such as community service orders. As in Ontario, it is clear that the project of change endured throughout the 1980s as BC penal institutions continued to make concerted efforts to improve the people in their custody.

The one notable difference between the trajectories followed by British Columbia and Ontario is the former's brief attempt to instil a regime of forced treatment. In 1978, British Columbia introduced the controversial and short-lived Heroin Treatment Act. The legislation, crafted as a response to the enduring problem of addiction in the province, allowed for the forced carceral treatment of heroin addicts. One heroin user described the "intake" method followed by police under the new legislation:

I was standing at a bus stop on Granville St. waiting for a bus to take me home to Kitsilano when a marked police car stopped in front of me. The police officers approached me and started looking me up and down. One of the officers asked what I was doing, I told them I was waiting for the bus to go home. They wanted to know where I had been and what I was doing downtown, if I had any drugs on my person and what I was going to be doing in Kitsilano when I got there.

After answering all their questions and after being searched by them, I was asked to roll up my sleeves. When they saw some fairly fresh needle marks on my arms, they informed me that under the new Compulsory Treatment Act, I was being placed on the Compulsory Treatment Program.

I was given a document informing me to report by a specified date to be processed by an alcohol and drug counsellor and a judge under the auspices of the B.C. Government. I would be taken into custody and transported to Brandon Lake to start my incarceration. Brandon Lake was nothing more than a jail for drug users who couldn't be arrested and put in a provincial or federal prison. Essentially a jail for the innocent.[35]

This man's belief that forced carceral treatment constitutes "jail for the innocent" was regularly brought to the attention of the government in the few months that compulsory treatment was in force. The act itself was struck down in less than a year by the BC Supreme Court, which found that it contravened civil rights.

Punishment in British Columbia today looks very similar to punishment in Ontario. The province has also adopted targeted criminogenic programming and offers substance abuse, violence prevention, and "respectful relationships" programs[36] as standard fare to prisoners and those serving community sentences.

Drug treatment courts (DTCs), which I describe in much greater detail in the following chapters, are also examples of the enduring commitment to the project of change. The courts currently in operation direct a good deal of state resources and energies in attempts to cure selected criminal addicts.[37]

Treatment prisons are still features of punishment in the United States (Coldren 2004). The US Federal Bureau of Prisons offers a long list of change-oriented programs for inmates, which includes substance abuse, parenting, vocational and educational training, mental health programming, and physical education.[38] Many of the state prison systems also continue to offer change programs to prisoners. In California, the governing authority is the Department of Corrections and Rehabilitation. California has an extensive substance-abuse treatment program as well as a number of pilot initiatives, including mother-child programs and vocational training.[39] Prisoners in New York State are also subject to substance-use interventions as well as to psychological programming to assist in arresting their criminal behaviours.[40]

Conclusion

Genealogy is a tool of disruption that unsettles assumptions of linear progression through time, where one thing naturally and inevitably follows from and to another. My analysis shows that the fixing of the criminal addict comes out of a particular political/epistemological moment, a time in which the co-emergence of welfarism and the medical model, alongside calls to humanize the prison system and in the face of growing concern about a "drug problem," created the perfect conditions in which to produce a criminal addict who can then be cured. When these conditions change, when social workers no longer play a central role in corrections, when the system is decimated by funding cuts and re-emerges as a sleeker, cheaper version of its old self, the criminal addict does not go away. She simply re-emerges as a substance misuser whose pathologies are replaced by errors of thought. She is able to emerge partly because of the endurance of concerns over the drug/crime nexus (see Chapter 3) and partly because the practices of cognitive behaviouralism are close cousins to the expectations of neoliberalism. Both are interested in working on the responsible, neoliberal subject.

There are no prisons left in Ontario that offer yoga and encounter groups as therapeutic practices, just as few institutions continue to run on the kind of strict disciplinary schedules found in the old treatment prisons. This does not mean, though, that the overall project of changing people went down with the ship, and it certainly does not support the punitive-turn thesis. The goal of changing people remains. The programs offered in the Ontario penal system today are just as change-oriented as they were in the past. What is different is the kinds of people meant to be changed (the rational rather than the pathological) and the practices used (targeted interventions rather than holistic care).

It is interesting to consider how various factors allow for this continuation. In theorizing the punitive turn, scholars point to a number of different variables that affect penal practice. The demise of the Keynesian state is a popular argument, taken up by Feeley and Simon (1992), Garland (2001), and Wacquant (2001). Similarly, Feeley and Simon point to the loss of expert-driven criminal justice practices in favour of managerialist discourses. Bauman (2000) links punitiveness and widespread social anxiety, and Garland points to the rise of populist retributivist sentiments as etiologically linked to the rise in punitive mentalities. Matthews (2005) does an admirable job of testing these theses against the material practices of punishment as a means of destabilizing these claims. My research supports Matthews' claims that the arguments for the punitive turn do not stand up to the material test.

The political and economic shifts to which Garland, Wacquant, and Feeley and Simon point are apparent in the rise of addiction treatment in Ontario and have notable results. The loss of Keynesian mentalities does not, however, serve to rupture change-oriented mentalities; rather, it redirects them. This redirection occurs because of the work of a collection of psychologists and bureaucrats whose sustaining influence challenges both Feeley and Simon's argument about the loss of the expert as well as Bauman's and Garland's claims about the influence of the populace. The criminal addict, because she is easily constituted as the rational subject, or, more specifically, because her criminogenic factor is most easily set outside the bounds of the social, is a salient figure here. Her criminality is totally individual, reduced to the solitary activity of choosing to use drugs. Her recovery, too, reflects this as correctional programs are organized around teaching her how to think properly so that she will be better able to make good, non-criminal decision in the future.

As I suggest in the Introduction, understanding governing practices and grammars is only one way of exploring the criminal addict. This figure and the system that would change her are all found in a particular cultural context that has distinct and long-standing ways of thinking about drug use. I now turn to considering how drugs, as clinical and cultural artefacts, fit into this picture.

3
The Personalities of Drugs

The intersection of drug use and the CJS is often thought of as a location of tension between two different sets of actors: drug users and the official agents who manage them. The drug/crime nexus does not, however, pivot on a binary relationship between users and officials. There is a third set of actors who contribute to the nexus: the drugs themselves. The US war on drugs (WOD) serves as a salient example of the centrality of drugs in generating practical responses to drug use and criminality. The iconic "this-is-your-brain-on-drugs" advertisements launched at the start of the US WOD do not pit users against the state. The ads feature an egg and a voice-over that says, "This is your brain." The egg is cracked and dropped into a sizzling frying pan. The voice-over says, "This is your brain on drugs." And as the egg flash fries in the pan, the voice-over adds, "Any questions?" The message of the advertisement is clear: drugs fry your brain. The user is notably absent from the advertisement; there is no person, simply an egg and a frying pan. It is not the action of drug use taken by the actor that wreaks damage but, rather, the drugs themselves.

Aldous Huxley makes a similar claim about the action of drugs, albeit in order to present a far more pro-drug message. In *The Doors of Perception* (1954), Huxley identifies drug use as a viable means of exploring heightened or alternate forms of awareness. Huxley (excerpted in Jay [1999, 24]), writes,

> Most people, most of the time, know only what comes through the reducing valve and is consecrated as genuinely real by the local language. Certain persons, however, seem to be born with a kind of bypass that circumvents the reducing valve. In others temporary bypasses may be acquired either spontaneously, or as the result of deliberate "spiritual exercises," or through hypnosis, or by means of drugs.

Drugs, to Huxley, are one of the keys to the doors of perception, entities that would lead the user to heightened awareness and spiritual awakenings.

Despite these observable actions of drugs in both pro- and anti-drug narratives, the role of drugs within the drug/crime nexus is rarely considered in academic literature. Drugs, however, play an active and generative role both in determining the nature of the nexus and establishing responses such as therapeutic initiatives. Through particular problematizations, drugs are given criminogenic attributes in official, popular, and marginalized discourses. Psychoactive substances have always been ascribed specific characteristics, often helping to shape understandings of how these substances contribute to criminal behaviours. The specific personalities of different drugs are important in reading how drugs come to be criminogenic, reifying the drug/crime nexus.

This chapter maps the personalities of four of the most salient substances in the Canadian drug/crime nexus – marijuana, heroin, cocaine, and crack – and critically explores the broader category of drugs as an actor in and of itself. Drawing on popular culture representations, scientific and social science literatures, courtroom observations in the drug treatment courts of Toronto and Vancouver, and interviews with key practitioners in these courts, I show the constitution of these personalities and how they play out and play into the drug/crime nexus. Within this discussion, I also show how knowledges of drugs help to shape and are shaped by these different personalities, making the point that these tropes about individual drugs play a central and generative role in influencing drug policy and in dealing with the "problem" of drug use in the CJS and in shaping therapeutic responses to their use.

The Personalities of Drugs

Actor network theory (ANT) attempts to provide a cartography of the scientific process around a given object. Specifically, the ANT researcher takes up the notion of the network. In deploying a network analysis, Latour (1987) suggests that the researcher can eliminate the hierarchies assumed to exist in a particular site. By erasing imagined distinctions between who (or what) has the ability to take action in a site, Latour suggests that we are able to see how all the actors have generative capabilities. Included here are objects. Taking the scallop fishery in St. Brieuc, France, as his site of study, Callon (1999) argues that, in dealing with a crisis in the fishery industry brought on by overfishing and environmental degradation, a process of translation occurred. Through a network formed of the fishers of St. Brieuc, scientists, and the scallops themselves, the practice of scallop fishing was problematized, alliances were formed, the roles of the different actors were negotiated, and, in the process of taking action, spokespeople were established to speak for the cause and the actors. The action (or rather inaction) of scallops not reproducing has an effect on the site, influencing the outcome of the activity and shaping the actions of the others participating in the network.

It is crucial that Callon places the scallops on the same level as the fishers and the scientists, affording them generative power within the process. The scallops, as Callon points out, are not just things; rather, they have characteristics, tendencies, and actions of their own. Neither the fishers nor the scientists know whether or not the scallops will accept relocation in a bid to increase their stocks. These things, these scallops, which we ordinarily think of as actionless objects contingent upon human intervention, are not silent. Their own actions are generative and central to the success of the entire initiative. The scallops have action.

The generative capabilities afforded to the scallops are not exclusive to animate things. Just as Callon observes and chronicles the generative qualities of the scallops, so Latour discovers and chronicles the generative qualities of inanimate objects like the diesel engine. Latour (1987) charts the development of the diesel, citing the vast network of engineers, inventors, and investors who all played a role in its realization. Included in this network is the engine itself. Latour charts how "bugs" in the workings of the engine originally designed by Diesel had a considerable effect on the engine's birth and generation. By not working in the way investors and other engineers envisaged, the diesel engine itself generated adverse responses to its creation, leading the project to be sidelined and all but abandoned until such time as other actors entered the network to work with the engine, rendering it realizable as a functioning machine.

In charting treatment programs aimed at the criminal addict, I include drugs as generative actors that shape the governing strategy. Drugs have particular pharmacological properties (not the least of which is that some of them can be addictive) that organize the ways in which criminal justice actors respond to their use. Paying attention to the bacciferous capabilities of the drugs (both as a generalized category and as singular entities) helps to forward understanding of why drug use is a ready target of criminal justice intervention.

In 1980, Winner (1980) asked, "do artefacts have politics?" Through his study of a bridge in New York, he concludes that political strategies are written into technological designs. The bridge, according to Winner's analysis, was contrived so as not to accommodate buses, a plan that granted access to the beach lying on the other side of the bridge only to those affluent enough to own cars (namely, middle- and upper-class white folks). The case of "Moses' bridge" set off a controversy in the realm of science and technology studies as scholars hurried to contest Winner's claims, revealing that buses could and did in fact cross these bridges and that people of colour and poor people did have access to the beach (Jorgess 1999). Jorgess' sharp critique of Winner's original study is followed by a rejoinder from Woolgar and Cooper (1999), who suggest that attempts to "prove" the rightness or wrongness of Winner's original claims about how we can know artefacts are met with inescapable complications. Woolgar and Cooper question whether the politics of the bridge is written in Moses' original design, in "legendary" understandings of the design, or in possible technological adaptations (such as changing the dimensions of buses so that they can now fit on bridges). Their point is that understanding the politics of the bridge cannot be reduce to merely amassing facts about it; rather Woolgar and Cooper, evoking the network, encourage us to pay attention to the "relational properties of the various artefacts involved in [an] episode" (443). This approach does not eschew realist accounts but, rather, opens them up for broader surveillance so that it is possible, returning to Winner's argument, to see that the politics of exclusion built into the bridge are substantiated by urban legends about the bridge and also countered by the addition of technology in the form of shorter buses – vehicles that are now imbibed with their own emancipatory politics.

I flag this debate because drugs are political artefacts whose meanings are as relational as they are real. Rather than trying to fix the "true" politics of substances through establishing their essential personalities, my intent is to show how these personalities are set relationally. The productive actions of drugs need to be understood as a combination of both clinical and cultural thinking about what they can do. Governing strategies are not shaped so much by the truth about the thing being governed as they are by a combination of factors, including the governmental rationalities I discuss in the previous chapter and the legacy of cultural understanding surrounding the thing. This chapter is not about the truth of drugs but, rather, the *truths* of drugs, the multiple ways in which drugs are ascribed actions and how those actions (real or otherwise) generate governing responses.

I am not the first to see the importance of centring drugs within a critical analysis of criminal justice responses to drug use. Thomas Szasz, in his formidable *Ceremonial Chemistry* (1985), centres drugs in his study of the rise of anti-drug laws in the United States through the twentieth century. Szasz, although a psychiatrist by training, takes a decidedly sociological and anthropological approach to drugs, drawing mainly from religious studies to show the ritualization of both drug use and its control. Szasz bemoans the centrality of "scientific" accounts of drugs permeating popular notions and narratives around drug use. He advocates a separation, suggesting that

> we distinguish more sharply than we have heretofore between the study of drugs and the study of drug use and drug avoidance. Organic chemistry, biological chemistry and pharmacology are all concerned with the chemical properties and biological effects of drugs. Ceremonial chemistry, on the other hand, is concerned with the personal and cultural circumstances of

drug use and drug avoidance. The subject matter of ceremonial chemistry is thus the magical as opposed to the medical, the ritual as opposed to the technical dimensions of drug use; more specifically, it is the approval and disapproval, promotion and prohibition, use and avoidance of symbolically significant substances, and the explanations and justifications offered for the consequences and control of their employment (xv).

While Szasz recognizes the importance of delineating drugs, drug use, and "drug avoidance" or the control of drug use, his attempts to extract classically scientific aspects of drug use from other cultural and social phenomena sets up a dichotomy based on the idea that the social or cultural is separate from the scientific or natural. As Latour (1993) articulates, these opposing realms, the social and the scientific, are best regarded as only contingently separate: there is no separation and no point at which one sits outside the other. In mapping the personalities of different drugs, the characterization and reification both of "drugs" as a monolith and of particular substances in their own right are not born solely of either science or cultural practices. Drug personalities are the progeny of a messy constellation of different kinds of knowledge and practice, using bits of different grammars to be constituted as criminogenic entities.

Klein (1993), in his study of cigarettes, makes a similar point. Klein focuses on the seductive qualities of cigarettes over the last century, arguing that cigarettes are rendered sublime through a combination of scientific and social knowledges about their "badness" and in relation to their fluctuating degrees of prohibition and repression. Like Callon, Klein sees cigarettes as having an active and generative quality separate from those who smoke them or those who try to control their being smoked. Klein quotes Cocteau's narrative on smoking :

> Il ne faut pas oublier que le paquet de cigarrettes, le ceremonial qui les en sort, allume le briquet, et cet etrange nuage qui nous penetre et que sougglent nos narines, c'est par des charmes puissant qu'ils ont fait la conquete du monde.

> [One must not forget that the pack of cigarettes, the ceremony that extracts them, lights the lighter and that strange smoke which penetrates us and which our nostrils puff, have with powerful charms seduced and conquered the world] (cited in Klein 1993, 4).

As subjects rather than objects, cigarettes have generative power, sexuality, nationality, and politics. It is through these various "seductive" characteristics, following Klein's argument, that cigarettes ensure their continued existence and use, even in the face of rising "healthism" and moral campaigns against smoking. Like cigarettes, drugs have also developed a cultural presence and have characteristics. Observing and examining these characteristics, it is possible to see the ways in which drugs have specific action.

Specific drug personalities also relate to how drugs are reified both culturally and by individual users. In *How to Stop Time: Heroin From A to Z*, Ann Marlow (1999, 280) ruminates on the importance of creatively understanding her own experiences through privileging her relationship with heroin:

> There's something arbitrary about looking at my life and our times through the lens of heroin. I might have picked tennis, or shoes or cooking, all of which have been important to me for years and have their own cultural resonances. From this angle, dope is just the lever I've chosen to move what I can. But no. Every thread would not be equal. Our culture has lent dark powers to narratives of drug use, more than to drug use itself, and I am taking advantage of them, like a painter using the severity of northern light.

In Marlow's case, heroin is the fundamental lens through which to understand and write about her life not because it has taken on any more of a generative role in her existence than have any of her other passions but, rather, because heroin has a cultural presence that, as Marlow describes, lends it a certain narrative power. This narrative power is not exclusive to heroin and can be extended to other substances (e.g., marijuana and cocaine).

These analytic concepts – supplied by Latour, Callon, Winner, and Woolgar and Cooper through the notion of the actor network, and by Szasz, Marlow, and Klein through cultural analysis – are useful in exploring the question of drug control from the perspective of drugs. The realm of drugs is a messy and rugged terrain made up of historical, cultural, pharmacological, social, political, biological, and psychological features. This being the case, a study proposing to take drugs as its subject must approach research with an eye to these complexities. It is for this reason that I am thinking here about the personalities of drugs. The personality is not simply made up of how we function as biological entities; it is also constituted by the ways in which others see and react to us. The conclusion that an individual is psychopathic, for example, is born out of a combination of biomedical observations made about the person (low serotonin, accelerated synaptic activity) as well as cultural understandings of the individual's behaviour (harming animals). The constitution of a personality, thus, is best understood through a combination of approaches that are able to take into account both science and the social. So, too, in the case with drugs. Drugs have never been simply physical entities. Reactions to drugs come as much from understandings (or alleged understandings) of their social presence as from understandings (or, again, alleged understandings) of their pharmacologies.

Risk and Drug Personalities

One of the main languages taken up in official attempts to rationalize controls over substances is the language of risk. Several key works (Beck 1992; Ericson and Haggerty 1997; Ericson and Doyle 2003; Leiss and Hrudey 2005; O'Malley and Valverde 2004; Valverde, Levi, and Moore 2005) highlight risk discourses in contemporary governing rationalities and illustrate how discourses translate into specific practices for managing risk. Castel (1991) describes the impact that replacing the language of dangerousness with the language of risk has on psychiatry. Talk of the dangerous individual, according to Castel, offered an imprecise profile that emphasized the essential unpredictability of mental patients. This model of unpredictability disallows the possibility of talking about prevention: how can we prevent what we cannot predict? Risk places prediction as its central goal and privileges calculability as a primary and attainable feature of a system of governance; thus, it holds strong appeal and lends a productivity to governance that dangerousness could not sustain. The same trend, moving from dangerousness to risk, is observable in relation to drugs. While classic narratives conjure drugs as dangerous, contemporary accounts tend to imagine drugs as risky.[1] This injection of risk into drug narratives influenced both the general term "drugs" and specific personalities. Risk here is most often used to embed these substances in the drug/crime nexus, thus justifying criminal justice responses. The language of risk is also taken up in initiatives oriented around resisting drug controls. Risk is mobilized in the harm-reduction movement, especially around opiates (cf. Erickson et al. 1997; O'Malley and Valverde 1999a, 2004). Also, law reform movements, particularly those focused on marijuana, strive to de-risk these substances, to extract the notion of risk from their drugalities (Young 2003). Within this discourse of risk related to drugs, the language of harm is applied most readily. Common representations see drugs as risky (or, conversely, attempt to de-risk drugs) by discussing the harms they do or do not evoke. These include physical, psychological, and social harm to the user as well as broader societal harm in relation to crime, health care costs, and the denigration of the social fabric.

Drugs

The term "drugs" requires special consideration as it takes on its own personality, distinct from those of specific substances. The "drug problem" is a recent phenomenon. When first problematized and rendered objects and subjects of legal regulation and sanction, substances were conceptualized as singular entities. It was not, then, a problem with "drugs" that led to

Canada's first anti-substance legislation, it was a problem with opium (Carstairs 2005). Significantly, Canada's first anti-substance law was the Opium Act, which, predictably, only set out prohibitions around opium. Opium was similarly problematized in other jurisdictions. For example, international conventions on opium held through the early 1910s were all concerned specifically with the opium trade. Historians writing about the turn of the twentieth century describe a globalized opium panic that spread across the northern hemisphere (Berridge and Edwards 1981; Goldsmith 1939; Morgan 1981). While the nature of the panic differed from jurisdiction to jurisdiction,[2] the target was almost exclusively opium.

As the purview of narcotics legislation expanded both in Canada and internationally,[3] the rhetoric around criminally controlled substances shifts, becoming more homogenous and generalized. Canada and the United States both organized narcotics control offices. In 1911, the Opium Act became the Opium and Drug Act. However, despite these moves towards adopting the umbrella term "drugs," substances were very much still problematized in their own right. Giffen, Endicott, and Lambert (1991) point to a series of moral panics around specific substances that directly contributed to their criminalization. Thus, the opium scares in Vancouver at the start of the twentieth century resulted in Canada's inaugural anti-drug legislation (see Chapter 2; Carstairs 1999, 2005). In 1911, cocaine panics in Montreal, focused primarily around youth, served as the catalyst for including cocaine in the drug schedule. Giffen, Endicott, and Lambert do not account for the inclusion of marijuana, but they speculate that it may have been interdicted as a result of the importation of panics from the United States.

Despite the inclusion of cocaine and marijuana in anti-narcotic legislation in the early part of the twentieth century, the primary target of intervention and problematization continued to be opium. Terms like "narcotics" and "drugs" meant opium. While other drugs came onto the schedule, all the histories of Canada's drug laws show that opium and its derivatives remained central to the problematization of substance use (Carstairs 1999, 2005; Giffen, Endicott, and Lambert 1991; Mosher 1998). Law enforcement resources were directed at the opium trade, and therapeutic initiatives were organized around opium users (Carstairs 2005; Giffen, Endicott, and Lambert 1991). In 1927, responding to debates about the division of law enforcement labour among different levels of police forces,[4] C.H.L. Sharman, appointed chief of the Canadian Narcotics Service in 1927, directed provincial and municipal police forces to concern themselves with policing "smaller narcotics cases," outlining the need to crack down on "the keepers of opium joints" (Giffen Endicott, and Lambert 1991, 131). Likewise, early references to attempts to treat addicts refer directly to opiates. Physicians writing about treatment options consistently refer to the need to give medical attention to individuals using "the drug." Often, these doctors advocated maintenance doses[5] of opiates to help wean the individual off of opium (ibid.). Carstairs (1999) shows that the expansion of drug laws through the 1920s stemmed mainly from concerns over the use of opium in Vancouver. In *The Black Candle*, Canada's first popular anti-drug text, Emily Murphy (1922) directs almost all of her concern and panic at opiates, designating a brief chapter each to marijuana and cocaine.

The 1960s, however, mark a shift in the discourse as the term "drug" comes to stand in for all sorts of substances that, by then, had been added to the Narcotic Control Act. The term "drugs" loses its plurality and, as a result, takes on its own personality, translating a vague collection of substances into one "super substance": drugs. Writers like Timothy Leary, along with "beat" and counter-culture poets and musicians, helped enshrine the existence of an entire drug subculture. For example, though he used LSD almost exclusively, Leary (1968) writes about his "drug sessions." Drugs in this counter-culture did not, however, include every substance that is now labelled a "drug"; rather, to the beat generation and the "flower children," drugs meant psychedelics or hallucinogenics like LSD, magic mushrooms, marijuana, and hashish. Leary's writings focused exclusively on psychedelics used for both spiritual and recreational purposes. Throughout the 1960s and 1970s, Leary (1983) organized his proselytizing around what he called "psychedelic" drugs, referring to LSD, magic mushrooms, and other substances with hallucinogenic properties. The folk-psychedelic music scene of the time confirmed the commitment to psychedelics. The Beatles' "Lucy in the Sky with Diamonds"[6] and Jefferson Airplane's "White Rabbit,"[7] for example, both chronicle and celebrate the use of psychedelics. "Lucy in the Sky with Diamonds" paints a utopian picture of an acid trip, where the drug takes the user "in a boat on a river, with tangerine trees and marmalade skies." "White Rabbit," drawing on Lewis Carol's *Alice in Wonderland*, offers a similar chronicle of acid and magic mushroom use, locating the user in Carol's mythical Wonderland, where one is directed by the dormouse to "feed your head." When other substances were incorporated into the counter-culture, they were more often critiqued than accepted. The Rolling Stones' "Mother's Little Helper" offers critical commentary on the use of Valium by housewives. The song, from the Stones' (1972) album *Hot Rocks*,[8] paints Valium as a drug proffered to bored and depressed women struggling to escape the doldrums of suburban life.

The Velvet Underground's "Heroin"[9] offers a similarly critical commentary on the use of heroin. The song concludes with a clear lament regarding the effects of heroin. Far from the celebratory and awe-inspired flavour of songs about psychedelics, songs about opiates display a far more insidious and menacing characterization throughout this period.

The plurality of drugs, however, acquires a very different and strategically important meaning for "mainstream" culture and, in particular, political and enforcement-oriented rhetorics. Drugs, particularly in policing narratives, came to be a noun of slippage as it translated into anything from marijuana to heroin. In his treatise on the evils and perils of drugs in the United States, Harry Anslinger, known in the United States as the father of the drug war, slides easily from discussing fears of opiates, to calling for widespread resistance, to calling for relaxing anti-drug laws. Anslinger (1961, 294) writes: "Much of the campaign for relaxing narcotic controls and setting up clinics emanates, in fact, from organized syndicate sources. Reefers and propaganda, too, go hand in hand." In using the term "narcotics," Anslinger easily implicates marijuana as being synonymous with the heroin trade (his reference to "syndicates"). Marijuana users also become linked to the same treatment programs that are used for heroin users (the clinics). The effect is that heroin and marijuana blend into the same substance: one stands in for the other. Fears about heroin, especially its links to trafficking and other drug-related crimes, become fears about marijuana. They become the same thing, a singular substance: narcotics – or, simply, drugs.

The event of this slippage was not solely a US phenomenon. Canada also had a strong counter-culture presence, and most major cities had a thriving counter-culture scene. Toronto's Yorkville, as Giffen, Endicott, and Lambert (1991) write, was the cradle of Canadian counter-culture and it mirrored US trends. Giffen, Endicott, and Lambert describe Yorkville during the 1960s as a "Mecca of freedom from social restraints [where youth had] freedom to live and love as they pleased, to 'turn on' with drugs and generally 'do their own thing'" (496). As they describe it, the Yorkville scene centred mainly on marijuana and, to a lesser extent, on other psychedelics (such as LSD).

Predictably, like those in the United States, law enforcement officials in Canada were quick to effect the same slippage as did Anslinger, extending classic, opiate-derived fears to the use of psychedelics. In particular, marijuana use in Yorkville was seen as a threat to young women, their sexuality, and their sexual safety. One *Globe and Mail* article from that period states:

> "The real evil of Yorkville is what is happening to these young girls, many only children. They came to the village as good kids, mixed up perhaps, and many from fine homes, and these beatniks grab them and within two days they are ruined," said Deputy Chief Bernard Simmons, in charge of criminal investigation in Metro. One officer termed sex in Yorkville "a communal affair. The girls are fed a little marijuana and in a few days they are passed around to everybody" (excerpted in Giffen, Endicott, and Lambert 1991, 497).

These fears about the effects of marijuana on women's sexuality and sexual safety are strikingly similar to the fears laid out about opiates forty years earlier. Emily Murphy (1922, 17) describes the effects of opium on women:

A man or a woman who becomes an addict seeks the company of those who use the drug, and avoids those of their own social status. This explains the amazing phenomenon of an educated gentlewoman, reared in a refined atmosphere, consorting with the lowest classes of yellow and black men. It explains, too, why sometimes a white woman deserts or "farms out" a half-caste infant, or on rare occasions brings it to the juvenile court for adoption.

Under the influence of the drug, the woman loses control of herself; her moral senses are blunted, and she becomes "a victim" in more senses than one. When she acquires the habit, she does not know what lies before her; later, she does not care. She is a young woman who is years upon years old.

Young women using marijuana in the 1960s in Yorkville face the same perils as did young women using opium in the 1920s. The drugs will cause them to jeopardize their sexual sanctity and place them in criminogenic spaces that threaten their safety.

The slippage effected through the use of the term "drugs" also facilitated the reading of all psychoactive substances as inherently dangerous as opposed to posing specific risks. The invocation of words like "evil" and "menace" in early and mid-twentieth-century anti-drug discourses ascribes an overall characteristic of threat to the drugality of drugs. There is no continuum or calculability of the harms posed by drugs; rather, the language relies on an absolute, moral message that drugs are bad. Sarah Graham-Mulhall's (1926) *Opium: The Daemon Flower* paints repeated portraits of the devastating effects of drug use, expressly on the morals and virtues of young men and women on college campuses. White slavery fears, popular in pre-Second World War North America, reinforced the inherent dangerousness of drugs. Particularly trenchant in racializing drugs, these tales had young women fall slaves to narcotics, then languish in opium dens or get raped by black men (see Campbell 2000; Valverde 1991).

It was the American declaration of another war on drugs in the early 1980s,[10] however, that truly reified drugs as having their own criminal existence. Reagan declared this war in 1986, installing his wife Nancy as the chief spokesperson for the initial "just-say-no" campaign. The campaign was intended to combat drug use by targeting the demand side. Images of school children surrounding Nancy Reagan on the White House lawn, all sporting "just-say-no" buttons were iconic. This "soft side" of the WOD accompanied a much harsher reality as US law enforcement targeted the supply side of drug use. The WOD heralded the most expensive and comprehensive offensive campaign against drugs in American history. Drugs emerged in the United States in the 1980s as the new enemy, replacing communists as the primary target of public fears and government resources. By 1995, billions of dollars had been mobilized in enforcement efforts both inside and outside its boarders (Marez 2004). Implicated in US military involvement in

Nicaragua and Columbia, the WOD gave the FBI a reason to gain international policing footholds across the globe (Nadelmann 1993).

On the heels of the United States, then Canadian prime minister Brian Mulroney declared his own war on 29 September 1986, two days after Ronald Reagan had made his declaration (Jensen and Gerber 1993). The Canadian drug war proved far less spectacular than its American counterpart, but it led essentially to the same ends: drastic increases in incarceration rates, particularly of members of marginalized communities; increases in law enforcement budgets; and law reform initiatives calling for tougher penalties. Canadian narratives of substances also embraced, and continue to embrace, the generalized term "drugs" to the same purpose as one finds in the United States. The RCMP, as well as provincial and local police services, have drug enforcement units. The legislation interdicting certain substances is called the Controlled Drugs and Substances Act. Perhaps most tellingly, all contemporary responses to substance use in the nation are meant to be guided by the Ministry of Health document entitled *Canada's Drug Strategy*.

In 1987, as a sort of Canadian alternative to the WOD, the federal government introduced the drug strategy – a more tempered response to the panics around substances that surfaced (or were conjured) in the 1980s (Hathaway and Erickson 2003). The drug strategy offers a collaborative response to the drug problem, incorporating criminal justice and health-based initiatives around drug use and drug dealing. Substances targeted in the drug strategy include "alcohol, medications (both prescription and over the counter), illicit drugs, inhalants and banned performance-enhancing sport drugs (as defined by the International Olympic Committee)" (Canada 2000, 2). The drug strategy is presented as targeting drugs generally, not just those that are illicit. However, underlying the strategy are core assumptions about drugs: they are addictive, criminogenic, and carry with them considerable costs, notably health care expenses, lost productivity, and law enforcement expenditures. The strategy links drugs, for example, to domestic violence and property crime. It also underscores the need for treatment for drug users, offering several treatment options, only one of which (methadone maintenance) relates to a specific drug. The only other distinction it identifies around drugs concerns alcohol, particularly drunk driving. It concludes with a statistical breakdown of drug use among youth and adults, which is intended to show a considerable increase in drug use in all populations. Despite these distinctions, no demarcation is made between different drugs.

Most recently, the Parliamentary Special Committee on the Non-Medical Use of Drugs (SCNMUD, 2002) was mandated to look at the non-medical use of drugs as a general category and make recommendations regarding the revision of the drug strategy. Like LeDain, the report rendered by the committee only distinguishes cannabis, treating the remainder of substances covered as homogenous.[11] The committee makes clear its position that drugs remain criminogenic. In its introduction, the committee outlines the harmful effects of psychoactive substances, noting health concerns like the spread of HIV/AIDS and Hepatitis C as well as social concerns like "family violence, prostitution, sexual exploitation, delinquency, crime, and child abuse and neglect" (5). Similar claims about the inherent criminality of psychoactive drugs are made by other government organizations. The RCMP cites the violence and greed that accompany drug use as forces that weaken the social and economic fabric of Canada. Borrowing from US, post-9/11 initiatives to reinvigorate anti-drug campaigns through links to terrorism,[12] the RCMP and the parliamentary committee both implicate drug use in terrorist activities. In his opening statement (quoted in the introduction of the committee report), Michael McLaughlin, deputy auditor general for Canada, states that "the sale of illicit drugs is a major source of funding for organized crime and for terrorism" (5). Likewise, the RCMP suggest that drug sales are a "major source of funding" for terrorist enterprises.[13]

This reification of drugs is directly apparent in attempts to cure the criminal addict. One salient example of this is the advent of drug treatment courts (DTCs). The courts are officially called drug treatment courts, using the term "drug" as a shorthand, even though they are only mandated to deal with crack, cocaine, methamphetamine (Vancouver only), and opiate use. Writing about the formation and practices of Toronto's DTC, Judge Bentley (2000), the presiding judge, presents the court as a response to the problem of drugs and crime. He underscores the failure of the CJS thus far to adequately and effectively address the problem of drugs, and he argues that, in finding ways for people to stop using drugs, the court is simultaneously improving the lives of its "clients" and protecting public safety. The specific substances targeted by the court are not described in the article until the fourth page. When Bentley does mention crack, cocaine, and heroin, he offers no explanation as to why these substances in particular are singled out by the court and only makes distinctions between them in two paragraphs, where he describes the different counselling services set out for different types of drug use. The description of these different programs only illustrates their existence, however, and does not offer any commentary on the personalities (i.e., drugalities) of different substances.

The Vancouver Drug Treatment Court (VDTC) deploys the term "drugs" in the same way. In twenty-five pages of executive summary spanning the three process reports released to date, there are only three instances in which specific substances are named. Even in these instances, there is an air of generality. In all cases, the reference is to "heroin/cocaine." The reports themselves follow the same trend of generality. Specific substances are almost never referenced, with the exception of descriptive, demographic data. In addition, unlike the Toronto Drug Treatment Court (TDTC), the VDTC offers no substance-specific programming. When I asked the VDTC's program designer about this, she explained that the orientation of the VDTC is to work with the disease of substance dependence. She argued that the disease does not discriminate between substances and, therefore, that there is no need to do so in offering treatment. The only exception is pharmacological, as heroin addicts may take methadone. This is the same sentiment expressed by one of the informants in Chapter 2. Drugs are generalizable, of interest only because of their iatrogenic effects. Even if the substances differ, the diseases (addiction, criminality) are the same.

The TDTC produced a promotional video in 2000 that offers an overview of the court program from the perspective of both the users and court personnel. When treatment court officials talk about substances in the video, they never mention a specific drug but, rather, talk in generalities about drugs and their adverse effects. The comments of the judge are instructive:

> They [drug users] feel they're not connected to society. They feel abused by society either because they have been abused or they feel they're abused. Many of them have mental health problems. Drugs are a release, an escape from their drudgery, from living in one-room tenements or living on the sidewalk. For these people the only way to get them out of drugs is to remove them from that milieu, the lifestyle, the people they associate with.

This judge presents a very clear depiction of the effect of drugs on people's lives. Drugs promise a way out of misery that only leads to further misery, an escape from which they later must be saved. As in other official narratives, drugs take on a slippery identity here, lacking any fixed meaning. Escapism is not attributed to any one substance but, rather, to an undefined mass – drugs.

By way of helpful contrast, the users featured in the video discuss their own drug involvement specifically. All of the users speak directly about their crack/cocaine use (there are no heroin users featured). They make specific reference to crack and cocaine, talking directly about the ways in which they use the drugs (typically smoking) and about the development of their respective addictions to crack/cocaine. Thus, while the judge speaks in generalizations about the effects of drugs on people's lives, the users are more apt to offer specific narratives about how crack affects them.

Exchanges in the courtrooms of both DTCs evoke the term "drugs" in a similar fashion. In the Toronto court, when clients are called before the judge, invariably one of the first questions asked is whether or not they have any drug use to report. Clients who have used since their last court appearance often offer the judge an account that specifies (typically by way of explanation) the kind of drug they used. The following is a typical exchange:

Judge: Any drug use to report today?

Client: Yeah, I smoked a joint the other night when I was out with some friends.

Judge: You smoked a joint ... Do you have any insight into why you used?

Client: I was out with some friends and they were smoking. It was no big deal. I didn't use crack or anything, just had a few hauls off a joint.

Judge: You've heard me say repeatedly in this courtroom that a use is a use. I know crack's your drug of choice and it's good to hear that you didn't use crack. A use is still a use. In this court we see all drug use as a problem. Smoking a joint is a relapse and, as you know, is one step away from using crack again.[14]

While the client is trying to distinguish between the meaning behind her marijuana use versus the meaning behind her crack use, the judge clearly resists this delineation. "Use is use," he insists, and recognizes little distinction between the use of one kind of substance and the use of another. All substance use, following the judge's logic, will eventually lead to the same ends: relapse and a return to criminal and addictive behaviours.

While I was conducting courtroom observations in the VDTC, the Crown indicated that court personnel are careful not to name specific substances in open court and asked that the court clients refrain from doing so as well. The Crown explained that the presiding judge felt that naming substances could function as a trigger for court clients. All drugs in the VDTC are referred to as "substances." Thus, reference in the court to a dirty drug screen might indicate that an individual used her drug of choice or that she took a sleeping pill. No effort is made in open court to differentiate between different kinds of substance use; instead, clients are reminded that all substance use is discouraged and is taken as reason enough to have them enrolled in a residential detoxification program.[15]

Similar generalities are made about drugs in programming initiatives offered to those already convicted of criminal offences. Correctional Services Canada (CSC) and the Ontario Ministry of Safety and Security offer core programming to individuals with identified substance-use problems (see Chapters 2 and 5). The programs are similar in philosophy and practice. They are standardized across the jurisdiction and are often mandated to anyone thought to have committed a criminal act either while under the influence of a particular substance or while seeking out a substance.[16] The programs themselves address drugs as a general category, offering ways for lawbreakers to "change their substance-use habits." While the educational portion of these programs often breaks down these different substances, especially their varying pharmacologies, the responses to their use are uniform. The focus of these programs is to help the individual curb his drug use via tools to manage cravings and avoid triggers.

CSC offers the same core program for substance use at every federal penitentiary. The Offender Substance Abuse Pre-Release Program (OSAPP), as described by CSC, offers no specific programming around individual drugs but, rather, programming for the estimated 80 percent of prisoners who exhibit problems related to "substance use or alcohol." While the use of specific substances is noted through the initial risk-need assessment conducted on every federal prisoner (see Hannah-Moffat 2001) and may elevate an individual's risk or need profile, the language of programming relies heavily on the generalization of the term "drug," as did the treatment court. The CSC program also incorporates alcohol into the drug problem. The program description begins with the general claim that "alcohol and drug use are highly associated with crime" (Lightfoot 2000). Lightfoot goes on to explain that there are notable variances in the roles alcohol and drugs play in the commission of criminal acts. These variances, however, she attributes to differences between individual people, not substances. Lightfoot, a researcher and program designer for CSC, suggests that these individual differences indicate a need to "match" people with treatment programs that will best suit their individual needs. These individual needs are shaped by learning style rather than drug of choice. Paradoxically, Lightfoot then describes the CSC's standardized, non-variant substance-abuse treatment regime, a regime that takes into account neither differences among different substances nor differences among individual users. Here, the criminogenic nature of any drug is firmly established in the practitioner discourse. In her program description, Lightfoot states clearly that "alcohol ... and drug use are contributing factors in criminal behaviour" (1). She explains that there are a "wide variety of ways" in which substance use contributes to criminal behaviour, including: association with social groups in which criminal behaviour is the norm, the lowering of inhibitions, and overreaction to stress on the part of intoxicated individuals.

Likewise, the provincial program, newly devised and implemented for the Ontario Ministry of Public Safety and Security, offers a generalized substance-use program. Like CSC, the Ministry program does not make distinctions between different drugs; rather, any form of broadly defined substance use falls under the purview of the program. The program, tellingly, is called the Substance Misuse Orientation Program. The program manual is explicit in stating that no distinctions are to be made between different kinds of substances. Cox (2001, 10), the program designer, writes:

> The type of substance abused is not a selection factor. Whether an offender has a severe alcohol problem, a severe cocaine problem or a severe heroin problem, the emphasis is on the "severe" and not on the substance used. Group members are able to relate to each other on the basis of the resulting life consequences of the substance abuse as opposed to the specific substance.

The substance-use patterns of the men I interviewed who had completed the Ministry program varied widely. Like the people in the court, when interviewed, the majority of these men wanted to make distinctions pertaining to their specific substances of choice, showing quite clearly that there is a difference between being a cocaine user and a pot smoker (see Chapter 5 for a more in-depth discussion). Still, their behaviours were understood as drug use by the Ministry and were dealt with as such.

Theorizing Generalities

The term "drugs" serves as a handy stand-in for a long list of problematized substances. However, the purpose of adopting the term is not just to provide a simple linguistic shorthand; rather, evoking the term "drugs," despite its vagaries, effects a strategic technique of generalization. This generalization conjures drugs as an overly broad, catch-all phrase that mobilizes considerable action and has particular consequences. At the start of this chapter, I suggest that some of the analytic tools laid out in ANT are useful in understanding the conjuring of drug personalities. I want to return to that proposition for a moment in order to unpack the mechanics of this technique of generalization.

In *Science in Action*, Latour (1987) pinpoints interests as an overarching motivator for the conducts of different actors within a network. Latour locates interests within the actor-network as lying in between actors and their goals. He describes several scenarios in which an actor's goals are achieved through alignment and realignment of interests. These he calls moments of translation. Reshuffling interests and goals to shift focus from explicit to implicit interests is one such moment of translation.[17] One of the techniques by which Latour renders the erasure of explicit interests possible involves the invention of new groupings within the network. Deploying the example of infectious diseases in the nineteenth century, Latour argues that the regrouping of people from members of socio-economic classes to potential carriers and transmitters of infectious microbes coordinated a realignment of interests, whereby members of different classes diametrically opposed with regard to questions of urban development and public health came to share common interests with regard to their mutual concern about contracting diseases like malaria, cholera, and tuberculosis.

Official discourses around drug control regroup particular substances under the umbrella term "drugs" in order to attain particular goals, some of which are more apparent than others. The reason for deploying the general term in the VDTC is most obvious. The judge refuses to name substances because he believes that specific names have a particular power and negative effect upon drug users. In this context, the use of the term "drugs" is meant to have the effect of diffusing the allure attached to words like "heroin" or "crack." In the VDTC, generalities are benign and specificities are triggering.

The reasons for adopting this generalization in the other sites I studied are not quite so clear. I suggest that official discourses prefer generalities over specificities when it comes to drugs because the former work far better than the latter at maximizing fears. Fear is pivotal to any campaign as it functions to justify actions and interventions as well as to reify the drug/crime nexus. Most recently, the strategy of wedding fears and generalities has played out on the world stage as the Western world's responses to terrorism continue to unfold. Following the attacks on New York, George W. Bush took up a campaign of generalities in order to justify the erosion of civil liberties, the invasion of Iraq, and the imprisonment without cause of thousands of people in military detention centres (Singh 2002). The same technique was used by world leaders following the 2005 attacks on London. For weeks following those attacks, Canadians were cautioned that the bombings in the United Kingdom constituted an attack on "our way of life." Newscasters and terrorism experts speculated publicly on the most likely Canadian targets for the threat of attack now looming over this country. These generalized fears had the desired effect of recruiting citizens into the war against terrorism, shoring up international support for US-led aggression in the Middle East as well as for acquiescing to the "need" to compromise human rights at home.

Changes in discourses surrounding specific substances (mostly marijuana) over the last forty or so years have worked to erode many if not most of the fears the public was originally trained to have. This I discuss in more detail below. Here, I want only to highlight a few key points. The LeDain Commission suggested that marijuana was far less harmful than its location on the drug schedule would suggest and called for its decriminalization. That same call was again made by senate and parliamentary commissions in 2003. While scientific communities continue to oscillate on questions about marijuana's harms (e.g., its addictive properties or the degree to which it impairs driving), if recent public opinion polls are any indicator, the scourge of marijuana does not factor prominently in the fears of most Canadians. The demystification of marijuana meant a loss of support for the WOD due to the erosion of alliances between the government, the (white, middle-class) citizenry, law enforcement, and health care (Moore and Haggerty 2001).

Regrouping specific substances into the catch-all category of "drugs" has the effect of reinvigorating those alliances. Parents who are unconcerned about their children's exposure to marijuana are very concerned about drug dealers in the schoolyard. The use of the term "drugs" renders all substances equally dangerous, harmful, and, significantly, criminogenic. In the TDTC, *all* drug use is a problem because *all* drug use places the user at risk of relapse. Likewise, the treatment and intervention programs offered by the federal and provincial governments see generalized drug use as criminogenic. This regrouping erases claims that substances like marijuana are not harmful (or are, at least, less harmful than others) because it categorizes them as one and the same as crack or heroin.

Alcohol is a sticky point in this narrative. While legally different from illicit substances, it is still recruited in some of these strategies as a criminogenic substance. This is achieved through its stated inclusion (i.e., "alcohol and drugs") as well as through the sideways and unclear reference to "substances." The term "substance abuse" often, but not always, includes alcohol. The inclusion of alcohol in the discourse makes it into a drug, inscribing it with the same general characteristics as other "substances."

Theorists argue that the ascendance of neoliberal regimes has given rise to new forms of targeted governance. Valverde (2003b), in her study of pharmaceutical drugs designed to target alcoholism, and Rose (2003), in his study of pharmaceuticals that target the action of certain brain chemicals, both show the emergence of "magic bullets." Rather than address the classic binary between normal and pathological, the search for magic bullets targets specific sites below the level of the whole organism. Valverde argues that the emergence of targeted governance, be it in relation to alcoholism, policing specific communities, immigration profiling, or brain chemicals, signifies a bid to govern more "modestly and specifically."

Such technologies are readily observable in the Canadian CJS. The rise of risk assessments and cognitive-behavioural therapy, as I show in Chapter 2, allowed correctional officials to hone in on specific thought processes rather than attempt to pathologize and treat the whole person. Substance abuse emerges as a main target of intervention. Still, as is the case with drugs, there are, within these targets, practices of generalization at play. Valverde observes the generalization involved in "smart drugs" aimed at alcoholism: these drugs were originally used to treat opiate addictions. The specific targeting technology can take on the qualities of a panacea, treating the general as it treats the specific.

Valverde and Rose also reveal links between the need for targets that are at once both specific and general and the need for greater efficiency and resource maximization. Techniques of generalization mass market various practices in bids to maximize resources in an age of scarcity. Rose observes that Prozac, a drug originally marketed only to address depression through the specific targeting of serotonin, is now used to treat eating disorders, panic, and obsessive-compulsive disorders. Rose (2003, 204) credits this to a marketization of targeted interventions:

> Biovalue, here, seems to demand constant innovation, and the cycling from the specific targeted cure – the magic bullet – to the wonder drug that will cure all seems endemic to marketing and perhaps to the very project of

commercial psychopharmacology itself. Yet, despite this cycling, in any of these phases, it is not the pathological individual that is targeted but a molecular anomaly.

In Chapter 2, I argue that interventions with drug users are readily shaped by the neoliberal bid for greater efficiency, the need to do more with less. Part of this quest for greater efficiency involves the need to paint as much as possible with one stroke (as with the generalizing of the term "drugs"). For there to be a magic bullet capable of piercing the larger problem, there must first be a larger problem, an amalgamated mass, to pierce. Just as Rose observes the rise of a panoply of mood disorders treatable with one targeted intervention, so too do we see the rise of a panoply of substances that can all be addressed with a small, homogeneous set of technologies. If the problem, at least from the point of view of governing bodies, is "drugs" rather than a profusion of different substances, then needed solutions can be generic. There is no need to offer separate (and costly) programming or to differentiate between the kinds of substances causally linked to crimes. There is no need to be troubled with burgeoning and often conflicting scientific evidence about harms, addictive potentials, or the behavioural effects of different substances because it is enough to know that all drugs are dangerous.

Specific Drug Personalities

As well as general substances, specific substances also figure into the lexicon of criminal addiction. These reveal the unique personality of each substance, attributing specific characteristics, criminalities, and pathologies to each different entity. I focus here on the four most salient substances: marijuana, crack, cocaine, and heroin. These specific personalities are crucial to the CJS as they inform not only law-making but also how the system approaches the users of these particular drugs.

Marijuana

Classic narratives present marijuana as the "demon" drug that spawned insanity and criminality. Marijuana was, to go back to Castel's distinction, a dangerous drug. One scene from the 1937 cult classic *Reefer Madness* shows a white couple sitting in their living room. The woman is smoking a joint and playing piano while the man, smoking his own joint, encourages her to play faster. The more she smokes the faster she plays, and the more he smokes the more insistent he becomes. Within a matter of seconds, both take on the classic "mad" visage, complete with a crazed expression, bugged out eyes, and strange facial ticks. Eventually, they both become frantic. Another man enters the room, and the first man beats him to death with a fire poker as the piano-playing woman stands by and watches with something between glee and horror. The piano player then leaps to her death (see also Carstairs 2005; Jay 1999; Sloman 1979).

Contemporary understandings of marijuana are far less pernicious. Although the religious right would have us believe otherwise, mainstream, or popular, conceptions of pot generally regard it as a reasonably benign substance. Pot smoking is rarely problematized in popular media and is often presented as a form of comic relief rather than a demon drug. Popular Hollywood films such as *American Beauty*, *Fast Times at Ridgemont High*, *Dazed and Confused* and the Cheech and Chong movies all present marijuana use as a harmless activity, offering comic relief rather than negative social commentary. There are rarely depictions of major marijuana trafficking rings. People who use marijuana never have to go into treatment and, if arrests for marijuana are shown (as happens periodically in some of the earlier Cheech and Chong films), they are presented as commentary on the futility of marijuana laws. In *American Beauty*, for example, in middle age, the lead character, Lester, develops a penchant for pot. The depiction of his marijuana use is synchronized with his reclamation of his selfhood. Lester's increased marijuana use is concomitant with his moves towards eschewing the empty materialism of middle-class America. He quits his job, starts lifting weights, finds himself attracted to teenage girls, and becomes more open-minded, all the while offering a narrative of how dead he was before initiating these changes.

In Canada, this low level of problematization with regard to marijuana is also found in legal arenas. Marijuana carries one of the lightest penalties under the Controlled Drugs and Substances Act (CDSA). Three official government reports (the LeDain Commission, the Senate Committee, and the Parliamentary Committee) advocate its decriminalization. The LeDain Commission's separate report on marijuana clearly calls for law reform and advocates the decriminalization of marijuana, arguing that, especially with regard to the offence of simple possession, the interdiction of marijuana proves costly and has a considerable negative impact on society.

The Special Committee on Non-Medical Use of Drugs (SCNMUD), struck by Parliament in 2001, took up a mandate and methodology similar to LeDain and mirrored the latter in offering specific consideration of marijuana. Originally, the committee was ordered by Parliament to revisit the same issues raised by LeDain thirty years earlier. In 2002, the committee's mandate expanded to include Bill C-344,[18] a private member's bill introduced by Esquimalt MP Dr. Keith Martin calling for the decriminalization of marijuana. Like LeDain, the Parliamentary Committee found that the effects of uneven law enforcement practices and of sanctioning on those found guilty of marijuana possession were far more harmful than were the effects of marijuana itself. The committee unhooks marijuana from the drug/crime nexus, placing it firmly within the context of health, not crime. In its final observations about marijuana, the committee writes, "smoking any amount of marijuana is unhealthy, because of its high concentration of tar and benzopyrene" (SCNMUD 2002, 131). The committee does not de-risk marijuana but, rather, transfers the harms associated with it. The claims that marijuana is linked to criminal activity are deflated as the alleged physical harms linked to the substance are given precedence. The committee continues on to underscore the importance of educating the public concerning the harmful effects of marijuana (particularly with regard to youth), including short-term memory loss and dependence. Former fears of marijuana leading to criminal activity or harder drug use via the "gateway" argument are absent.

The Senate Special Committee on Illegal Drugs (SSCID), chaired by Senator Claude Nolin in 2002, took on a mandate that focused exclusively on marijuana legislation. The Senate Committee reached conclusions similar to both LeDain and the Parliamentary Committee, calling for law reform and the decriminalization of marijuana and contradicting the Parliamentary Committee in discounting common fears about the pernicious effects of pot. The Senate Committee concluded that there was insufficient scientific evidence (from both social and clinical science) to support claims that marijuana had any remarkable, long-range, or deleterious effects on users. Couching LeDain's conclusions in the contemporary argot of risk and harm,[19] the committee concludes that, "used in moderation, cannabis in itself poses very little danger to users and to society as a whole, but specific types of use represent risks for users" (SSCID 2002, 42). It is, in the committee's eyes, not the substance itself that poses harm or risk; rather, risk associated with marijuana consumption is linked to the user (e.g., developing emphysema) and the manner of use (i.e., smoking is thought to be more carcinogenic than eating or drinking).

These official government responses (in contrast to the generalizing ones outlined above) work to de-risk marijuana as a threat to public safety and to reduce the perception of threat to public health. In Canada, marijuana has shifted from pariah to panacea. The medical marijuana movement gives pot new credibility, even in the face of the federal government's botched attempts to become a dealer itself. In *R v. Parker,* the Ontario Court of Appeal found that the medical benefits wrought by marijuana far outweighed the harms it caused (Young 2003).[20] Beyond this, the appellate court made strong claims about the benign nature of marijuana. Justice Rosenberg, writing the court's unanimous decision, describes the court's view of marijuana:

> Consumption of marijuana is relatively harmless compared to the so-called hard drugs and including tobacco and alcohol and there is not "hard evidence" that even long-term use can lead to irreversible physical or psychological damage. Marijuana use is not criminogenic (i.e., there is no causal

relationship between marijuana use and criminality) and it does not make people more aggressive or violent. There have been no recorded deaths from consumption of marijuana.[21]

Rosenberg's only cautions regarding marijuana are that it should not be consumed while driving and that it could contribute to bronchial ailments. After the landmark case, the federal government launched a pilot project offering exemptions from anti-marijuana laws to those who could prove a medical condition ameliorated by marijuana use. Under the *Marijuana Medical Access Regulations*, introduced in 2001, Canadians with exemptions could possess and cultivate their own medical supply of marijuana. The government also began to grow its own supply of marijuana, with the intention of distributing it to those with exemptions.

The possession of marijuana, however, remains illegal in Canada,[22] giving it a unique personality: on the one hand benign, benevolent and curative, while on the other, malign, threatening, and in need of strict control. In light of this illegality, it is interesting to look at the ways in which marijuana is characterized in the treatment courts by court officials. Marijuana is the problem child of the TDTC, championed by some and lamented by others as court affiliates fall on all sides of the decriminalization debate. The court is mandated only to deal with individuals proven addicted to cocaine, crack, or opiates, but it monitors clients for all drug use and offers sanctions for undisclosed drug use of any description (including marijuana). Clients cannot graduate if they continue to test positive for marijuana.

When marijuana is raised in the court directly, it is ascribed particular attributes within the drug/crime nexus. These attributes do not render marijuana criminogenic directly; rather, the court actors tend to take up the gateway argument about marijuana, supposing that its use leads people to other, more serious drug use. The following comes from my research journal,

> Karen is called next. She admits that she smoked pot and drank (had one shot) over the weekend. The judge goes on then about the importance of not drinking. Karen argues that she's never had a problem with drinking or smoking pot and doesn't see why she shouldn't drink. Bentley responds that drinking can lower your defences and make you more likely to relapse. He then reminds her that abstaining from alcohol is a bail condition.

> Mike is called after Karen and he also admits to smoking dope. The judge asks who he used with (clearly Mike and Karen are a couple). Mike responds that he was with friends, going to see a movie. The judge responds by saying, "The comments I made to Karen apply to you too. I urge you not to smoke marijuana for that reason." This, I suppose, means that marijuana

can also lower your inhibitions and therefore make you less resistant to triggers.

Interestingly, the judge here conflates marijuana and alcohol, painting them both with the same brush, rendering them, at the same time, non-criminogenic but disarming.[23] Still, this particular risking of marijuana, a judgement of its effects familiar to the DTC, has the consequence of criminalizing marijuana by proxy, making it guilty by association. It is not the marijuana per se that is a problem but what it might lead to. The worst thing that marijuana can do to you, according to the court program, is to weaken your resolve to not do other drugs.

This particular view of marijuana – that it is a bad influence – is echoed by some of the key actors in the court. One Crown counsel painted a similar portrait of marijuana:

> From a therapeutic perspective just watching what was happening, for some people or a majority of people, I don't know, but for some people the use of marijuana usually leads them eventually to using cocaine or heroin; especially for people who were addicted to cocaine or heroin before anyways. I mean by certainly coming they are addicted and I don't know what they were using before. But we found that to be a cycle that occurs. And so from a therapeutic standpoint, without necessarily getting into the philosophical aspect of whether marijuana is good or bad ... perhaps we should be a bit tougher on marijuana.

While the gateway argument is built into the rationales of the court and serves as one of the primary justifications for the interdiction of marijuana, it remains contested within academic literature. There is wide disagreement among academics as to the merits of the gateway theory. Some maintain that marijuana serves as a gateway to other forms of drug use, while others maintain that it is impossible to isolate marijuana use from other factors contributing to substance use.[24] Despite the continual debates over the "truth" of the gateway theory as it relates to marijuana, it is an old and familiar characterisation that is readily taken up as a justification for criminalizing the substance. Giffen, Endicott, and Lambert (1991) chronicle the use of the gateway argument on the part of prohibitionists throughout the 1960s and 1970s Canadian debates about decriminalizing marijuana.

Other actors in the court adopt a different view of the personality of marijuana. For the most part, they take a harm-reduction approach to drugs in general and set up a hierarchy of harm among the different substances addressed in the courtroom. While the definition of harm reduction is contested across disciplines and organizations (see Erickson et al. 1997), the philosophy, as it has evolved over the last twenty years, is organized around basic principles more or less commonly shared among those who take up a harm-reduction approach. White's definition of harm reduction captures these basic principles. He suggests that harm reduction is

> posited on the belief that some alcoholics and addicts are for some extended periods of their lives incapable of sustained sobriety, and that no viable intervention technology exists that can immediately alter this condition. Therefore, intervention strategies are recommended that enhance the quality of life for addicts while reducing the personal and social costs of addiction (White 1998, 292).

The court explicitly assumes a harm-reduction program. Still, despite the overt presence or acknowledgment of harm-reduction practices, those actors in the court whose work aligns them closely with treatment aspects of the court program adopt the language of harm reduction in trying to imagine marijuana. When asked how they characterized and understood the role of marijuana in the court, most therapists acknowledged the continued illegal status of marijuana and recognized that its use could not be condoned by the court. At the same time, marijuana is read by these people as a qualitatively different substance than, say, cocaine. A client who stops using cocaine but continues to use marijuana has, in the majority of their opinions, exhibited positive change in her substance-use habits. One therapist states:[25]

> If a client were to come into treatment and report a marijuana use because they had cravings for cocaine, they had [a] craving they wanted to use so they smoked a joint, okay – harm reduction, right? You didn't go out, you didn't use crack cocaine. You smoked a joint. It's lesser on the scale of harm reduction, right?

Another takes an even more liberal approach to marijuana use among clients in the court:[26]

> We were noticing that there were some people doing really well. They were off of the crack, off of the heroin or whatever they were doing. They were participating in the program. They were making all of their appointments ... They were doing all the things that we said at the beginning we needed them to do; that we expected of people. Yet they were still smoking pot. The system was being positive about marijuana. So you can't say the marijuana use is bad when you look at it in terms of the big picture and you see that this person is really improving. You know some people can argue well maybe [with regards to] marijuana if they had been without it, they would be improving even more. But who's to say? Maybe they would. Maybe they'd

be crash[ing] and burning more because they'd be smoking more crack or something.

Even though the majority of the therapists place marijuana on a harm-reduction continuum, agreeing that smoking pot is an improvement over using either crack or heroin, they are all quick to point out that there are still harms associated with marijuana use. Another therapist,[27] who described herself as leaning more towards an abstinence-based model, offers her opinion of marijuana use among court clients:

> Well, I think the message is – and I've heard this from a lot of clients – is that it is okay to smoke weed or have a drink, you're not going to get in as much trouble as you are with cocaine. I think if the message was from the beginning, "don't use this [marijuana]" and it's equally punishable as cocaine, then people would look at it differently. But I think it's an opening for a client. The therapists, some of them think it's not as bad. I have issues with, you know, if there is a pregnant woman. My first impulse is to get her into detox because she's smoking weed or whatever. I mean a lot of the effects of marijuana are known, but I would really struggle with having somebody continue who's pregnant.

The idea that there are still a lot of unknowns surrounding the effects of marijuana, and that it is because of this that therapists especially should err on the side of caution with respect to condoning marijuana use, is echoed, albeit less strongly, in the comments of other therapists. One of these people,[28] discussing her views on harm reduction in relation to marijuana, stated:

> It [taking up a harm-reduction approach] doesn't mean there isn't any harm, though. So the struggle is in terms of addressing marijuana use. I mean it's really quite fascinating when you are in a group and people start talking about crack cocaine. You swear to the negative consequences of crack cocaine use, and they are, you know, a hundredfold. But when you ask, "What are the negative consequences of marijuana use?" there's no hands going up. People don't see harm. You know as a result of it because the consequences aren't as immediate, right? We think they're further down the road, for the chronic users. And no one really knows for sure what it can do.

There is concern that marijuana is not sufficiently well known through science for the court actors to allow a liberal response to its presence.

By way of contrast, the VDTC does not deal with marijuana at all. The Vancouver court is mandated to deal with heroin, crack/cocaine, and methamphetamine addiction (a substance Toronto is working to add to its roster as well). The interdiction on mentioning substances in the court means that the courtroom is free of the kinds of discussions detailed above in relation to the Toronto court. Like the TDTC, the VDTC incorporates drug testing into its programming. However, the court does not test for marijuana use in the regular drug screens; THC (the active ingredient in marijuana) is only tested for in the final drug screen preceding graduation. Testing positive for marijuana use does not preclude court participants from graduating, only from receiving an "honours" designation.[29] None of the people with whom I spoke in the VDTC identified marijuana as a concern or alluded to any struggles among themselves over marijuana use by court clients.

Marijuana is the person at the party who elicits a different reaction in everyone she meets. Some are offended and threatened by her, some see her as harmless, and others enjoy her company. A contested drugality, like a contested personality, can give rise to conflict and struggle.

Opiates (Heroin)

While marijuana elicits ambivalent responses from actors in different locations, opiates, particularly heroin, garner a consistent and practically uniform response. Opium was the original demon drug, the reason for the nascence of Canada's drug laws, and the centre of moral and racial panics that lasted well into the twentieth century.[30] Over the last sixty years, opium came to be replaced by heroin, its synthetic cousin, as the most problematic of substances.[31] While opiates have remained hugely problematic over the last century, their personality has not remained consistent. Opiates were originally depicted as highly racialized substances that led to moral degeneration. Contemporary thinking about opiates offers a far more medicalized characterization, suggesting that they pose certain risks of harm to the user. Consistently, however, opiates are implicated in criminogenic harms and are directly, causally linked to criminal behaviour.

The case of opiates is perhaps the best documented in Canadian drug history. But while a small yet significant body of Canadian work addresses the problem of opiates, as with the wider literature on drug laws, little of it deals with the substance itself. Writers tend rather to focus on the laws surrounding a substance or on accounts of the users (Boyd 2004; Carstairs 1999, 2005; Comack 1991; Giffen, Endicott, and Lambert 1991). While these accounts are limited, it is possible to piece together a thumbnail sketch of how opiates were characterized at the start of the twentieth century. Emily Murphy (1922, 42) offers a concise summary of opiates in the 1920s:

> But in whatever form these drugs are taken, they degrade the morals and enfeeble the will. No matter what their status has been, inveterate users of drugs become degraded. All are liars; nearly all become dishonest. Being

deprived of the drug, they will go any length to get it, even to thievery and prostitution.

Opiates are implicated in both moral denigration and criminal behaviour. Murphy goes on to describe how opiates compromise the purity of white women, reaching into xenophobic concerns with illustrations of white women in bed with black men, sharing an opium pipe. Opiates, to Murphy, are the vehicle leading women, especially, on a downward slope ending in criminality, moral degeneracy, and compromised motherhood.

The dangerousness of opiates, particularly heroin, has come to share space with notions of their risks. The harm-reduction movement, which began in the 1980s around the "discovery" of the HIV/AIDS connection to injection drug use, lent to heroin the language of risk (Erickson et al. 1997). Risks posed by heroin are usually expressed as health risks. Fears of HIV/AIDS, Hepatitis C,[32] and overdose inform much of the current discourse around heroin. Heroin, however, is rarely read directly into these narratives; instead, discourses refer to "injection drug use."

Still, despite the fact that heroin is often presented in medical terms, it also retains a criminogenic identity in so far as it triggers a compulsion to use that is so strong the individual is driven to criminal acts. The 2000 film *Requiem for a Dream* is a prime example of this. The film tells the story of three friends, all of whom are heroin dependent. It focuses predominantly on their heroin use, depicting them engaged in theft, prostitution, and fraud all to obtain money with which to purchase heroin. The Scottish cult classic *Trainspotting* offers a similar depiction of heroin use.[33] Again, we see a group of friends compelled, through their common addiction, to acts of debauchery. In *Trainspotting*, violence, theft, black-market drug trading, guns, and child neglect are all linked to heroin use.

Official accounts of heroin use reinforce the criminogenic properties ascribed to it in popular depictions; however, the criminogenic nature of heroin is often presented in more economic than moral terms. The LeDain Commission (1972, 321) reached the following conclusions about opiates:

> There are very few legitimate ways in which most individuals can afford to meet illicit market prices. Consequently, when tolerance pushes the cost of drug use above what the user can afford legitimately, he is forced into a decision – either quit the drug and go through withdrawal, or turn to criminal methods of acquiring the necessary money ... many [users] turn to petty crime, small robberies, shoplifting and prostitution.

Thirty years later, the latest Parliamentary Committee (SCNMUD 2002) pays passing attention to the criminal attributes of heroin. In its focus on heroin, the Parliamentary Committee addresses heroin's criminogenic properties by providing a list of the drug's ill effects on users. This list provides the percentages of heroin users who are incarcerated, have criminal records, or have committed crimes.

The Drug Strategy sees opiate use primarily as a health concern, something that poses a threat to public safety only through its role as a conduit for HIV/AIDS and Hepatitis C rather than through crime. The Directions and Priorities section of the Drug Strategy raises harm reduction to an elevated position in the government's approach to drug use as it sets education and research as primary goals. Even official police representations of heroin use tend now to focus more on its health concerns than on its criminogenic nature. The film *Through a Blue Lens*, produced by the Vancouver Police Department, chronicles the activities of Vancouver's Odd Squad, a special unit of police officers assigned specifically to police the Hastings and Main district. The Odd Squad takes on a hybridized role, combining law enforcement with a public health agenda to help residents of the area find shelter, medical attention, and, ultimately, address their heroin habit. The documentary never shows one of the residents of the Downtown Eastside being arrested; rather, it shows police intervening in an overdose and residents talking with high school kids about the social and health implications of their heroin use (loss of family, tooth decay).

A combination of factors are at play to contribute to this reshaping of heroin's personality. It is much easier to establish a direct, causal link between HIV/AIDS or Hepatitis C and heroin than it is between heroin and crime; and, thanks to the diligence of public health workers since the mid-1980s, there is a great deal of public concern in Canada over stopping the spread of HIV/AIDS (Erickson et al. 1997; Fisher 1997). Also, the alleged link between heroin and crime has been proposed and reproposed throughout the twentieth century (Allen 2005; Carstairs 2005; Giffen, Endicott, and Lambert 1991). It is almost intuitive to simply assume that heroin use is criminogenic. The ability of popular media to continually present heroin as inherently criminal is testament to this. Heroin's personality is constituted, especially through the language of harm, as *both* criminal *and* iatrogenic. Opiates are the only schedule-one substance under the Controlled Drugs and Substances Act, commanding the highest penalties for possession and trafficking.

This multifaceted portrayal of heroin's drugality is readily observed in the drug treatment courts. The courts are organized around a common assumption of heroin's (and cocaine's) inherent criminality, and they are mandated to address drug-related crime. This, of course, is another instance of generalization. Given the courts' strictly limited menus of targeted substances, drug-related crime really means crimes linked to heroin, crack/cocaine, and (most recently, in the case of Vancouver) methamphetamine.

Heroin is not often discussed directly in the Toronto court room. When it is raised in Toronto, it is typically by the court clients as they report to the judge that they have used the substance. The response of the judge in these instances varies considerably, depending on the individual circumstances. Commonly, he will ask the individual why she used and will point out that she does not look well or is slipping back to her old ways. These comments, however, are not specific to heroin. The judge tends to make the same kinds of comments when individuals report crack use. And these comments are not specifically about the substance. The judge is inclined to focus more on the behaviour of the person than on the behaviour of the drug. In fact, none of the legal actors in the court, either in the day-to-day goings on or in interviews, offered much in the way of substantive comments related directly to heroin. The Crown, judge, and duty counsel all tend to talk about individual behaviours rather than specific substances. My interviews in Vancouver bore out the same results.

Despite the lack of discourse around heroin in either courtroom, the TDTC (unlike the VDTC) offers separate programming for heroin users and cocaine users. When asked about this, the legal actors in the TDTC were inclined to deflect the question, saying it was a "treatment issue."[34] Members of the treatment side of the TDTC team emphasized the importance of understanding the specific personality of heroin. Often the distinction was an attempt to set heroin apart from crack/cocaine. Largely, this distinction is made around the temporality (and, to a lesser extent, the pharmacology) of the different substances.

Because heroin arises in the TDTC far less often than do crack or cocaine, many of the therapists have only limited experience counselling heroin users. Still, they are quick to point out that heroin allows people to lead relatively stable lives, making it, in some ways, the easier drug to manage. One therapist describes her impression of dealing with opiate users:[35]

> The heroin clients that we have, you know, they'll go out, they'll get enough for that day to last them the twenty-four hours. I mean, basically the clients that have come into the program as opiate users, they're at the point where they're addicted and they need it in order to function, right? They need it in order to get through the day because if they don't use they're going to be experiencing some serious withdrawal symptoms.

This therapist goes on to describe heroin use as a solitary activity: "You go out, you get your drugs, you go back home for the day." The long-lasting effect of heroin has a specific impact on how heroin is understood by the therapists. Another comments,[36] with the opiates, you can maintain a job for many years before things get really out of hand because you only need it once or twice a day. They [users] can maintain a place to live, they can even maintain certain relationships ... The opiate users usually have somewhere because they haven't lost everything to the drug.

The only problems consistently raised regarding heroin users in the court program concerned initial periods of withdrawal and stabilization on methadone maintenance. One therapist described her work as follows:[37]

I used to do a group primarily where everybody was methadone maintained and they were on the nod all the time.[38] So it's really challenging to do a group because this is the difference [between opiates and cocaine]; it's like in their head, and because the substance is a sub of opiates, everybody kind of like kicks back. When you're methadone maintained, especially while you're trying to get your dose regulated or if you're taking bennies on top, that certainly has an impact and you kind of get dozy.

The treatment workers in the court tend to paint a picture of a drug that is far less volatile than popular media depictions of the substance would have us believe.

In recent years, heroin and opiates have undergone a conversion. Whereas, in the early twentieth century, opiates were cast as demon drugs (Carstairs 2005; Giffen, Endicott, and Lambert 1991; Murphy 1922), they are now read more benignly. Their ability to incite criminal behaviour is still present, especially when they are described by individuals directly involved in the CJS. Those who do not enter into discussions of drugs through the door of crime, however, describe a different substance. From the point of view of users and therapists as well as law reformers, opiates, like marijuana, are better understood as substances that are far more threatening to individual health than to public safety.

Crack/Cocaine

Crack continues to be the most criminogenic of all illicit substances. Reeves and Campbell's (1994) study of the rise of the crack panic in the mid-1980s demonstrates how crack was criminalized in a way that had never before been applied to cocaine or a cocaine derivative.[39] According to Reeves and Campbell:

A pleasurable substance that was once the province of the wealthy had finally trickled down to the lower levels of the American socioeconomic racial order. In this violation of taste distinctions, cocaine would not only lose some of its value as a status symbol, but it would become associated with a mode of drug abuse that is more a matter of desperation than recreation. In the symbolic inversion, the preferred purifying solution to the cocaine problem would shift from the therapeutic branch of the medical-industrial complex to its armed disciplinary forces (129-30).

The move from cocaine, a drug of status and upper middle-class self-indulgence, to crack is instructive as it reveals just how generative the personalities of drugs can be. Cocaine was (and still is, in certain circles) a drug of privilege and recreation reserved for the rich and self-indulgent (Jenkins 1999). Accounts stemming from the 1970s onward paint cocaine as the ultimate party drug (Jenkins 1999; Reeves and Campbell 1994; Reinarman and Levine 1997). While not represented as unproblematic,[40] it was also not particularly criminogenic, at least not in the street crime sense of the word. Even when crimes were associated with cocaine use (violence for example), it was rarely with the thought that some sort of criminal justice response would ensue. The criminalizing of cocaine was reserved largely for the high-level dealers (see, for example, the film *Blow*).

Crack, on the other hand, is deeply criminalized. The iconic crack house is perhaps the most salient example of this. Although Reeves and Campbell (1994) read the fascination with and focus on the crack house as a shadow image of Reaganomics gone awry, it is also apparent that the crack house, as defined solely through its affiliation with the substance, came to epitomize, particularly in the United States, the burgeoning threat to public safety posed by the rise of crack (Bourgeois 2003; Williams 1993).

The criminogenic nature of crack is not only linked to the crack house. "Gangsta" rap music, birthed in Los Angeles in the 1980s, continues to have a strong following today. Much of this music constitutes a form of resistance to the criminogenic targeting of black communities, which emerged out of the crack panics. "Night of the Living Baseheads" by Public Enemy offers a cogent rejoinder to the rise of crack use and arrests in Los Angeles through the 1990s and serves as a good example of this kind of resistance. While offering critical commentary on justice system responses to crack use, the song still underscores the criminogenic nature of crack. While crack users and sellers might be "run" by the justice system,[41] the bigger problem is the crime linked with the drug. In one verse, burglary is referenced; in other verses, the problem of black-on-black violence is raised.

Phillippe Bourgeois' (2003) enthnographic study of crack dealers in East Harlem offers a concentrated illustration of the links between crack, violence, and other kinds of crime. Bourgeois focuses on one organization of crack dealers who operate out of a mocked-up street-corner business. His descriptions of the relationships between members of this network show strong social connections set against a backdrop of violence and threat. Bourgeois is careful, though, to avoid the overly simple conclusion that the crack is the cause of the neighbourhood's troubles; rather, he points to the area's lengthy history of poverty and racism, citing the establishment of the crack economy as a rational survival strategy. Still, the link between crack and crime is palpable throughout his study. Bourgeois chronicles stabbing, murder, violence against women, theft, armed robbery, police brutality, and burglary as commonplace in the crack-based street culture. At the same time, running counter to the narrative, Bourgeois also paints a picture of a close-knit, caring, and visionary community in which people help each other out, imagine and plan ways to improve their condition, and offer hospitality to visitors. This idea that crack-using communities could be anything other than utterly dysfunctional is shunted to the side in much of the prevailing discourse.

This view of the highly criminogenic nature of crack use is supported by actors in the TDTC. During our interview, the Crown counsel argued strongly that the distinction made between heroin and crack/cocaine within the CDSA is erroneous: they are both equally harmful. According to this individual,

> the crack cocaine addict is usually out of control. And it really surprises me, having worked in the criminal justice systems for as long as I have, in dealing with criminal matters that I have no idea how bad crack could actually be. I mean heroin can get you into penitentiary quite easily ... whereas crack you get a month. I mean, for you to get a number of years with crack, you have to have a lot, a lot of crack. So I mean, the disparity, I mean in terms of the impact on people, you know, has really surprised me.

Observations concerning the "out-of-control" nature of crack are also made by other practitioners in the court. Several of the therapists describe the crack lifestyle as one filled with "chaos." One therapist described crack as follows:[42]

> I think the chaos associated with crack use is tied to committing the crimes to support your habit, and you use it more frequently. You're using more regularly. You're going out every couple of hours unless you've, you know, got a lot of money and you scored a lot of crack. You're going out every couple of hours and, you know, boosting something else to get more crack and back and forth, back and forth.

Crack, according to both the legal and the therapeutic actors in the court, breeds an instability that is readily linked to gendered criminal behaviour. The short high crack gives creates a brief cycle of using and seeking, fuelled by a desperation that leads to break-and-enters among men and to prostitution among women. Dealing drugs is also seen as a way of getting money; however, as one therapist explained, dealing is not conducive to the chaotic crack lifestyle because it requires a certain amount of organization and planning as well as an ability to not use the drugs you are selling.

The crack baby is another iconic symbol of the destructive character of crack. Images of malnourished, allegedly drug-addled infants (almost always black) were featured on North American television screens throughout the 1980s and 1990s. The scare over crack babies is perhaps the best known drug scare of the latter half of the twentieth century. This, despite the fact that there is little evidence to support popular claims that a mother who used crack during her pregnancy was automatically placing her foetus at risk (Boyd 2004; Logan 2000; Murphy and Rosenbaum 1999). The criminalization of these women was particularly fierce as they were painted as threats to their children (born or unborn). Often, these women were and are accused of child abuse and neglect and face the loss of their children (Boyd 2004).

Coming of age in the early 1990s, I was exposed to the height of crack panics and the last dribbles of cocaine pleasures. As a teenager and young adult, cocaine was always one of those drugs that was around, on the periphery – a drug that one encountered from time to time and, less frequently, might try. Crack, however, was a leper, completely untouchable. For those of us who dabbled and more in recreational drug use, crack was as low as you could go. We left parties when crack appeared, knowing that merely being in its presence would jeopardize the tenuous social capital inherent to middle-class white kids in the suburbs. Crack retains this untouchable status, remaining the drug of desperation and demise.

A Note about Crystal Methamphetamine

As this book goes to press, I am keenly aware that the text is haunted by methamphetamine, or crystal meth, even as it never really enters into my analysis. In 2007, crystal meth is only starting to enter into the awareness of both government and the public. The VDTC deals with the substance, although it is never talked about. In the wake of heightened public awareness about the growing use of crystal meth, the federal government recently elected to elevate its position on the drug schedule to Schedule 2, making it legally similar to crack/cocaine. At the first conference of Canadian drug treatment courts held in Edmonton in October 2006, the spectre of crystal meth hung heavily, framed as a looming social crisis. The conference's plenary session included several speakers who focused on the allegedly emergent crystal meth epidemic. We were thoroughly versed in the evils of the drug, and the dire circumstances of children living in homes where meth is manufactured were emphasized. The Alberta government has taken such warnings to heart, enacting a new piece of legislation to force teens using meth into treatment. These growing concerns over crystal meth make it the drug to watch; however, meth's arrival on the scene is too recent to give it adequate attention here. I want only to acknowledge its emergence as a drug of growing public concern and flag its status for further inquiry.

Conclusion

Following Woolgar and Cooper (1999), understanding drugs as (possibly political) artefacts means approaching them with ambivalence. The personalities of drugs are constituted through an array of epistemologies and representations, each of which has its own particular effects. The cultural and scientific properties of drugs, both specific and general, cast their personalities. These personalities are reflections of what these drugs do and what they are thought to do. As Latour (1987) reminds us, the lines between the social and the scientific are not particularly clear. As a result, the "truth" about substances is less important than is what is thought to be true. The personalities of drugs change because the social understandings of the "truths" of these substances change. Studying drug personalities from the point of view of popular, official, and clinical discourses illustrates the material "legends" pertaining to their personalities. These personalities play a part in sculpting criminal justice responses to drug use.

Drugs, then, have a hand in shaping the CJS. The close link between drugs and crime underscores the need for a criminal justice response to drug use. The deployment of the generalized term "drugs" works to paint all drug users with the same brush, constituting a singular, governable subject who is inherently criminogenic. At the same time, drugs also have their own unique properties, dictated by both cultural and clinical understandings of their effects. These specified personalities are also generative. An increasing acceptance of marijuana as a benign substance informs law-reform movements, moving it closer and closer to decriminalization. In the DTCs, marijuana, while still criminogenic, is nowhere near as problematic as are other substances. Marijuana is ambiguous. It is neither harmful nor harmless, depending upon which knowledges about the substance one is citing. Heroin is both benign and insidious. Its capacity to render people addicts, coupled with its troubled and vilified history, makes it the most criminalized of all substances. Still, despite this criminalization, there is a steadiness to heroin, afforded through its pharmacodynamics, which renders its users manageable. While cocaine raises less ire (than crack), crack is the maligned target of most concern and anxiety within the CJS. The crack user is unpredictable and volatile, and the crack lifestyle is highly criminogenic.

The ability to see these generative capabilities is facilitated through the use of Latour's notion of the actor-network. In allowing for the potential action of objects, I show that attempts to regulate and cure drug addiction are not only shaped by social and political factors but also by the ways in which substances are imbued with social and political meaning, enabling them to take on personalities that give them generative capabilities. These personalities are not only political and social. If heroin and cocaine use did not cause addiction, a disease that most people imagine is curable, then there would be no reason to act on people who use these substances in the first place. Further, the addictive properties of both these substances shape the criminality attached to their use, tailoring criminal and therapeutic responses. Attempts to understand mentalities of rule benefit from the ability to see the generative capabilities of all the actors involved in the site. The criminal addict is not only born of a set of governing rationalities but also emerges from a cultural/scientific context within which drugs themselves have a guiding hand. This does not mean that the drug/crime nexus is "real" but, rather, that these interpretations of the actions and personalities of drugs have real effects. And these are what shape our responses to users.

4

Translating Justice and Therapy: The Drug Treatment Court Network

During an observation session in the Toronto drug treatment court (TDTC), the judge calls the court to attention. He is addressing a specific client but makes it clear he wants the entire court to listen. He proceeds to reiterate the goals of the court, concluding: "The purpose of this court is to cure addiction; the closer he (the client) or anyone is brought to cure the better." The promotional video produced in 1999 for this same court illuminates this goal. Both the judge and the Crown attorney explain that the mandate of this court is to "close the revolving door on crime" by treating drug addicts.

Psy disciplines, actors, knowledges, practices, and curative goals are stock features of Western penal systems (Arrigo 2002; Kendall 2005; Pasquino 1991; Rafter 2004). In Chapter 2, I outline the rise of psy in the Ontario penal system. In the current penal context, prisoners and probationers are actuarially assessed through psychologically based risk prediction tools and offered cognitive behaviourial programming to target criminogenic factors. Those convicted of criminal offences can lower their risk levels (and, therefore, the levels of control to which they are subjected) if they address their criminogenic needs by, for example, taking part in substance-abuse programming and developing "pro-social" relationships. Thus far, I have built the case that these initiatives are deeply political and cultural, born out of strategic governing and popular thought about the causes of and cures for crime. The politics and culture of punitive substance-abuse treatment relies on links between law and psy disciplines (Kendall 2000; Simon 1993).

In keeping with my broader genealogical project, I want to turn now to a closer consideration of these links by exploring how psy and legal knowledges are assembled in justice settings to effect a project of change tailored to "cure the offender." I use the drug treatment courts (DTCs) as sites in which to study these knowledge assemblies. Taking my cue from Rose's (1998) work on psy knowledges and Latour's (1987) work on the actor-network, I show how expert knowledges are freed from expert actors within these settings.

This uncoupling allows for the translation of the goals and interests of legal and therapeutic actors involved in the courts, translations that affect the ways in which both justice and therapy are imagined. On a practical level, these translations have implications for questions of due process and the ethical treatment of court clients.

Undisciplined Knowledges

If, following Foucault, we accept the assemblage of power/knowledge, then knowledges become important sites of study because "if knowledge is power, so too, are power relations also knowledge relations" (Valverde 2003a, 1). The power/knowledge lens is a particularly useful tool in developing a critical understanding of the treatment courts because it is precisely the arrangement of knowledges in those courts that shapes their disciplinary effects. It is because of the exceptional coordination of psy and legal knowledges within their apparatuses that these courts can take "to cure the offender" as their governing mantra.

Mannheim (1970), the "father" of the sociology of knowledge, sets out a clear theoretical and methodological approach to the social study of knowledge. Relying heavily on tools and ideas born of colonialist anthropology, Mannheim outlines the different ways in which sociologists can think about and research the link between the social and ways of knowing. Mannheim's account of the sociology of knowledge is premised on the assumption that research can draw discernable boundaries around different kinds of knowledge, understanding different knowledges as having distinguishing levels of "purity." He outlines these distinctions in aligning knowledge with art:

> Just as in art we can date particular forms on the ground of the definite association with a particular period of history, so in the case of knowledge we can detect with increasing exactness the perspective due to a particular historical setting (115).

Knowledge, according to Mannheim, is something to be neatly sorted and categorized. It can be placed into certain specific genres and disciplines. He is right, of course: these are the ways in which we think about different knowledges. As students, we are taught "modern thought," "Greek philosophy," and "the Enlightenment." Each of these categories of knowledge, like the different subjects students take in school, is separate.

Law, as both an epistemology and a discipline, has never been pure. This is what the law and society and legal realist movements have been teaching us for the better part of a century (Tomlins 2000). Noting the ways in which the social seeps into legal arenas, legal philosophers such as Pound (1921) were quick to point out that law is driven not only by legal knowledges or processes but also by social factors (including knowledges). In the earlier realist tradition, this way of seeing law tended towards normativity and positivism, with an eye to reimagining the juridical project as deeply socio-logical. More recent incantations gesture towards the descriptive and ge-nealogical, looking at the role of law in society and of society in law (see Ewick, Kagan, and Sarat 1999). In this chapter, I build on knowledge of law's impurity by focusing specifically on the circulation of knowledges and actors.

Legal settings offer a number of different opportunities to explore know-ledge relations. One might address, as does Valverde (2003a), the connec-tion between expert and non-expert knowledges and people. In her study of law's "common" knowledges, Valverde uses the terms "high-status knowledges" and "low-status knowledges" to mark the difference between epistemologies.

Concentrating specifically on the relationship between law and the ex-pert, scientific knowledges, Jasanoff (1995) charts the long-standing alli-ance between law and science – an alliance born of their mutual truth-finding endeavours. She shows the increasing centrality of science in the court-room and illustrates how legal practice develops to facilitate the incorpora-tion of scientific knowledge into legal proceedings. Kendall's (2005) erudite work on psy interventions with women in conflict with the law illustrates how epistemologies of women's mental illness injected into criminal jus-tice practices fuel the endurance of age-old stereotypes of the criminal woman as mad or bad, reinforcing women's inherent pathologies over the possibil-ity of alternate rationalities.

Rose (1998) offers a different perspective on knowledges. He is occupied with the productive nature of power/knowledge. In studying the role of psy knowledges in governing projects, Rose charts the devolution of expertise "from above" to facilitate governing at a "molecular" level as carried out by mid-level practitioners such as probation officers or even individual selves. Contesting Mannheim's claims, Rose contends that expert knowledges are not bound to experts; rather, he observes the strategic, downward move-ment of knowledges, which is firmly located in broader trends of rising neoliberalism accompanied by increased individualized responsibilization and "governing at a distance."

Like Rose, I am interested in what happens to knowledges when they are liberated from their disciplining experts and the DTCs' attempts to cure the criminal addict. I don't imagine that the treatment courts are the first or the only legal sites in which this liberation happens. What sets the treat-ment courts apart, then, is not their interdisciplinarity but the obviousness of it and the non-hierarchal arrangement of legal and non-legal expert knowledges.[1] In these courts, there is no pretense that law sits outside of other epistemologies; rather, law's contamination is explicitly mandated and acted out. The kinetics of knowledge in the treatment courts do not lend themselves, however, to the hierarchical knowledge model hitherto observed. Law and therapy are meant to share space in the courts without one being privileged over the other. As such, knowledge circulation in this site is best thought of as occurring latitudinally. For this reason, Latour's (1987) notion of the actor-network proves useful.

In Chapter 3, I use Latour's notion of the network as a means of understanding the generative capabilities of drugs. In this chapter, I recall and expand this approach. Latour suggests that we can comprehend complicated assemblages of experts, knowledges, and objects by looking at them as networks that revolve around objects and scientific inventions. In light of this, I do not imagine that his methodology can be or, indeed, ought to be directly imposed on governance sites such as the DTCs. Still, the analytics of the actor-network afford a useful perspective that allows me to unhook the apparently well-soldered links between experts and knowledges without having to map their movement on a vertical axis (Valverde, Levi, and Moore 2005); instead, these knowledges and actors rest on a horizontal axis. Knowledge is understood as operating within a network alongside (not born of or disciplined by, as in Rose's model) other actors that are both people and things. Seeing knowledges and actors on the level means that they may circulate without either gaining or losing "status." Within the actor-network, these circulations are enabled through "translation," by which Latour means the ways in which knowledges, actors, objects, goals, and interests are brought together. He argues that, within a network, there are moments of translation that take on a number of different forms. One way that translation occurs is in the redefinition, or "reshuffling," of interests and goals. Network actors often have disparate goals and interests. The inventor wants merely to have her invention manufactured, the investor wants to make money, and the purchaser wants a product that will perform a certain function. When these different goals and interested are located within a network, according to Latour (1987, 114), there is a move to "*do away* with explicit interests so as to increase [the] margin for manoeuver" (emphasis in original). This "doing away with," for Latour, means that network actors shed individual goals and interests to facilitate a move towards a collective enterprise that includes shaping collective goals.

Translations are also contaminating. The network shrinks the significance of disciplinary barriers erected around epistemologies. Thus, the researcher can question familiar separations, such as those between science and politics, in order to see the intermingling of seemingly distinct categories. Pure distinctions become less viable analytic tools when differences, although still noticeable, are minor.

The dynamics of knowledges and actors in the DTCs are well understood through the lens of the network. Flagging Rose's work, the courts recruit psy knowledges in a project of governing. In fact, the equal status of psy knowledges within the courts is celebrated as their most redeeming feature. Once introduced into the court, psy knowledges are no longer bound by disciplinary actors; instead, expert knowledges are shared among court actors (both legal and therapeutic). In the DTCs, therapeutic knowledge cohabits with legal knowledge. Through mingling, these knowledges remain in the realm of expertise. The courts are designed specifically to bring together experts and expert knowledges to target a specific problem – drug addiction. In order to participate in the treatment court, the actors must undergo translations through which they realign their own personal, disciplinary, and institutional goals and ideals with those of the broader court.

Therapeutic Jurisprudence and the Drug Treatment Court

Psy knowledges, practices, and actors are not new to courtrooms. Court support workers, introduced into the legal system in the 1970s, often take on a therapeutic role, especially in offering support and on-the-spot counselling to female and child witnesses (Mugford 1987). Even seemingly more innovative approaches to law, such as the DTC, are not particularly new. An alcoholism treatment court for criminal offenders operated in the city of Hamilton, Ontario, in the 1970s. Though short-lived, this court followed an approach similar to that followed by current DTCs. There is precious little archival information on this court and, in fact, I was only able to find a six-month evaluation report on it (Archives of Ontario 1975). While not enough to offer a good analysis of its activities, this report does confirm the court's existence and offers an overview of its practices. The alcoholism treatment court emerged under the direction of – and largely, it seems, as a result of initiatives taken by – Judge D.M. Steinberg, who wanted to offer "treatment and/or counseling as an alternative to the usual incarceration or almost meaningless fines ... for individuals with apparent need of intervention" (ibid.). The court offered community-based alcohol treatment under court and probationary supervision. Despite the glowing reports it received after its first few months of operation, both in terms of its ability to "mend broken lives" and to save the justice system money, the court inexplicably folded some time in 1975.

Specialty courts designed for social engineering and remaking people are an even older feature of justice. Emily Murphy, Canada's first female magistrate, ran a specialty court for women and girls (Mander 1985). Also, Roscoe Pound took aim at early twentieth-century specialty courts (for vagrancy, juvenile delinquency, etc.) in developing his notion of sociological jurisprudence (McLean 1992). These earlier "problem-solving courts," although not drawing on psy knowledges, blended the law and forms of therapeutic knowledge in order to instrumentalize personal transformation.

DTCs are part of a broader contemporary phenomenon – one born out of a theoretical movement known as therapeutic jurisprudence (TJ). Coined by David Wexler and Bruce Winnick (1996, xvii), the term "therapeutic jurisprudence" refers to

> the study of the role of law as a therapeutic agent. It is an interdisciplinary enterprise designed to produce scholarship that is particularly useful for law reform. Therapeutic Jurisprudence proposes the exploration of ways in which, consistent with principles of justice, the knowledge, theories and insights of the mental health and related disciplines can help shape the development of the law.

The notion of TJ emerged out of the realist tradition in response to the observed need to provide extra support to individuals who were in conflict with the law and who also had mental health problems. The movement rapidly expanded to encompass all kinds of issues, including drug use, domestic violence, labour conflicts, young offenders, and sex offenders. The expansion of the ideal of TJ is so profound that a search for "therapeutic jurisprudence" on any university data base reveals hundreds of hits.[2]

TJ, as it is written about in the fecund literature, is not limited solely to advocating for the establishment of special courts organized around addressing therapeutic issues; rather, TJ is applied to all kinds of legal practices in which a crossover between law and therapy is possible. The most definitive text on TJ, Wexler and Winnick's (1996) edited tome, *Law in a Therapeutic Key*, features debates on long-standing legal doctrine, including the insanity defence (Perlin 1996), the tort doctrine of standard of care (Shuman 1996),[3] and the court's in loco parenti responsibility to under-age participants (as either litigants, victims, or accused) (Shiff and Wexler 1996). Those aspects of TJ that do centre on the courtroom, however, offer accounts of courtroom dynamics and reforms to legal processes that mandate the interplay of legal and psy knowledges. Courts focusing on issues of mental health, family violence, and drugs all seek to reinvent the courtroom as a place of healing.

The DTC arm of TJ enjoys giddy popularity throughout the United States and, increasingly, through the Western world. The first DTC opened in Miami in 1989 (Goldkamp, White, and Robinson 2001). Now there are over six hundred DTCs in the United States, and more are operating and/or slated to begin operations in Australia, Great Britain, Guam, the Cayman Islands, Puerto Rico, and Scotland (Belenko 1999).

DTCs in Canada
The first Canadian drug treatment court opened in Toronto in 1997, and the second opened in Vancouver in 2001. Both courts are mandated to deal

with people convicted of non-violent crimes for which they would other-wise receive a custodial sentence. An accused person wanting to apply to the court programs must undergo an assessment to show an addiction of at least three month's duration to either heroin, crystal methamphetamine (in Vancouver only), or crack/cocaine. Potential "clients" are also evaluated for violent histories, mental health issues, and levels of motivation (i.e., with regard to actively engaging in an addiction treatment program). Once accepted to the program, successful court clients cascade down through levels of supervision as indicated by frequency of court appearances and participation in treatment. Through their time in the program, clients are placed on a special bail specific to the treatment courts.[4] They must also sign a waiver acknowledging that their sentencing will be delayed and fore-going a number of other rights and protections (see below). Clients consid-ered to be high risk must enter a guilty plea in order to be admitted to the court program. Clients who successfully complete the program are guaran-teed a non-custodial sentence. The DTCs follow a system of sanctions and rewards. The sanctioning systems in the two courts are quite different and are discussed independently below. In both courts, clients are rewarded for consistent attendance and for showing progress in their treatment (as de-fined by periods of abstinence or decreased drug use). Rewards include eas-ing up on bail restrictions, decreasing court appearances, and praise from the judge and the court.

The differences between the courts are as considerable as are their simi-larities. The primary difference has to do with the location of the courts and the different cultures of drug use from which they emerge. Vancouver boasts one of the largest and most visible drug-using populations in the world. The acuity of Vancouver's drug scene means that responses to drug use in that city evolved in very specific ways. Vancouver is the first Canadian city to have a safe injection site, a needle exchange program, and a harm-reduc-tion hotel. The drug scene in Vancouver has had a huge influence on polic-ing in the downtown core, rendering the area a de facto decriminalized zone for small-scale drug possession and prostitution. At least one mari-juana café operates in the Downtown Eastside without much reported po-lice intervention.

The Vancouver Drug Treatment Court (VDTC) is shaped to fit the con-tours of its surroundings. The court itself is located in the heart of the Down-town Eastside, thus placing its clients in the thick of the drug trade on a regular basis. Its program tempers this by offering a "one-stop shopping" day treatment centre for court clients that is deliberately located outside of the Hastings and Main neighbourhood. Clients are either encouraged or mandated (depending on their status in the court) to attend the treatment centre daily, especially at the start of their participation in the program. The centre offers addiction-related programming, social programs, individual therapy, a methadone clinic, and a breakfast and lunch program. Clients also have access to a physician, nurse, housing, and a children's advocate (who offers support around parenting and information regarding child custody and access) through the centre.

As I explain in Chapter 3, drug use is more silenced in Vancouver than it is in Toronto. As a result, all the courtroom exchanges take on a veiled and obscure quality. The judges in Vancouver never ask clients directly about drug use or name substances out loud; instead, they initiate conversations with court clients by asking, "How are things going?" Clients, aware of the court's interdiction on directly naming a substance, might respond, "I'm having a rough time" – phraseology that, in this context, means: "I started using heroin [or cocaine or crystal methamphetamine] again." In response, the judge often orients the conversation around urine screen results, allowing the language of the "dirty screen" to serve as supporting evidence to the client's surreptitious admission of having used a particular substance.

In Vancouver, the court and some treatment centre programs are gender segregated, an initiative that attempts to alleviate the gendered exploitation and victimization often faced by drug- and street-involved women. Largely because of the de facto decriminalization of downtown Vancouver, the court does not, for the most part, deal with simple possession charges; instead, almost all its clients face possession for the purpose of trafficking charges or property offences. Sanctions in the VDTC are typically placed on clients who fail to appear either in court or at the treatment centre. The sanctions most typically used in this court include issuing a warrant unique to the VDTC that mandates treatment centre attendance or places clients in custody. Geography is a major focus of the VDTC as energies are directed towards extracting court clients from the Hastings and Main corridor. At the same time, the court appears to recognize that drug-using communities are communities nonetheless, complete with intimate relationships, social supports, and familial ties. The court does not expect clients to immediately extract themselves from these connections, and court clients are encouraged to maintain those relationships that are deemed healthy (i.e., relationships with others who are becoming or are drug free). Finally, the VDTC does not demand total abstinence from all substances in order for a client to graduate. Clients need only test negative for six months for the three mandated substances.

The drug scene in Toronto lacks the truculence of Vancouver, although, as a large urban centre, Toronto hosts a considerable amount of drug trafficking and use. Crack, cocaine, crystal methamphetamine, and, to a lesser extent, opiates, are all common in the city. The scene in Toronto, however, is geographically dispersed, lacking the dramatic, palpable concentration found in Vancouver. The city has a needle exchange program, methadone clinics, and is one of the sites for the current prescription heroin trials. The Toronto Drug Treatment Court (TDTC) does not have gender-specific programming or a comprehensive treatment centre (although the Centre for Addiction and Mental Health does serve as a hub for the treatment program). Abstinence is a requirement for graduation in Toronto, and, in general, the TDTC tends to take a harder line on drug use than does the VDTC. In the Toronto court, there are two kinds of sanctions available: (1) community service orders (CSO), through which the individual is mandated to perform a set number of hours of community work (ranging from food preparation at homeless shelters to tearing posters off of phone poles), and (2) bail revocation, referred to as "therapeutic remand." CSOs are given far more often than are therapeutic remands. These orders are assigned to clients who miss treatment groups and urine analyses and who do not "process" relapses well.

Exchanging Knowledges in Practice

The physical layout and positioning of actors in DTCs is instructive. The courtroom is filled with "clients" (not defendants) who are waiting to be called before the judge. In Vancouver, a liaison from the treatment team holds a permanent position in the witness box, and several other treatment team members are present in the courtroom, moving back and forth across the bar. In Toronto, a probation officer and two therapist liaisons sit alongside the duty counsel at the bar. The presence of treatment people in a courtroom is not particularly curious; certainly, therapists, psychologists, and psychiatrists are called into court on a regular basis to provide testimony, report on assessments, and offer support to victims. The DTC treatment people are not, however, invited into the courts as witnesses or to offer court support; instead, flagging the oddity of these courts, treatment people participate directly in legal processes. In this venue, legal knowledges and actors do not act as filters for other kinds of expert knowledges; rather, legal knowledges share space with clinical (mainly psy) knowledges and experts.

In both DTCs, each of the clients has to go before the judge in order to report in. On one occasion in the Toronto court, a man who had been on methadone maintenance for a few weeks was called up. When the judge asked him whether he had any drug use to report, he admitted that he had been using heroin fairly regularly for the last week. The judge thanked him for his honesty, as he always did, and then asked him why he used. The man responded that he had been craving heroin and had been unable to overcome those cravings. The judge refused to accept this response, relying on clinical knowledge to justify his position. The judge said: "Look, the whole purpose of methadone is to stop you from having cravings. That's why you're on methadone is so you don't feel that need to use the heroin anymore. That's how methadone works." The judge went on to explain that the court encourages heroin users to get on methadone so that they can stabilize their lives, learn and practice coping mechanisms. "And," he concluded, "it's dangerous to mix methadone and heroin." This judge considered the pharmacological properties and clinical purposes of methadone as well as the psychological techniques of addressing and attempting to remedy drug addiction (e.g., in talking about cravings and coping mechanisms) (White 1998).

Another example from the TDTC solidifies this point. A woman named "Jane" had been enrolled in the DTC program for about six months, the point at which treatment court practitioners (mainly judges) claim to have established a relationship with court clients. From various comments made in court, it would seem that Jane, a heroin addict, was also suffering from long-term health concerns. Jane had been clean for a long time but then had a relapse. When she arrived in court after her relapse, the judge gave her an extended lecture about why she should not use. He offered the typical arguments, but then gave Jane a clinical analysis of the interaction between drug use and her "condition." He said: "Using heroin isn't going to make your other medical problems better, it's going to make them worse. The Jane before me today is not the same person who was in this court a few weeks ago. You look worse, tired. Your eyes are sunken in and you look haggard. I can see the change in you." Again, the judge produced his own clinical assessment of Jane based on his own knowledge of effects of continued heroin use on an individual with a chronic medical problem. The judge was able to draw on his cumulative knowledge of Jane in order to make his assessment. In this interaction, the judge, rather than exerting judicial power, used available clinical knowledges to position himself as a nurturing therapist, offering care and advice for the client as well as gentle reprimand.

Similar knowledge exchanges are carried out in the VDTC. The following excerpt from my VDTC research journal illustrates the nature of these:

> Tim is next called. Tim opted to detox himself rather than go to a residential detox centre. The judge asks the therapist to call [the treatment centre] and see if Tim's urine screen came back clean. Tim (and the whole court) wait as the call is made. When she gets off the phone the therapist comes back and tells the judge that Tim's urine tested dirty for both heroin and methadone. The judge takes the presence of heroin in his urine as indication of a possible slip back into drug use. She tells Tim she will watch him closely for the next week and cautions that if he continues to turn in dirty urine screens she will force him into detox.

While this discussion is not as explicit, particularly on the part of the client, as are those that typify the TDTC, the judge engages in a similar kind of clinical assessment about the client's addictive state. The threat of incarceration (either in jail or a detox centre) is a way to manage what the judge sees as Tim's risk of relapse. Significantly, the judge is able to apply the power of judicial sovereignty in chorus with her clinical assessment as a means of forwarding Tim's therapeutic process.

The judges in both courts not only engaged in clinical assessments but also took up psychologically based treatment knowledges in dealing with clients. After listening to Paulo explain his reasons for wanting to be admitted to the VDTC, the judge offered an assessment of his level of motivation to actually change his drug-using behaviours:

> I think you are very sincere about wanting to get treatment and wanting to get clean, but I am not convinced by your plan so far. I want you to go to develop a tight plan that will get you into a recovery house.[5] Come back and show me you've done this and that will show me your commitment.

In addressing Courtney, a man who had been having recurrent problems in the program, a judge from the TDTC stated:

> I have never seen any period of time when you weren't in conflict with the program. It would seem at first blush that you really don't want to change, but there is some part of you that does want to change. You come to court and you go to your programs. You know you're looking at significant time if you don't do it [the program]. External pressure is fine, but at some point the internal pressure has to come to make you want to change. You'll have to make decisions to work with your counsellor to make a treatment plan, but if you don't follow your plan you're looking at serious time.

The judges are referring to the body of knowledge around recovery on which the court program is based. Motivation-based psychology holds that, before you can expect someone to change a set of behaviours, she has to be motivated to change it (Prochaska et al. 1988). Programming can start to foster those motivations by using external forces such as the sanction-and-reward system followed by the court. At some point, as the theory goes, the individual begins to internalize motivations, and programming no longer needs to rely on external incentives to get her to want to change.

The judge's ability to bring his own psy knowledge into the courtroom does not merely serve the purpose of providing lectures directed at clients: it also serves to justify the legal actions the judge takes vis-à-vis those clients. In the TDTC, a set of standard bail conditions is placed on each client. Invariably, one of these conditions is alcohol abstention. This condition is interesting, given the court is not mandated to deal with alcoholism, and, for the most part, the clients who come in to court do not have problems with drinking. Still, alcohol is one of the drugs screened for in the drug tests, and drinking (particularly to the point of drunkenness) is sanctionable behaviour.

In one example, Mark was called before the judge and reported that, over the last week, he had smoked crack and marijuana. The judge asked what happened, and Mark replied, "I was clean for so long I guess I just got overwhelmed by it. I went drinking with some friends and one thing led to another." To this, the judge responded, "That's why we have in the bail no drinking. It's not because we want the liquor companies to suffer but because drinking alcohol often makes people relapse." The judge revoked Mark's bail, placing him in custody for the night. The judge justified this action by saying, "You're not being sanctioned for your use but for your failure to attend treatment and missed urine screens. I want to be sure that you know how important it is to engage with the program."

Two days later, Mark was back in court, this time in custody. When he was called up, the judge asked him whether he had had any time to think while in custody. To this, Mark replied, "I made a mistake." The judge asked, "Do you have any insight into why you relapsed? Do you see now how risky it is to take even one step back into your old ways?" Mark replied that he did and that he was sorry. The judge released Mark from custody. At the outset, when the judge initially imposed the sanction on Mark, it was presented as a need to "teach him a lesson." The judge also believed that sanctioning serves therapeutic ends. In fact, in the TDTC, these kinds of sanctions are known as "therapeutic remands." Mark is sanctioned, not because he broke the law by using drugs or breaching his bail but, rather, because his actions indicated a decreased level of motivation. The sanction served as an external incentive rationalized through therapeutic ends.

The VDTC, like the TDTC, also uses therapeutic justifications to rationalize legal actions. This court has a number of technologies at its disposal for dealing with low motivation among court participants. Unlike the program in Toronto, the program in Vancouver has its own treatment centre, which, five days a week, offers comprehensive programming to court clients during normal working hours – an approach the treatment providers call "one-stop shopping." At the treatment centre, clients attend social groups, eat breakfast and lunch, organize and obtain social support payments, undergo their random drug screens, receive health care and methadone, and participate in both individual and group treatment. The treatment program consists of three phases, each of which requires clients to attend the centre for a certain number of hours each week. A client's failure to attend the treatment centre as directed is reported to the judge, who, in turn, questions the client about her absence. Absences for legitimate reasons or occasional mishaps such as over-sleeping are not sanctioned. However, if a client shows a pattern of being absent from, or arriving late at, the treatment centre, the judge typically reads this behaviour as a sign of her waning motivation to participate in the program (and, ultimately, to become drug free). On reaching this diagnosis, the judge most often offers the remedy of adding the client's name to the warrant list, thus making attendance at the treatment centre one of her bail conditions or, more precisely, giving police reason to arrest her if she does not attend the treatment centre.

The judge's rationale for placing a client on the warrant list draws on therapeutic principles. For example, in responding to Shae-Lynn's admission that she was having a hard time getting to the treatment centre, the judge suggested that perhaps being added to the warrant list would help her with this problem. When Shae-Lynn agreed, the judge confirmed the decision by saying, "I'll give you that motivating factor then." The warrant list is used to respond to treatment court transgressions beyond not showing up at the treatment centre. Clients who breach their bail by being found in restricted areas,[6] or by not attending their residential treatment programs, may also be placed on the warrant list as all these behaviours are equally read as indicators of decreased motivation to participate in the program.

The question of motivation is central to the therapeutic orientation of the DTCs. The DTC programs are based on a branch of behavioural psychology that holds that individual motivation is crucial to effecting any sort of change within an individual. Motivation is generated through both external and internal factors, and the courts work on the premise that individuals need a balance of both external and internal motivations to stop using drugs. External motivations (like reducing court appearances and mandating community service hours) are used, but the clients themselves must also exhibit internal motivations. The client can express these to the court in a number of ways, including being vigilant around court appearances and program attendance, showing a positive and optimistic attitude while in court, and producing negative drug screens.

Clients who fail to express adequate internal motivation are often given negative, external motivators by the judge. The following excerpt comes from my research journal:

> Dean came into court late and sat at the back (which he has never done before). He is called before the judge shortly after he enters and as he approaches the Crown details how Dean has been absent from the court for a week, breached his bail, and clearly has had a relapse. The judge asks Dean what happened. Dean starts crying and says that he relapsed using bennies, coke, and morphine. He explains his relapse was a reaction to the fact that he got rejected by an old girlfriend. He also describes how he checked into

a hospital on a suicide watch. Dean then explains to the judge that his use was a "one day thing." The judge interrupts him and starts to go over the reports from Dean's therapist as well as the drug screen results. The judge makes Dean go through systematically every day since he was last in court. Dean recants his original "one day thing." He is forced to admit that the reason why he missed court, treatment sessions, or urine tests for an entire week is because he was using for that entire week. Once this story comes out the judge asks the Crown for his submission. The Crown asks for revocation of bail, arguing that Dean clearly needs time to rethink his commitment to the drug treatment court program. The defence counters this claim by saying that Dean has shown in the past how well he can do in the program, and his track record alone shows that "there is hope for him and he deserves a second chance." The judge asks Dean if he has anything else to add. Dean says, "I know why I relapsed and I know I will get help, I want to get help and work through this relapse," to which the judge responds, "the fact that you have insight is a positive first step. You can go forward when you have insight. Still I'm going to ask you to step into custody not because you used but because I think you have lost focus in the program, and I'm hoping that this will give you some time to think about how you're going to re-engage. When you come back to court on Thursday I want you to have written me a letter about your relapse, showing you know why you relapsed and how you're planning on dealing with it."

In another instance, this time at the VDTC, custodial sanctioning is presented as a form of child-protection.

Sky is called next. The judge finds out she has a dirty urine screen. Sky tested positive for cocaine. The judge says, "You are pregnant. This is a very bad thing" [it is not entirely clear whether the bad thing is the pregnancy or the drug use]. The judge threatens to remand Sky to prevent her from using. "I am really upset, it's not just you, it's this kid. The next time I'll be upset enough to remand you to custody." The judge berates herself for not having remanded Sky the last time she appeared. It is decided that Sky will go to a residential treatment centre. The judge concludes by saying, "I want this to work for you, for you and your child."

In this rather troubling instance, sanctioning is presented as a way of curbing drug use and, thus, protecting both the user and the foetus. Given the widespread questioning of the "crack-baby" phenomenon, as well as the clear Canadian precedent against the forced confinement of pregnant, drug-using women (Boyd 2004; Logan 2000),[7] one can argue that the judge is deploying folk rather than clinical knowledge here. Still, the implication of the judge's statement is that the mother's drug use will have adverse effects on the foetus and, thus, must be curbed. Incarceration is offered as a remedy for this woman's not being motivated to curb her own drug use and thus jeopardizing her unborn child. There is, obviously, also an argument against putting someone in a detention centre or provincial prison as a means of isolating her from illicit drugs.

In the DTCs, the legal act of punishment is translated into the therapeutic goal of motivation. Increasing surveillance and the possibility of arrest and incarceration is decidedly punitive, akin to sanctioning through heightened probation conditions. Through translation, exercising a warrant in the DTC becomes a way of applying the external motivating forces described above. The act itself remains unaltered, but its purpose is modified by rationalizing it through therapeutic rather than legal knowledges. These same sorts of translations are observable in the increasing use of conditional sentences as a means of mandating people to participate in treatment programs (Fisher et al. 2002).

Crowns and duty counsel also use clinical knowledges. This is most clear when an individual is facing expulsion from the program. Lying to the judge, breaching bail conditions, dealing drugs to other program participants, and having new criminal charges are all grounds for expulsion from DTCs. Clients can also be ejected if they consistently show a lack of motivation to change their drug-using behaviours. While ejection from the program does not occur that often, when it does happen, it is typically on the grounds of lacking motivation. For example, Karen, a client in the TDTC, faced ejection because she was consistently using heroin. The Crown took her repeated use as evidence of her low motivation, and its submission claimed that she "has shown poor quality and quantity of effort in her own recovery and clearly doesn't want to be here." The duty counsel submitted that Karen could complete her recovery and should be able to remain in the program. Karen, she argued, simply needed time in detox to sort herself out. Again engaging in translation, the Crown is not concerned with legal issues such as Karen's threat to public safety or criminal culpability. Karen's failure to comply with directions set out by a criminal court is not evidence of her dangerousness or blameworthiness; rather, her actions speak to her status as a viable recipient of addiction treatment. Ejecting Karen from the program is not presented as a punitive measure but, rather, as the clinical best practice for a therapeutically non-responsive patient.

In another example, Bruce, a client of the VDTC, faced remand to custody and possible expulsion for failing to admit to drug use in the face of a urine test that showed positive for cocaine and marijuana. Bruce vehemently denied his use, arguing that he was around other people who were smoking marijuana but that he did not, himself, use. The Crown countered that Bruce's explanation failed to account for the presence of cocaine in his system. In allegedly lying to the court, Bruce, according to the Crown, was displaying low motivation and ought at least to be detained for a few days as incentive to increase his motivation to participate in the program.

This exchange of knowledges is not unidirectional. As I mentioned at the outset, the treatment team plays a significant role in the court. Most often, its role is supportive: it offers comments to the judge on a client's progress, on-the-spot counselling for those in crisis in the court, and finds other resources for court clients. But the treatment team also uses legal knowledge. Often, it is in the position of making recommendations and, in some cases, legal decisions regarding clients. Typically, one sees treatment team members advising the court on sanctions against clients.

In the TDTC, there are two kinds of sanctions available: community service orders (CSOs), whereby the individual is mandated to perform a set number of hours of community service (ranging from working at a homeless shelter to tearing posters off of phone poles), and bail revocation (i.e., the therapeutic remand). CSOs, which are given far more often than are bail revocations, are assigned to clients who miss treatment groups and urine analyses and who do not "process" relapses well. Often, when such issues arise, the judge asks the court liaison for the treatment team's recommendation regarding sanctions. The treatment team recommends a number of community service hours, which it typically justifies according to punitive mentalities rather than therapy. A client missing a treatment group offers a typical scenario. Again from my research notes:

> Jess is called next. When the judge asks her if she's used she says no. Then the judge looks down at her file and says, "I see you missed a group last week." "That's right," responds Jess, "got the times mixed up." One of the members of the treatment team stands and addresses the court, saying, "Your honour, I can confirm that Jess did miss her appointment on ——— and we are asking for two hours of community service as a sanction for this. We further want to remind her of the importance of attending groups and that it is her responsibility to be clear on the timing of appointments."

The therapist justifies this sanction based on deterrence: Jess is sanctioned as a means of "reminding" her to attend groups.

An exchange around another client shows not only how treatment uses legal knowledges but also how therapeutic knowledge is taken up by the legal actors:

> Sam is next to be called before the judge. I have never seen Sam fail to report drug use in the court and today is no different. Sam is new to the program, so his continued drug use has always been excused and he has typically been commended for being forthright about having used. Today

though, Sam also admits that he missed a treatment group and a drug screen. A member of the treatment team stands immediately to speak. She indicates that the treatment team is concerned about Sam missing a group and that his case management officer has recommended that he do four hours of community service in order to make up for the group. She adds that the treatment team feels that it is very important for Sam to learn how important it is to attend groups. The Crown is next to speak and argues that, in fact, Sam's continued use coupled with his failure to attend groups calls into questions Sam's motivation to be in the program. The Crown calls for a revocation of Sam's bail in order to have him think about his motivation. The defence argues that it is still early days for Sam and that he has been upfront with the court about his use as well as his failure to attend groups. The judge decides to revoke Sam's bail, taking the Crown's position that Sam needs to show greater motivation and that perhaps having a strong external motivation like being placed in custody will help him to commit to the program. Sam is taken into custody and led away.

Here a therapeutic actor takes up the legal practice of sanctioning not to achieve therapeutic ends but, rather, to encourage both Sam as well as the other court participants not to miss groups. On the other hand, the Crown counsel takes up a therapeutic discourse about Sam's levels of motivation, voicing his concerns not about Sam's status as a law breaker but, rather, about his level of commitment to changing his substance-using habits. Just as therapeutic actions and knowledges need not be altered to be conscripted by legal actors, so, in the treatment courts, punitiveness can translate into therapeutic practice without removing itself from that most literal place of punishment, the prison.

The VDTC uses custody, the warrant list (described above), and increased court attendance as forms of sanction. Another "soft" sanction readily marshalled in the VDTC is residential treatment. Clients who are clearly struggling in the program, as evidenced by their inconsistent attendance at the treatment centre or their relapse into drug use, can be "recommended" by the treatment team to stay for a period of time at any one of a number of residential treatment centres in the Vancouver area. While it is not particularly surprising to have a therapist recommend that a client investigate a certain kind of treatment, typically, these recommendations are not accompanied with warrants that effectively remand individuals to residential treatment. In effect, these residential treatment centres become extensions of the penal system. Even if the recommendation is made by the therapist, clients are directed to attend by a criminal court judge (based, at least in part, on a therapist's recommendation). If the client fails to attend or leaves the treatment centre without permission or without having completed her period of treatment, she can be arrested and face further criminal sanction for breach of bail.

The Team

Translation is formally designed into the unique structure of the DTCs. The judges and lawyers do not claim to be addiction experts, and the treatment people do not present themselves as legal authorities; instead, the court actors I interviewed explained that the team structure of the court allows everyone in the court to have a certain amount of knowledge.[8] There is little variation in the court actors. The same judges, lawyers, and treatment people are there almost every day. The teams go on "development retreats" together and take classes and workshops specializing on addiction and treatment courts. They also meet together before every court session in what is called pre-court. The purpose of pre-court is to discuss each of the cases that will come before the court that day, notably without the presence or direction of the actual clients themselves. I was not permitted to attend the pre-court meetings in either the VDTC or the TDTC, but all the accounts of those I interviewed indicated that the actions carried out in court were decided upon in pre-court by the team. The use of the term "team" is purposeful and important because it troubles the disciplinary distinctions made between different actors in the courtroom. It is not the legal team versus the treatment team, just the team. This, in turn, helps to explain how knowledge is shared in the court.

In attempting to understand the dramaturgy of the team, Goffman (1961) underscores the importance of team dynamics and diversity of team members. Although the presentation of the team blurs distinctions between team members, Goffman observes that team membership does not indicate internal homogeneity; rather, each member of the team has a particular role or set of characteristics that is needed in order to build the team and help it achieve its collectively desired ends. At the same time as the team depends on these individualities, it must also function as a cohesive unit, sharing what Goffman calls a "script" but what I would suggest, invoking Latour, can be interpreted as a set of knowledges and goals. The point being that team membership does not mean absorption or erasure of the individual but, rather, a duality of being whereby each individual must, simultaneously, be both an individual and a team member. In treatment court terms, this means that all the court experts can come together as part of the DTC team because each brings her own individual expertise to the table. The teaming, as described by those whom I interviewed, enables the exchange of knowledges and ensuing translations.

The team is quite clearly the most distinguishing feature of the DTCs. It is the structure that formalizes the marked intersectionality of the courts. Nolan

(2001), in his study of American DTCs, also notes the importance of this, reading it as a dramaturgy. Nolan's descriptions do not suggest the kind of non-hierarchical knowledge exchanges I note here; rather, he describes the American courts as judge-centric, requiring the lawyers to surrender their authority to the pre-eminent relationship between the judge and the client. This is not the dynamic I see in the Vancouver and Toronto courts. These courts, to be certain, relay a curative drama of justice. However, despite her obvious hierarchal position as a judge, the judge does not enjoy a particularly elevated status; instead, the emphasis is very much placed on the team.

Distinctions between law and psy, while still apparent, become less significant as legal and psy actors and their knowledges become part of a networked team. Lawyers still identify as lawyers and claim expertise on legal knowledges. The same can be said for psy actors. Team membership does not erase these distinctions; rather, it diminishes their importance. Translating individual interests into team or network interests, as Latour (1987) describes, means holding less tightly to disciplinary distinctions. This also means that, contrary to Latour, individual interests are not "done away with" through translations and network participation. The practitioners in the DTC report translations that allow them to maintain their original goals and purposes while still aligning with those of the DTC.

Translating Actors

The personal goals of the actors need to be translated so that they can join the team and become part of the network. These realignments do not unfold in the same way Latour (1987) describes. While Latour's network lens offers a valuable technique for mapping and explaining varying constellations of actors and knowledges, his approach is presentist. The immediacy of Latour's method erases the important consideration of the historical narratives of the actors involved in the network. This perspective is valuable as it allows a fuller understanding of the mechanics of translation. The interests of the actors within a network pre-exist the development of the network. The actors enter into the network not with the sole purpose of developing new interests but also with an eye to better serving the interests they already have. These interests are not, pace Latour, done away with; instead, actors in the network rationalize involvement in the DTCs as a way of changing the avenues by which they attain their goals while maintaining their original interests.

Traditionally, the goals of those involved in substance-abuse treatment programs are to assist the user as much as possible both to alter her substance-using behaviours and to improve her life (cf. Webster 1990). Often, this means helping to keep people away from conflicts with the law. The traditional, imagined goals of criminal courts are to protect public safety, establish truth, and administer justice (Roach 2000). In traditional justice settings, it is not uncommon to find treatment people and legal people at odds with each other, offering notably different views on how to deal with an individual. Many of the treatment practitioners I interviewed talked about how, before they came to work in the DTC, they spent a good deal of time resisting the efforts of courts and the legal process. Likewise, legal actors I interviewed (the Crowns in particular) were quick to point out that, in regular criminal court settings, treatment people are often read as acting contrary to the Crown in advocating for lower sentences and non-custodial sanctions. The DTCs are not the first instances of rupture with regard to these distinctions; it is arguable whether or not these distinctions "really" exist in any material sense. What sets the DTCs apart, then, is not the blending of different knowledges but, rather, the fact that the distinctions between law and therapy are formally and explicitly ruptured, that the court actors are organized so as to deliberately collaborate around a particular and collectively agreed upon goal: curing the offender.

The Crown in the VDTC explained that the DTC's unique arrangement offers an opportunity to address addiction issues in a meaningful way – an opportunity not available in the regular criminal courts. This was of personal importance to this Crown counsel. Having dealt with the addiction of someone close to him, he wanted very much to "do something that mattered" in dealing with addiction so that he could "help stop the cycle."[9] Working in the VDTC allowed him to realign his goal of fulfilling a personal need to pro-actively address addiction, making it the same as the treatment court's goal of breaking the addictions of people in conflict with the law.

The coordinator of the DTC in Toronto offered a perspective on his own realignment around his involvement with the drug treatment court. He became involved with the DTC through his community work with homeless, substance-involved men in Toronto's downtown core. In 1997, he heard about the plans to propose a DTC for Toronto, and, working on the "hunch" that a DTC might offer an opportunity to address some of the problems he faced in his own work, he joined the DTC steering committee. While the coordinator expressed his own concerns with the operation of the DTC, he rationalized his involvement by virtue of the fact that, to his thinking, the DTC served his goal of increasing access to housing and social services for marginalized people.[10] In participating in the DTC network, the coordinator participated in translation. He expanded his own interests to reflect those of the team (i.e., to ultimately help people stop using drugs) while still maintaining those interests (i.e., to better serve marginalized populations of the inner city).

Where the court coordinator sees the court as an opportunity to provide better continuity of services, the Toronto Crown counsel opted to enter into the DTC network because he felt it better allowed him to pursue his goal of ensuring community safety and security. He explained that he served as a criminal prosecutor for thirteen years before becoming involved in the DTC. During that time, he became increasingly frustrated with what he saw as the "revolving door," whereby he prosecuted the same people repeatedly. The DTC, according to him, was a chance to "break the cycle" by offering a comprehensive treatment program that would, in turn, help people to arrest their drug use (and thus their own criminality).[11] The Crown counsel, in aligning his interests with the DTC, participated in translation. His goals of protecting public safety as well as breaking the cycle of drug use and crime were absorbed into the goals of the DTC network. The treatment court, for the Crown counsel, was a space where his interests were served even as he changed the techniques by which he pursued them, moving from traditional prosecution to the curative approach of the DTC.

This realignment of interests through the network of the DTC is extended to the therapists. One therapist, for example, saw her role in the TDTC program as a way to forward her vision of a more critical and radical system of social service delivery – a system centred on the notion of empowering clients and breaking down barriers that surround marginalized groups.[12] She reflected on her decision to become part of the DTC program:

> The last place I thought I would see myself was working in court. I have always been one to stand on the outside of systems and critique them for being disempowering, for being about coercion ... But the other piece I get that really kind of made me decide to go for it was that I'm still working with people in the system and I have even less power than a therapist in the community-based agency to impact the system at all from that place [i.e., working outside of the traditional social service system]. And my clients' lives are wrapped up in those systems. So I can stay in the system with them and try to make some of those changes. Or I can stand outside the circle and remain somewhat powerless along with them. So I thought, "Well heck, let's go, I'll do it." So I applied for the position and I got it.

For this therapist, the DTC offered an opportunity to work within a dominant system to effect the kinds of social and individual changes she felt were important. Her goals of working for more radical reforms and empowering individual people translated into working on the DTC team to introduce that radicalism from the inside.

The network constituted through the DTC also offers the opportunity for institutional goal realignment. The Department of Justice (DOJ), Canada's federal agency charged with addressing issues of public safety and crime prevention, is the major funder of the DTCs. The DOJ features Canada's two DTCs as examples of its most innovative developments over the last decade. It presents the DTCs as a way to "prevent crime by attacking root causes."[13] Following the logic of the drug-crime nexus, the DOJ asserts that its goal of crime prevention is well served by supporting the DTC initiative:

> By helping non-violent offenders overcome their addictions and improve their social stability, the [DTC] program reduces that criminal behavior associated with substance abuse. By addressing the root of the criminal behaviour – the addiction – we eliminate the need for the criminal behaviour.[14]

Again interests are translated. The DOJ goal of crime prevention, a goal traditionally served through law enforcement and punishment, is, through the DOJ's participation in the DTC network, served through attempts to cure addicts.

Contaminated Laws

This network analysis offers an opportunity to retheorize law vis-à-vis the rise of therapeutic jurisprudence (TJ) over the last fifteen years. TJ is aligned with the normative and ideological schools of thought that imagine law as an institution that can promise (and deliver on its promise of) truth, justice, and reform. This conclusion starts from the premise that, in studying the DTCs, there is something to be learned about the effectiveness of law. Actor-network theory, combined with the historical perspective granted through the use of narratives, gives another premise from which to form questions about the DTC and the notion of TJ. We can ask questions about how this network operates and, in turn, address the question of how interests are served, defined, and redefined through its practices. More broadly, then, it is possible to ask how it is that law and justice travel into curative realms. What are the epistemological and institutional conditions that make this journey possible? In answering such questions, it is clear that the DTC is not only a venue with the purpose of curing addiction but, through the exchange of knowledges and the realignment of goals, it is also an arena in which social justice is created, foetuses saved, public safety protected, access to social services facilitated, and punishment effectively carried out.

The network formalizes the muddiness of law. In helping legal actors and institutions to redefine their goals and to see their interests represented in different ways, the DTC network takes law from its imagined position as a pure discipline and makes it into something explicitly impure and contingent, connected through varying relationships to diverse actors, interests, and goals. The purity of law is not the only thing sullied through this network. The DTCs contaminate the purity of therapy and the therapeutic process, again working to redefine goals and interests and to change the practices of the "discipline." Indeed, the network shows that "we have never been modern."[15]

But what does this lack of modernity, this unrestrained sullying of the pureness of law and of therapy mean for each of these practices? We have a society that holds out the promises of due process on the one hand and sound therapy on the other. I show above how the goals of actors working under each of these paradigms are realigned through the network so that they fit with its goal of curing addiction while still maintaining pre-existing individual and organizational goals. In these shifts, it is clear that the mythology of the purity of the discipline vanishes. This being the case, how do the actors within these networks understand this realignment of their goals and interests while acknowledging that they no longer conform to the contours of their respective disciplines?

Procedural Fairness

Boldt (2002) argues that the adversarial mode of decision making favoured in Western criminal proceedings runs counter-intuitive to therapeutic practices. The adversarial system is based on the premise that fairness is ensured by appointing someone to act only on behalf and in the interest of the client and by having opposing "sides" in a legal hearing. One of the goals of this type of structuring is to offer procedural protections and assurances of fairness to those who come before the law. In Canadian criminal law, the adversarial system is meant to enshrine notions of procedural fairness – rules that are supposed to protect the most vulnerable from the overarching power of the law. So, for example, a client's confidentiality is to be protected, a lawyer is mandated to work only on her client's behalf and in her client's best interest, and she is expected to take direction only from her client. These protections are laid out in the codes of professional conduct for most bar associations (cf. Law Society of Upper Canada 2000). Boldt suggests that, when therapeutic ends are invested in the adversarial system, the principles of fairness are compromised to serve the emergent therapeutic goals. Law and therapy are antithetical, in Boldt's estimation. The legal actors in the courts acknowledge that their alignment with the court could conceivably transgress professional expectations to fairly represent and protect their clients. Still, their own interpretations of their actions intimate a notably different reading of procedural fairness within the DTCs.

The DTC network compromises many promises extended by law to accused persons in order to ensure that they are fairly dealt with before the courts. Clients enrolled in the DTCs are asked to sign a waiver. In doing so, they give up the right to plead not guilty to charges against them; the right to a swift and determinate sentence (in most cases, clients would have spent less time in custody than they would in participating in the DTC program); and the right to confidentiality (from both attorney and therapist). In addition to these forfeitures, clients also give up, through their agreement to participate in the urine screen, protections against unreasonable search and seizure. Clients must participate in a random drug screen program, whereby they have to produce a urine sample for drug testing at least once a week. Drug screen results are released in public court.

The actors within the DTC are aware of the aspects of the program that compromise the promise of procedural fairness. The importance of procedural safeguards, meant to protect the interests of the accused, is eclipsed by the broader court goal of curing addiction. The duty counsel for the Toronto court spoke to this issue:[16]

> You know, it's probably the biggest thing that comes up is the whole issue are you acting in your client's best interest? If you're acting in a program where you're representing the clients but you're also part of this whole realm, then how do you balance that? ... But I don't actually see it as a problem because basically what I say to people is that my role hasn't changed. Yes, I'm part of this team, and when we have a meeting I'm going to discuss the client as part of that team and I'm going to have things to say. But basically, when it comes down to it, I'm not going to do what the team wants me to do. I'm going to talk to my client and I'm going to do what the client wants me to. After I've instructed them, after I've given them my advice about something, and after I've gotten instructions from them, despite what the team wants me to do, that's where my interest is.

Here the duty counsel conveys the idea that she privileges the interests of her client over those of the court. Earlier on in this same interview, she defined her own notion of the client's best interest. This definition is closely aligned with the interests of the court (i.e., to get an individual to stop using drugs) rather than the case-by-case interests of each individual client:[17]

> If I'm acting in their [the client's] best interest, then one thing I'm doing is doing everything I can to get them into the program and, if I am successful in getting in the program, if I am continuing to act in their best interest, then I'm doing everything I can to keep them there and help them through the program.[18]

The defence counsel's duty to act in the best interest of her client is redefined through the operations of the network. The client's best interests are no longer served through seeking acquittal or a lesser sentence; rather, they are served by being helped to overcome her addiction. There is an assumption that keeping the client in the program is in the client's best interest. This best interest justifies the erasure of the client's rights and protections promised through law.

The duty counsel for the VDTC gave an equally interesting account of how he saw his client's rights protected in the court:[19]

A lawyer's job is to get the results his client wants. The goals of most of my clients are to stop their criminal behaviour. So this [the DTC] is a chance to marry those two goals. If my client can kick his habit then he can stop doing crime.

He continued on to explain that legal practice in the treatment court does not differ considerably from practice in a regular criminal court. The one big difference, however, is that, in the pre-court meetings, he has to engage in client advocacy without his client's being present. In justifying this action, the duty counsel emphasized that he knew that his client wanted to stop using drugs and so his advocacy, regardless of his client's presence, is always meant to facilitate and support that desire. He added that, ultimately, decisions made in pre-court can change in the actual court and that he is bound, in the final decision, to take his client's direction.

Justice Bentley (2000), penning an early description of the DTC program, argues the DTC is structured to make the role of defence counsel almost irrelevant. He writes, "Unless the judge is considering a revocation of bail or expulsion from the program, defense counsel does not attend court and duty counsel contributes simply as a member of the team" (268). The constitution of the duty counsel as "simply a member of the team" indicates a breakdown of the traditional adversarial roles taken by Crown and defence counsel in criminal proceedings. The adversity of the criminal process in Canada is meant to ensure procedural fairness by designating a party to work solely on the behalf of the defendant. That party, the defence counsel, is absorbed into the team, working as part of a larger whole within the network rather than (as in the adversarial system) as an independent representative of the accused.

The legal actors in the court justify transgressing the procedural protections of their clients by placing their ethical obligations to them on a hierarchy. Maintaining confidentiality is usurped by the "ultimate" best interest of getting the client off drugs. Here the fixation of the drug/crime nexus is felt most acutely. Getting someone off drugs means stopping their criminality, an action that can only be in the best interest of all the parties that, in the adversarial system, are traditionally in opposition. The cured addict is no longer a threat to public safety or to herself. Organizing around this "win/win" goal facilitates the erosion of procedural safeguards (Boldt 2002).

The Ethic of Care
The changes that the DTC networks have wrought on goals and interests are not specific to the realm of law. Those involved in the DTC teams as

treatment people are also engaged in a process of realignment. Traditionally, therapeutic initiatives work directly with and for the individual and have their own procedural safeguards and ethical best practices. Paramount are guarantees of client confidentiality and the idea that the therapist works in the best interests and under the direction of the client.

The newly developed Ontario College of Social Workers outlines a code of ethics for all social workers and social service workers employed in the province. The code guides the behaviour of social workers in a number of different areas and places primary importance on ensuring an ethical relationship between social workers and their clients. The first principle states: "a social worker or social service worker shall maintain the best interest of the client as the primary professional obligation" (Ontario College of Social Workers and Social Service Workers 2000). The code expands on this premise, explaining that working in the best interests of the client involves including her in decision making, facilitating her ability to self-determine, and privileging her interests above those of all others when working with her in an organizational setting (Ontario College of Social Workers and Social Service Workers 2000). Similar operative guidelines exist for psychologists employed in the province (College of Psychologists of Ontario 2004) as well as for psychologists and social workers in British Columbia.[20]

The majority of therapists working in the DTCs are either psychologists or social workers, and all are bound by such codes. Their location within the DTC network effects their realignment. I show, in the above section, that therapists are often placed in the position of participating in making legal decisions about their clients, including, from time to time, recommending sanctions. Like the counsel involved in the court, the therapists are also keenly aware of the ways in which their participation in the DTC team indicates a shift in their professional practices. One therapist observed that her role had changed considerably since she had joined the DTC. She reasoned that presenting a united front to clients was vital to her ability to do her job well. This was a practice in which she did not have to engage before coming to the DTC. She explained that, even if she disagreed with the way a client was handled in court, she would not directly advocate for him within that setting;[21] instead, she would take her dissatisfaction back to the DTC team for discussion. "We make decisions as a team and only as a team," she explained.[22] Likewise, another therapist recalled the first few times she watched a client of hers taken into custody based on her recommendation. She felt "awful" but learned to accept this part of the client's therapy (spending up to five nights in a detention centre), and now she has few reservations.[23] The head of the treatment team in Vancouver maintained that "the only time you should sanction is to engage people in treatment."[24] She justified this approach to dealing with criminal addicts by saying that coercion must be used in addiction treatment programs outside the court as well. She explained that people are always coerced on some level, whether the coercion comes from a partner who threatens to leave, a child protection worker who threatens to take children away, or a police officer who threatens to arrest a user if she does not go and get help.

The lack of safeguards for clients participating in the DTCs raises particular concerns for women clients. One therapist explained how the lack of a guarantee of confidentiality distresses many of the women involved in the DTC because of their fears of either losing children currently in their custody or jeopardizing attempts to regain custody of children who have already been seized. Another therapist explained that the women with whom she deals are often reluctant to actively engage with the therapeutic aspects of the DTC program because they see the therapist as a barrier between them and their children:[25]

> Ultimately I do the report to the court. If, you know, one of my clients is trying to get her kids back in a year, what I have to say is going to make an impact on that. I've got the power. I've got the power to recommend her being discharged from the program. It's a team decision but I make the recommendations. That scares a lot of women.

If any client does not actively engage with the treatment aspects of the DTC program, this is grounds for her expulsion from the program. It may be determined that an individual is not actively engaged with the program if she exhibits reticence during treatment. The realignment of goals sets up gender-specific barriers for women enrolled in the DTC. Successful completion of the DTC program is often a large factor in deciding when (or if) a woman will regain custody of her children. Being expelled from a DTC program does not bode well in attempts to regain access to one's children.

Above, I describe an instance in which a pregnant woman was remanded by a DTC judge for the sake of her foetus. Throughout the course of my research, this happened three times to two different women in the VDTC. In each of these instances, the judge and the Crown clearly translated the goals of the treatment court so as to include the elusive goal of child protection. In an instance involving Gigi (who had turned up a dirty urine screen), the Crown counsel was careful to avoid actually naming her pregnancy as the core concern with her continued use; instead, he refers to Gigi's "health problems," a phraseology that gestures towards familiar discourses that pathologize pregnancy more generally (Petchesky 1990). Given that his reference to health was markedly uncharacteristic of his typical courtroom discourse and that Gigi was obviously pregnant, the deployment of "health" as a euphemism is clear. Gigi's case spurred an uncharacteristic moment of adversarialism as the Crown counsel asked that Gigi be returned to the detention centre. For her part, defence counsel claimed this would be unfair, given that clients are not supposed to be punished for using drugs. The judge finally decided to "release" Gigi from custody but placed her on the warrant list and sent her directly to a residential treatment centre. Effectively, the woman was incarcerated, not released. While she was not being held in a prison, the warrant served to hold her in the treatment centre, making it illegal for her to leave.

In *Winnipeg Child and Family Services (Northwest Area) vs. G. (D.F.)*,[26] the Supreme Court decided that courts did not have parens patriae jurisdiction over foetuses. The case concerned a pregnant woman addicted to glue. The lower court ruled that courts had a duty to protect foetuses and thus could order a drug-addicted pregnant woman into treatment. Both the Appeals Court and the Supreme Court maintained (in keeping with abortion law) that foetuses are not persons and, therefore, not worthy of legal protection. Following this decision, to force a pregnant woman into treatment to protect her foetus ought to constitute, in Canadian law, a rights violation. There is no justifiable reason under law to limit a woman's freedoms in this context. Apparently, however, this same legal principle does not apply to women in conflict with the law. Women facing or already under criminal sanction can easily be confined for any number of actions that do not, in and of themselves, constitute crimes. Breaking bail conditions accounts for a huge proportion of custodial admissions in Canadian detention centres. Criminal courts are well located to take on a parens patriae role vis-à-vis foetuses despite the Supreme Court decision because, through the warrant and bail systems, they have an entire grey area of control available to them. This is especially true in the DTCs, where criminal sanctions, as I show above, are meant to serve therapeutic purposes.

The goals of the DTC to stop the cycle of addiction and crime easily translate into the goal of (unborn) child protection. Forced treatment is part of the DTC ethic and is the reason for the network of therapeutic and legal knowledges within the courts. The normalization of forced confinement within the DTC networks greases the doorway, allowing practices of foetal protection to slide in.

Involvement in the DTC network has notable and distressing procedural effects on those involved. Consistently, narratives of the practitioners, both therapeutic and legal, involved in DTCs reveal that they rationalize their participation, thus allowing themselves to change their practices while maintaining their original goals. The modification starts with what is "best," an ill-defined proviso whose shifty nature easily translates into a wide range of practices. What happens is that the changes effected through the DTCs work to alter the procedural safeguards set out in the realms of both law and therapy. These safeguards are meant to protect subjects of therapeutic or legal practices, especially those who are most vulnerable to the negative impacts of malpractice. From a practical point of view, flags are worth raising whenever we see actors' changing practices while attempting to maintain the same goals. These changes find team members in situations that, they freely admit, often constitute drastic deviations from how they felt they were meant to practise or imagined themselves practising prior to their involvement in the DTCs. It is worth cautioning against holding that somehow, if actors stayed within their assigned roles, justice would be done. This is a realist, positivist position. Legal practice does not exist in a vacuum, sealed off from social (and epistemological) influences. This being the case, one is hard pressed to find a process that involves "purely" legal decision making. If law cannot be crystallized, then it is impossible to realize due process free of the contaminants of the everyday world. What we find in the DTCs is a chance to explore situations in which the goals of purity are clearly sidestepped and to see how actors translate themselves and their practices so as to justify overriding those promises of purity.

Conclusion

The DTCs are not particularly new or surprising innovations in criminal justice practice. The marriage between law and therapy is one of long standing. Even if they lack novelty, they are very interesting. The appeal of the DTCs, I think, comes out of the high visibility of the relationship between law and psy. When one walks into the drug treatment court, one is meant to actually see justice curing the offender through the performance of the team. Also visible are the negotiations of power and knowledge that shape this performance. In revealing the network of knowledge exchanges in the court, it is possible to see yet another layer of court interactions. The knowledge exchanges and translations in the DTC effect a particular style of governing, which closes ranks on the court clients. This makes the DTC akin to other therapeutic settings in which people are worked upon. The DTC is not dissimilar to the team at Goffman's asylum, which is collectively organized around the goal of working on people who, themselves, are not invited to participate in designing or implementing the project; rather, they are entreated to participate only in so far as they are agents in realizing a predetermined notion of their own best interest.

The DTCs are places in which roles, knowledges, and goals are redefined, and the boundaries surrounding knowledges are permeable. These courts represent networks in which therapeutic and legal knowledges are exchanged among the different personnel, rendering them, at the same time and often in the same breath, spaces of both justice and therapy. Members of the network undergo processes of translation whereby their goals and interests shift. These translations do not indicate the erasure of individual goals and interests that pre-existed DTC involvement; rather, participation in the network allows the actors to maintain their old interests but to redefine them so as to have them met through the technologies and practices of the DTC.

These changes have notable effects at the level of both theory and practice. In the DTCs, knowledges are integrated into different practices, working to sully the purity of individual disciplines. At the level of practice, this sullying has certain concerning effects. While law's promises of due process and procedural fairness, on one hand, and the therapeutic pledges of working in a client's best interests and protecting client confidentiality, on the other, may never have been realized, the practices of the DTCs formalizes the schism between promise and practice. The DTCs build the removal of many rights of due process into their operations. The courts also work on an ill-defined and obscure notion of a client's best interest – a best interest that includes removing clients' confidentiality protections.

Placed against the geneaological backdrop of the rise of penal addiction treatment in Canada, and within the cultural context of the inherently criminogenic nature of the substances targeted in these courts, this networked analysis of the DTCs serves as an illustration of criminal justice responses to drug addiction. The DTCs rest on the sure knowledge that drugs lie at the heart of criminal activity and, following this, that treatment is the necessary, right, and just response. Couched as a critical response to the futility of incarcerating drug addicts, court-supervised therapy serves as the perfect answer to the question of criminality: the revolving door of crime will be closed because the addicts will be cured. The network analysis facilitates the exhibition of the DTC as an arena in which knowledges are unhinged from actors, liberating the flow of legal and therapeutic expertise within the courtroom. The team approach is meant to offer the best possible blend of court supervision and addiction treatment. The result is a series of goal translations on the part of both legal and therapeutic actors.

Michel Callon (1999, 82) makes the following observation about the relationship between translations and power relations.

Translation is the mechanism by which the social and natural worlds progressively take form. The result is a situation in which certain entities control others. Understanding what sociologists generally call power relationships means describing the way in which actors are defined, associated, and simultaneously obliged to remain faithful to their alliances. The repertoire of translation is not only designed to give a symmetrical and tolerant description of a complex process which constantly mixes together a variety of social and natural entities. It also permits an explanation of how a few obtain the right to express and to represent the many silent actors of the social and natural worlds they have mobilized.

Following Callon's description, translation is unmistakably about negotiating power. In the context of the treatment court, translations work to silence the interests, desires, and rights of the treatment client. When they see it for the first time, many people remark on the rabid paternalism of the DTC, amazed at how clients are infantalized by the clear "father/mother-knows-best" attitude that pervades the courtroom.[27] This is an apt description. The injection of practices of care into practices of control starts to sound markedly similar to the combination of epistemologies meant to guide child rearing. As parents, we are meant to care for and discipline our children. This combination gives us an awesome power over our kids, who are, regardless of how many choices we give them, deeply subjugated through the status of being children. Adults are afforded protections against this degree of power. The potential for subjugation inherent in the relation between either a therapist or a legal actor and a person in conflict with the law is substantial enough that governing structures of both legal and therapeutic professional bodies (as well as the law itself) place checks and balances on these relationships. The formalized uncoupling of therapeutic and legal knowledges in these settings translates into the formalized uncoupling of checks and balances on the relations of power. Recalling Valverde's observations that knowledge relations are also power relations, the liberation of expert knowledges in this court is also the liberation of expert powers. The result of this is the formation of a network of actors with the potential to engage in a heightened degree of subjugation, all of which is excused by the inarguable goal of curing the offender.

Caring for the Addicted Self

So far, I have attempted to weave together a narrative of the rise and current practices of criminal justice addiction treatment. From what I have discussed, it should be clear that attempts to cure criminalized drug addicts are deeply political. I also make the case that our notions of drugs and their dangers are as much products of culture as they are of science and that neither of these leads us to any objective reality about harm, its assessment, or its effects. Finally, with any luck, it should also be apparent that state attempts to "do better" by criminalizing drug users occur through epistemic translations that allow punitive practices and actors to reiterate themselves under the guise of therapy and vice-versa. Translations are worked into the apparatuses of power, effecting a coalescence of law and psy designed to cure the criminal addict. These are key points in my attempt to disrupt widespread assumptions that drugs are dangerous, their use criminogenic, and addiction treatment inherently progressive. So far, though, I have been largely silent regarding the users who are subject to and criminalized through these interventions.

This chapter is about those users. I am interested in four things: (1) how users are identified and made governable in these initiatives, (2) how they fit into and care for themselves within state-mandated efforts to change them, (3) how they act to resist state attempts to intervene with them, and (4) how authorities make sense of and respond to that resistance. In crafting this narrative, I argue that users are rendered governable through the discovery and assignment of the criminal addict identity. Through this identity, users are initiated into varying practices of self-care (Foucault 1978, 1994) designed to have them engage in personal regulation (Cruickshanks 1996). Being made governable in this way does not, however, reduce the users to docility, despite the sizable power to subjugate that engulfs them (Bosworth 1999); rather, they take active roles in this governing project, caring for themselves by both embracing and resisting governing regimes. These actions generate governing responses that frame almost all actions (both compliant and resistant) in a therapeutic discourse. The end result is a complicated map of power, resistance, and governing in which practices of self-care emerge not only as exercises of subjugation but also as attempts at subversion.

To make my argument, I draw on two research sites – the DTCs and the Ministry program. I do this for two reasons. First, while the people in conflict with the law in these settings share the experience of being identified and then acted on as drug addicts, they also have marked differences. The DTC population, for the most part, is comprised of people who have extensive criminal justice involvement and relatively uncontested addiction issues. In contrast, the men I interviewed through the Ministry were serving their first or second sentence and were more inclined to reject the addict identity.[1] Working with research from both these populations offers a good opportunity to explore issues of identity, self-care, and resistance at different moments of intersection between drug use and crime,[2] revealing how they are differently iterated by individuals at different points of involvement within the CJS.

Second, drawing data from both sites compensates for some of the limits of this research. I was not able to conduct interviews with DTC clients, nor was I able to observe the actions of probationers in the Ministry groups. In combining the DTC observations and Ministry interviews, I can explore data on both the performance of addiction recovery (as illustrated through the DTCs) and personal narratives (gleaned from the interviews with probationers). The ability to approach questions of self-governing using a variety of experiences and research techniques is beneficial as it allows for a rich and varied account of the ways in which interventions are managed by their targets. This approach also warrants the necessary caution that the two sites are different. While it is helpful to have data on both performance and narrative, I want to underscore that one does not fit seamlessly with the other. I am working with different kinds of information gleaned from different moments of intervention. My goal is not to craft a seamless account of how people in conflict with the law manage attempts to govern them through the addict identity; rather, my goal is to draw on these differences to capture the complicated nature of these initiatives and the intricate and varied negotiations of power therein (Gubrium and Holstein 1999; Valverde 2005).

I want to take a moment to briefly describe the research I completed with the Ministry. Between September 2002 and May 2003, I interviewed ten men serving terms of probation in Ontario. All the men completed the Ministry's Substance Misuse Orientation Program and were still serving their sentences at the time of the interview. The men ranged in age from twenty-four to sixty-eight. The offences for which they were sentenced included assault, possession of weapons, driving under the influence of alcohol, and sexual assault. Four of the men had never been in conflict with the law before, while the other six had criminal records. Of these, three had spent time in prison on previous convictions. Seven of the men reported a wide range of experiences with different substances, citing three or more different kinds of substance use within the last year (including alcohol). Half of the men interviewed had postsecondary educations and self identified as middle class. This group represents a minority of people in conflict with the law, and it is not representative of the racial demographics of the CJS. All of the men I interviewed were white.

Making Governable Subjects

In *History of Sexuality*, Foucault (1978) focuses on how particular identities are "discovered" at defined historical moments in order to facilitate a practice of governing. The homosexual, for example, is unveiled in the late Victorian era as an object of fear, threat, and needed intervention. The discovery of the homosexual does not mark an actual unearthing of a previously unseen kind of man;[3] rather, this character is found in an arrangement of social, scientific, historical, and cultural factors. By the end of the nineteenth century, a set of behaviours (mainly sodomy) becomes a subject (the homosexual). Foucault (1965) takes similar aim at medicalized discoveries of madness as a scientifically knowable (and curable) disease. His point in both these instances is to disrupt the taken-for-granted nature of these identities, showing that they (the homosexual, the mad person) emerge under specific historico/political conditions and, through particular power/ knowledge arrangements, are reified as objective facts. These identities are subjective rather than objective and, more important, become subjectifying technologies through which to govern individuals (Lupton 1997). The homosexual is not a materially true identity. Homosexuals do not exist in nature; rather, the homosexual is constituted through the strategic arrangement of a set of behaviours (in this case having sex with men) that, when arranged in a specific order, come to stand for the homosexual (Foucault 1977).

The drug addict and, by extension, the criminal drug addict are also discovered. Addiction is a modern discovery, not a natural truth. Social histories of drugs indicate that the addict was exposed at much the same time and under much the same circumstances as was the homosexual (Berridge and Edwards 1999; Carstairs 2005; Courtwright 2001; Morgan 1981; Musto 1973). A range of behaviours such as injection drug use and the administration of cocaine to relieve the strange sickness that emerged as a result of no longer taking opium (all aptly and wholly unproblematically described by Sir Arthur Conan Doyle in the Sherlock Holmes series) are rearranged alongside xenophobias, concerns about the chastity of white women, labour shortages, and class unrest to form a new identity: the drug addict. Once identified as such, an individual could be subject to a wide and varying range of interventions, guided as much by socio-economic status, race, and gender as by the nature of her "problem" (Berridge and Edwards 1981; Carstairs 2005). Upper-class white women and (to a lesser extent) men went the way of medicine, confinement, prayer, and rest in the country (Carstairs 2005). "Others" (the poor, people of colour, immigrants) were criminalized, forcibly confined, incarcerated, and disenfranchised (White 1998).

The addict identity, as I show in Chapter 2, gains much purchase as an explanation for undesired or unlawful behaviours, becoming a prime account of crime. In this chapter, I describe change-oriented interventions carried out on people in conflict with criminal law. Criminality, even if it is the reason these people become subjects of intervention, is not the target of these interventions. The target is addiction. Directing curative interventions at addiction rather than criminality is politically strategic. I have already argued that the most recent iteration of the addict in contemporary criminal justice initiatives is particularly felicitous. The addict identity reifies neoliberal narratives about social ills: addiction (not social inequality) is the root of criminality. Addiction is also a product of individual choice. The individual makes a conscious decision to use a particular substance and, therefore, is personally and (most important) solely responsible for all the negative outcomes of that act (including, of course, the criminality). There can be no social explanation or cure for crime because crime is a product of individual choice rather than of social ills. The addict chooses to put the needle in her arm, thereby consciously opting for the criminal lifestyle that must, by definition, accompany her drug use.

This story about the etiology of crime is advantageous for governing because, in locating the addict at the core of criminality, it allows crime to be easily solved. Widespread social change is not necessary to eliminate the crime problem. What is necessary is getting people off drugs. If people start using drugs because of the choices they make, we need to teach them how to make different choices. The newly cured, choice-making, and, most important, self-regulating subject is then liberated from her addiction and is free to navigate her life making good, non-criminal choices (Hannah-Moffat 2000; O'Malley and Valverde 2004; Rose 1999; Valverde 1998b). The effect is that criminality is, in many ways, irrelevant to these governing initiatives. Crime is not the object of intervention, and its elimination is the secondary goal of these projects.

We cannot, of course, throw the criminal baby out with the therapeutic bath water, however, because, as much as criminality is backgrounded in these settings, it plays the crucial function of control (Hannah-Moffat 2000; Kendall 2000). The discovery that an individual is a criminal is the key to unlocking other kinds of interventions. In other words, one must be known as a criminal before becoming a criminal addict, just as one must find oneself incarcerated before one's criminal abnormalities can be revealed (Castel

1991; Foucault 1977; Pasquino 1991). Blending treatment and criminal justice creates the sense that curing the criminal addict is doing good at its finest. Obscured beneath this aim is the reality that these people have all been (or are about to be) convicted of crimes. The status of a convict is, by definition, a subjugated one (Bosworth 1999; Foucault 1977). People in conflict with the law are under control that, at the end of the day, is meant to oppress and punish them, even as it may also try to remake them into better people.

The notion of control is well veiled, though, in the quest for the happily-ever-after of curing addiction (Moore and Hannah-Moffat 2002). To reach the happy ending of a crime-free society, all we need to do is to get rid of the evil villain, the drug addict. The choice of addiction over criminality to play the villainous role in the narrative is important. Criminality suffers the flaw of vague definition, making it hard to see, measure, and, more important, eliminate. Addiction, on the other hand, is a deft villain. It is easily seen (through drug testing), measured (through actuarial assessment), and eliminated. Technologies such as drug tests make it possible to be sure that the source of the problem is totally eliminated (Moore and Haggerty 2001). Thus, the start of this happily-ever-after ending is the discovery of the addict. Addiction becomes the tidily defined problem that must be solved (Foucault 2001). Naming the addict is crucial to mobilizing any initiative that would cure criminality by curing addiction. Once she is found, the addict must know (or be shown) the truth about herself. I turn now to exploring how addicts are revealed in the CJS.

The Criminal Addict and the DTC

The discovery of the addict in the treatment courts is fairly easy. As I describe in Chapter 4, to be accepted into the DTC, a person must show a history of being addicted to one of the targeted substances, although the operational definition of this history is unclear. Written and interview descriptions of the intake process leave a clear impression that the establishment of addiction is not a particularly complicated, time-consuming, or rigorous feature of intake; rather, intake in both the VDTC and the TDTC is driven largely by the Crown counsels, who screen potential files, weeding out unsuitable candidates with histories of violence, weapons offences, or high-volume drug trafficking. When I asked the Crown counsels how they know whether or not a potential DTC client is an addict, they gave similar responses. The addict is known by "typical" addict behaviour, such as a long history of property, possession, and (for women) prostitution offences, street knowledge (mainly from police), the Crown's familiarity with her, and her own admission of addiction. In this sense, the decision is very much one of common sense rather than one that emerges from clinical, expert observation (Moore 2000; Valverde 2003b). Potential court clients identified as addicts and successfully screened by the Crown are referred to a DTC therapist for assessment. This screening process is designed not to establish or confirm the presence of an addiction but, rather, to "determine program suitability" (Orbis 2003, 4-3). The VDTC describes the purpose of this first screen.

Issues such as degree of substance abuse problems, participant motivation, ability to fit within the existing group composition, and general suitability for the treatment regime are taken into consideration at this stage. While not a formalized process, this screening allows the program director to have the first contact with the new participant and to identify any potential impediments that might result in an early termination for the participant or constitute risks to the functioning of the court.

Notably, this screening process lacks the actuarialism central to most penal rehabilitative initiatives (see Hannah-Moffat 1999). The screen, as it is described, appears to be more about ensuring that people who will likely succeed in the DTC are chosen to participate. When I asked the program coordinators about the purpose of the initial screen, they both confirmed that it is intended to ensure that clients who would "do well" in treatment court are chosen. The addiction of the potential client is taken as more or less unproblematic.[4] Over the course of my research in the VDTC and the TDTC, I never saw an open debate in court about an individual's addiction status.[5] Nor did I ever see a court client contest the addict identity. Furthermore, establishing the addict identity raised no concern in interviews.

Once potential court clients have undergone the initial screens and assessments, they are brought into the DTC for formal intake. As with most aspects of the DTCs, these intakes serve both legal and therapeutic purposes. Clients are called before the judge. Following traditional criminal court procedures, the charges and police disclosure are read. At this point, for most clients, a guilty plea is entered. In the less common instances in which clients are not entering guilty pleas, they are accepted into the court on bail with a delayed trial. The judge then questions the potential client about his motivations for participating in the court. Typically, the questioning involves asking the client how long he has been an addict, why he wants to stop using drugs, and why the DTC is going to help him. The following is a typical account of these interactions:

> Donovan is called next on intake. The Crown introduces Donovan to the Court, telling us that Donovan is thirty-eight years old and has been using crack for twelve years. Donovan is also a pot smoker. When the judge asks him why he wants to be in the treatment court, Donovan responds "I'm tired of being an addict." The judge asks Donovan if he has even been in treatment before. Donovan says no. When the judge asks him about his motivations for participating in the program, Donovan responds, "I recognize a lot of the people in the body of the court and they look pretty good.

I want to be like them." The judge seems satisfied and admits Donovan to the program.

In this interaction, the truth about this man, that he is a long-time drug addict, is revealed and uncontested. It is vital to the intake process that the potential court client reveals this truth about himself rather than having others unveil his addiction for him. In a move reminiscent of Alcoholics Anonymous (see Valverde 1998b), speaking these self-truths is an act of supplication and surrender to the higher power. The difference here is that the higher power is a judge, not a god. The effect, however, is the same. In AA meetings (as well as Narcotics Anonymous and Cocaine Anonymous) participants must start by admitting their addictions because, in the absence of the revelation of those truths, it is not possible to change. AA operates, as Valverde points out, through the alcoholic identity. This is why members introduce themselves at meetings through the refrain: "My name is Dawn and I am an alcoholic." In the DTC, this truth of the addict identity must also be revealed. Addiction is the essence of court clients.

In mapping the centrality of identity as a technology of governing, Foucault (1994, 87) suggests that it is helpful to ask, "How were the experiences that one may have of oneself and the knowledge that one forms of oneself organized according to certain [governing] schemes? How were the schemes defined, valorized, recommended and imposed?" Exploring these questions leads to particular insights into the nature of governing regimes that place the self at the locus. In response to the first question, considering the particular context of the DTCs, the entire scheme of the DTC rests on the addict's own personal knowledge of her addiction. Without that self-knowledge, she is in denial. While, as I show below, the state of denial does not negate the possibility of intervention, it does call for a different kind of interference than that offered in the DTC.

The mere admission of addiction is not sufficient to facilitate the governing scheme of the DTC. I could admit my addiction to the court and have no interest in doing anything about it. A lack of desire to change myself, to alter my habits, precludes me from entering the program. Here is the (partial) answer to Foucault's second question. Governing through the addict identity in the DTC can only happen if the user accepts the governing and surrenders to the imposition. This places the DTC initiatives squarely within long-standing practices of treating addicts (Valverde 1998b; White 1998). The video advertising the TDTC shows a therapist meeting with a potential court client in prison. The therapist begins her initial assessment by asking the client a number of questions. She then explains to him the litany of obligations that accompany DTC enrolment. She concludes by underscoring how busy he will be as a result of participating in the program, asking him whether he is sure he wants to do this. After he assures her several times that he does want to participate in the program because he is desperate to get off crack, she says that she agrees that he can enrol in treatment court.

Potential court clients must also show a high degree of personal motivation, a notion derived directly from the psy traditions I describe in Chapter 4 (Prochaska 1999; Prochaska et al. 1988). The assessment of personal motivation is fundamental to the court process. If the offender does not have personal motives to change, then the court is powerless to act on her. The judges in both DTCs often underscore this point in dealing with offenders whose motivations appear to be waning. In these instances, judges make comments such as, "we can't do this for you" and "you have to want to change for yourself." More important, as the above examples show, motives are always in question during the intake process. In the first example I describe, Donovan has to show some degree of personal motivation to change his substance-use habits. In addition to having court clients express their motivations in court, judges might also ask potential clients to write letters to the court explaining why they want to come into the DTC program. The judges do not read these letters out loud but will often comment on them in court, saying things like, "wanting to get your kids back is a good goal" or "sounds good, sounds like you're ready for all the hard work ahead of you." In the second example I offer, the assessment of motivation is also the therapist's goal. In the video, she deploys a tactic not unlike the one I use when attempting to weed students out of overcrowded classes: she exaggerates the amount and difficulty of the work ahead in an attempt to ensure that the potential client is "serious" about wanting to change.

Finding the Addict Probationer

The probation officer (PO) does not enjoy the ease of dealing with people who display the kinds of ready self-realization found in the treatment courts; instead, probationers enter probation offices largely unknown,[6] both to themselves and to the PO. For the probation service, knowing these individuals is crucial as they cannot be acted upon until the PO is able to identify what kinds of action are needed. The probationer's abnormalities must be revealed. Actuarial and clinical assessments are deployed as part of the process of uncovering varying criminal factors, including addiction.

Under the Conservative government that held power in Ontario from 1995 until 2003, the province's penal practices underwent a process of renewal (see Chapter 2; and Moore and Hannah-Moffat 2002). Part of the renewal project was the introduction of the Probation and Parole Service Delivery Model (PPSDM) in September of 2000. This document set the groundwork for standardizing the "business of offender management" through "empirically based approaches which have been shown to have positive impacts on the rates of recidivism," and which would "focus more on those criminogenic factors known to correlate the highest with recidivism" (OMCS 2001, 1). The PPSDM sets out a process of standardized assessment and intervention techniques by which the PO can most effectively manage each probationer's case.[7] Under this model, case management takes the form of identifying each offender's "needs." According to the PPSDM, there are five kinds of programs designed to respond to core criminogeninc issues: anger management, substance abuse, anti-criminal thinking, sex offenders, and spousal abuse.[8] During the time I was completing this research, only programs devised to target substance abuse and anger were operating anywhere in Ontario. The substance-abuse program is the longest-running and has the highest enrolment. The training manual outlines a detailed process through which probationers are selected to participate in the program. The process is two-tiered. On the first level, the PO uses actuarial and clinical assessment techniques (including a series of actuarial assessment tools designed to assess levels of substance abuse) to determine whether an individual needs programming targeting substance abuse and poses a high enough risk of reoffending to warrant intervention. This, coupled with determining whether the probationer's sentence allows enough time for the probationer to complete a program, constitutes the first cut-off. From this short list of potential program participants, the facilitator selects people through an interview process that assesses their motivation to participate in the program. As in the DTC, a good candidate exhibits an interest in changing his substance-using behaviours and expresses a commitment to completing the program.

While the PPSDM suggests that self-knowledge is an asset to enrolment in the program, in practice, it appears to be wholly irrelevant to participant selection. My research indicates that very little of the selection process set out in the PPSDM is followed. Even though the PPSDM suggests that criminal pathologies are arrived at through actuarial assessment and self-disclosure, probationers enter the substance-abuse program not as a result of a detailed and systematic selection process but, rather, as the result of a much more random path. In interviews, probationers indicated that they found themselves in the program because the sentencing judge recommended that they seek treatment or because their supervising probation officers "thought it would be a good idea." None of the probationers I interviewed indicated that they had disclosed an addiction to their POs or requested assistance with dealing with substance-abuse problems; instead, they reported having had only brief conversations about substance use with their POs, resulting in the mandate from their PO or in the PO carrying out the judge's direction that the probationer participate in the program.

The ethos of the program supports the notion that the entire initiative is designed to assist probationers to realize the truth about themselves rather than to support them in active choice making. The program is called Change Is a Choice and is based on the Stages of Change (SOC) therapeutic model pioneered by Prochaska and DiClemente (DiClemente and Prochaska 1998). The SOC model was developed to motivate smokers to quit but has since been adopted in all manner of "lifestyle modification" initiatives, treating eating disorders, obesity, compulsive shopping, and addictions. The model, closely aligned with CBT and drawing on the same ethic as the DTCs, starts with the problem of motivation. In order for an individual to change a particular habit or behaviour she has first to want to change (Prochaska et al. 1988). Following this, individuals are assessed at one of four stages of "change readiness": precontemplation, contemplation, action, or maintenance. The role of the practitioner within the SOC paradigm is to meet the individual in whatever stage she currently resides and to deploy therapeutic techniques to facilitate movement along the continuum. The person is expected to proceed linearly through different stages until she arrests the problematic behaviour. She then works to continuously maintain her new lifestyle.

The Change Is a Choice program targets probationers in either the precontemplative or contemplative stage of change; it is designed to respond to people who have not yet thought about changing their substance-using behaviours or who are thinking about changing them (Cox 2001). In actuality, this means that the program is almost exclusive to men who firmly deny having substance-use problems. Once a PO arrives at the truth of a probationer, the latter's self-identity as a non-addict is irrelevant. If the probationer denies addiction, then he is in precontemplation (what we might otherwise call denial). The goal of the program, in dealing with these precontemplators, is to help them to see the truth about themselves and, thus, to develop their own motivations for changing their substance-using habits.

One participant[9] explained his experience of coming into the program as follows:

> When I was talking to [the PO], he did my pre-probation [report] and because I've never been in the legal system before I answered questions honestly. And you know, I told him exactly the same as you, that I drink and sometimes I use other recreational drugs. And then I saw my other PO, and she asks the same thing and I tell her the same thing. And on my presentence report it says that he conceals his problem [with substance use] well. So when I met with my PO I said I've got to ask you a question, "Does [my other PO] drink at all?" and she goes, "No." And I said, "Well do you?" She goes, "No." And I said, "Oh, I guess I understand why, you know, my being honest, I'm considered with an alcohol or drug problem."

This individual felt that, in the eyes of his POs, admitting drug use immediately rendered him a drug addict. He explained that the sentencing judge and the PO both acknowledged he had not been under the influence of any substance at the time of his offence,[10] but the link between his drug use and his criminal activity was made nonetheless.

Another probationer told a similar story. He felt that the judge and PO both based their conclusions that he had a problem on his previous convictions for driving under the influence. His current charge was domestic assault, and he claimed that the circumstances around his case never involved any substance. Still, in his own words, "They decided I had a problem the moment I walked through the door. All they had to do was to look at my priors [past convictions] and that was enough for them." These men cannot escape the truth about themselves, even if they do not feel that it is accurate. The addict selfhood, once discovered through the CJS, becomes their true identity.

Foucault points out how important the realization of self-truth is to any liberalized regime aimed at changing people. For Foucault (1994), liberal self-change is effected through the development of a personal ethic and practices of self-care.[11] Foucault suggests that, in the development of a personal ethic, there must be an element of confession, a full disclosure of one's selfhood, particularly of the "darker" side of the self: desires, compulsions, and the like. The use of the SOC model delivers a framework within which to develop the desired ethic of the criminal addict. The probationer's denial of his substance-use problem is not only anticipated but also forms one of the key bases of the program. Significantly, unlike with the DTC, the goal of this program is not to cure the addict but, rather, to move the individual through the stages of change. This means that the program's goal is to get the probationer to admit, or consider admitting, a truth about himself that is already apparent to the probation officer: that he has a substance-abuse problem. This truth, we are told, needs to be arrived at by the individual and (at least at the level of appearances) by the PO. A scripted sentence provided for POs in the training manual reflects the importance of self-truth telling within the program. The sentence, meant to be read during the first session of the program, has the PO saying (Cox 2001, 34), "These sessions are designed to give you information to help you determine if alcohol or drugs may be a problem for you. Many offenders have at some point had problems with drugs or alcohol and these problems may have contributed to their criminal behaviour." It is not the role of the PO to tell the probationer he has a substance-use problem; rather, this is a truth the probationer (it is hoped) arrives at on his own, although the PO works as a guide on this journey. While appearing to take a value-neutral stance towards the probationer's addict identity, the PO participates in the process by teaching the probationer about substance use and giving him the means to discover the truth about himself (in this case, a self-assessment form). The probationer who is already prepared to confess to his substance-abuse problem is ready to move through the stages of change, take action, and eventually change his behaviours.

The self-assessment form given to probationers in the first Change Is a Choice session is instructive. All the questions asked on the self-screen are personalized, directing the probationer to think of his own substance use over his lifespan. Answering "yes" to even one question indicates, according to the screen answer key, that the individual is in the early stages of addiction. The questions paint a specific selfhood of the criminal addict. Question 8, for example, asks the probationer about his feelings of guilt, while Question 11 is concerned with evasion and excuses. As the probationer moves through the screen, the impact of substance use increases, as does the indicated severity of addiction. Questions asked in the latter part of the test concern prison time, health concerns, compulsion to use, chronic use, anger, and loss of control. If a probationer responds positively to any of the last twelve questions, the answer key indicates that he is in the late stages of addiction.

The individual composed through this screen is far from the neoliberal, choice-making subject (Rose 1998). He is, instead, a beleaguered, troubled man so desperate he considers turning to God to seek salvation (Question 34 asks about turning to God for salvation). He cannot make his own decisions or control his own emotions. He has no consistency in his life, is angry, and lacks initiative and ambition. This person has lost his freedom (Valverde 1998b). Drawing on classic narratives of drug use, it appears that addiction has enslaved him to the drug and caused his own personal decay, as is indicated by his criminality, failing health, and discovery of faith (Berridge and Edwards 1981; White 1998). The self conjured here is a slave, kept from freedom because of his substance use and unable to reveal his true self, to be ethical, and, ultimately, to be free (Valverde and O'Malley 2004). This self is moralized through subtle and not so subtle silences. At the same time, the criminal addict does not *really* have the choice of whether or not he wants to change (Hannah-Moffat 2000). There is no chance that, once filling out the screen, an individual could be comfortable with his drug use and feel no need to address it. This is because even as the screen is designed to place the addict on the path to liberation, it also firmly fixes him as the kind of person who simply cannot make choices. Question 24 of the self-screen, for example, helps the probationer to identify his inability to make decisions, preferring to "wait until things happen." The "choice" to not address addiction is just another indicator that one has an addiction. All paths lead to the same point. It is crucial that this picture of the criminal addict emerge out of a self-screen rather than an assessment conducted by the PO (even if it was the assessment that landed the probationer in the program in the first place). In completing the assessment on their own, probationers are made to take responsibility for their own truth telling and arrive at their own conclusions about the nature of their selves. This responsibilized subject is a touchstone of neoliberalism (O'Malley 1996) – one who is able to embrace self-subjection as a means of initiating self-government and self-care (Cruickshanks 1996).

The addiction discourse deployed in these settings is such that it is impossible not to be known. Each year I give the students in my "Drugs" class the same self-test that is administered to the probationers. Each year a goodly portion of the class (usually more than half) turns up with serious addiction issues. When they laugh, I tell them they are in denial and they start to see the trap. Trapping people in identities in order to make them governable is a familiar strategy, particularly when dealing with people deemed in need of normalization because of their (usually moral) deviations from an imagined norm. Goffman (1961, 159) makes this point in relation to studying people's personal histories in order to make them up as mental patients: "It might seem also to be true that almost anyone's life course could yield up enough denigrating factors to provide grounds for the record's justification of commitment." For Goffman, it is not that assessments and examinations work to form lies constructed by stringing together a series of untruths about a particular person's history. The project is far more subtle and nuanced. Assessments work through cobbling together selective truths, a practice Goffman names "social reworking." The goal is to organize people's histories in order to arrive at particular governable identities.[12] Recalling both the DTC Crown counsel's review of case files and the more individualized use of the self-assessment in the probation program (the one that asks probationers to consider their entire lifespan), Goffman argues that the social reworking of the mental patient's history through careful selection of "important" facts serves as the primary justification for the degree of power exerted over the individual upon commitment to a mental hospital:

> The case history construction ... placed on the patient's past life ... [has] the effect of demonstrating that all along he had been becoming sick, that he finally became very sick, and that if he had not been hospitalized much worse things would have happened to him (145).

The establishment of the mental patient as a mental patient serves the important purpose of initiating and facilitating the interventions carried out on the individual (regardless of whether or not there is any truth to the claim that a person is mentally ill). So, too, in the context of curing addiction, people's personal histories are examined and reworked to establish particular governable identities.

The same holds true in relation to the addiction assessment process. The students in my class may well have drunk themselves into oblivion on more than one occasion, snorted too much cocaine at a party, taken bad acid, or mixed ecstasy and alcohol, any one of which could result in hospitalization, sharp reprimands from friends, the invocation of spiritual assistance, or a brief convalescence in a jail cell. At the same time, other personal truths are not revealed through this assessment, such as dedication to their studies, immediate proximity to finishing a degree in higher education, and reasonably regular class attendance. These factors may well reveal the majority of my class to be hard-working undergraduate students rather than serious substance abusers teetering on death's precipice. Similarly, the Ministry clients have self-truths that are not revealed through the Ministry assessment. Three of the men I interviewed were professionals, five had stable families and postsecondary educations, and four had never been in conflict with the law before. There is no space for these truths, however, in the personal narrative solicited through the Ministry assessment, and tools like the self-test are meant to reveal certain aspects of personal history that work to "identify" addiction issues.

Caring for the Self

Once the addict identity is established, it justifies all manner of interventions and exertions of power. The kind of power exercised is meant to facilitate the act of self-governing through the development of a particular ethic. If a person comes to accept her assigned identity, then she can be recruited in her own project of change through learning how to care for herself. Both Goffman and Foucault point to the importance of practices of self-care in governing strategies.

Rabinow (2003, 9) defines Foucault's notion of the care of the self:

The care of the self, then, was not just a state of consciousness; it was an activity. Furthermore it was not an activity appropriate just for this or that occasion; rather, it was an essential dimension of a whole way of life. It was a constitutive element of a form of life. Thus, in one sense it was part of a broader pedagogy ... However, the care of the self was more than that; it was more than a stage (or set of stages) one passed through. The care of the self was also a form of critique, a critique of the self that entailed perpetual self-examination, an unlearning of bad habits as well as the forming of good ones ... The care of the self was an essential aspect of how a moral existence had to be lived. Although this preparation and this exercise focused on the care of the self, it was far from being a solitary affair. In fact, the practice of the care of the self passed through an elaborate network of relationships with others. The care of the self was highly social, and it was oriented from the self outward to others, to things, to events, and then back to the self.

Foucault (1994) locates self-care squarely in the art of governing. The care of the self is a strategy of rule, part of Western governmentality, with its roots in ancient Greece. Developing an ethics of the self is a political project tied closely to building populations and maintaining power structures through particular social relations. To carry out this project, the self must be known by the individual through careful study and reflection. Once the self is known, it must be cared for. The care of the self is "not just a preoccupation but a whole set of occupations; it is ... employed in speaking of the activities of the master of a household, the tasks of the ruler who looks after his subjects, the care that must be given to a sick or wounded patient" (50). Thus, the care of the self is an active and life-long process of governing that focuses on the individual but is guided either directly or indirectly by governing authorities.

The practice of self-care is shaped by particular identities. The self-care of the psychiatrist is different from that of the patient. These identities are the aspirations of the practice. The "common goal of these practices of the self, allowing for the differences they present, can be characterized by the entirely general principle of conversion to self" (Foucault 1994, 64). Self-care is about self-change, coming into one's self, realizing a particular identity and then acting to govern oneself in accordance with the prescription set out through that identity. This changed self is clear in his role and capable of carrying out his duties, sure in his ability to continue to self-examine and self-regulate, thus locking in the continuing ability to adjust oneself as the need arises (Cruickshanks 1996).

Foucault's notion of self-care is readily taken up by Rose (1998) in his work on the genealogy of psychology. Rose's work is incredibly valuable in terms of locating Foucault's ideas in sound empirical research, illustrating how practices of self-care relate to practices of governing, and, most useful for my purposes, how psychology has managed to graft itself onto other practices and institutions, locating itself firmly in contemporary strategies of rule. In the last chapter, I note that Rose gives us a hierarchical model of knowledge through which expertise can only flow downwards. My impressions, using the network approach, are that knowledges can circulate on a flattened plane among expert actors. I now take up this same argument in relation to self-care. For Rose, self-care is top down: practices of the self are iterations of larger governing strategies. Some of what I describe below supports Rose's model. Self-care, when viewed through the lens of official discourse and governing practice, does flow from the top down. At the same time, however, people engage in self-care practices that are meant to subvert or at least work against the governing strategy. In the following two sections, I build this argument, starting with a consideration of self-care as a form of top-down governing and then looking at "low-level" practices.

Governing practices, as Rose (1998) shows, promote practices of self-care. This is also O'Malley's (1996) point in revealing the role of personal responsibility in current risk management schemes as well as Cruickshanks' (1996) in her argument that self-esteem is a technique of governing through self-care. For these scholars, the self is recruited in a governing project that still succeeds in making bodies docile even as it has the appearance of making them free. Self-esteem, for Cruickshanks, is part of a broader political project that seeks to effect widespread self-regulation. O'Malley's point is similar. He locates the individual at the centre of disciplinary power, pointing to the rise of governing through risk as an example of a governing scheme that encourages self-action and self-regulation as an extension of that disciplinary power.

Goffman (1961) also considers the art of self-care as an extension of governing strategies. He outlines the "moral career" of the mental patient, choosing the term deliberately to capture what he sees as the fundamentally important relationship between the self and the governing structure. The mental patient is entreated to "succeed" in the hospital (thereby securing release) through effecting certain practices of self. Acquiescing to the new relations of power and suggestions of selfhood found in the hospital, engaging in hospital routines, and showing regret for past actions are all signs that a patient is "settling in." The goal of the mental hospital is not to force these behaviours on people but, rather, to bring the mental health patient to a heightened state of self-awareness so that he adopts these behaviours himself. That does not mean that the regimes of the self found in the mental hospital are void of disciplinary techniques. Goffman points to the ward system in the mental hospital as an example of how particular selfhoods are rewarded through the provision of greater creature comforts in more hospitable surroundings.

The model of addiction recovery that drives both the DTC and the probation program starts with acknowledging the addict identity. Once this selfhood is realized, the next stage of intervention is to teach the individual to care for herself. This self-care is composed of three aspects. First, the individual must be vigilant about knowing herself (this is what Rabinow [2003] refers to as pedagogy). In other words, she must be aware of what triggers her craving for drugs. Second, she must be aware that self-care is not only about self-knowing. It is also, as Foucault (1994) states, about developing an active ethics of the self: self-care is about doing. The criminal addict must act on this self knowledge. She must learn to deploy particular self-care techniques in order to "cope" with her triggers and to avoid situations in which her resolve to use drugs might be weakened. Third, she must be willing to remake herself.

Self-Care and the DTC

Because the DTC client has, by virtue of claiming her addiction without contest, embraced the notion of selfhood necessary to begin her metamorphosis, much of the emphasis in the DTC is placed on developing and sharpening practices of self-care. This does not mean, however, that the practice of self-knowing is thought to be completed through the admission of addiction and criminal guilt. Self-knowledge is constantly evolving (Rabinow 2003; Rose 1998). In the DTC, the pedagogy of the self is routinely negotiated as court clients are encouraged to engage in ever deepening self-examination.

The DTC invites clients to know themselves in a number of different ways. As I describe above, on intake they are called on to exhibit self-knowledge both in acknowledging their addictions and also in expressing the degree to which they are motivated to change their substance-using habits. Another moment in which self-knowledge is crucial to a client's successful navigation of the DTCs is in processing relapses. Relapsing back into drug use is expected in the DTCs, and thus does not, in and of itself, result in immediate sanctioning. What is sanctionable, however, is a client's failure to adequately process or reflect on a relapse. A client is thought to successfully navigate a relapse if she shows insight. An example from the TDTC illustrates this point:

> George is called before the judge to account for his full-blown relapse. George tells the court that, in the wake of breaking up with his girlfriend, he went on a bender, using an array of substances, including cocaine, codeine, sedatives, and morphine. In addition, George has been absent from treatment court for the last two weeks. The Crown is keen to come down hard on George and proposes a bail revocation. The judge invites George to respond to this proposal. George says that he deserves a second chance. George explains he has "processed [his] relapse," has "a clear understanding of [his] triggers and why [he] used." He also tells the judge that he is very committed to his own recovery and is confident that, with the assistance of the support people in the court, he will "work through this relapse and get back on track." The judge responds that he is pleased to see George's level of insight but nonetheless feels George would benefit from some time in jail to "further process" his slip.

Recalling the knowledge network, it is important to note that, in this exchange, George deployed the same argot of addiction recovery that is used by the experts in the court. He used key words such as "triggers," "relapse," and "processed." In light of both the popularization of therapeutic languages through the rise of the self-help movement and George's repeated exposure to treatment settings, it is not surprising that he deployed this language. Therapeutic knowledges are not only uncoupled from therapeutic actors in the DTCs. Languages concerning addiction and recovery are increasingly part of the everyday world. The bookstore section that used to be designated as "self-help" is now parcelled off into specific genres, including addictions and recovery. "Triggers," "motivations," and "processing" are all part of the vernacular.[13] George marshalled this lexicon to illustrate his own self-knowledge. While he "slipped," he had taken care to process the relapse, to gain insight, and to show motivation to recover from this setback. This example also shows that evidence of self-care is not a guarantee that the court client will be released from the overarching governing powers of the court in order to self-govern; rather, the court decided to provide George with the "structured" setting of a jail cell in which to gain additional insight into his drug use.

To yield recognition from the court, self-knowledge does not have to be packaged in the language of therapeutic recovery. For example, in the VDTC, Skip arrived in court for a second attempt at completing the court program. When the judge asked him why he thought he would succeed in the program this time round, he responded, "I am to the point that I don't like where I'm at, and I want to leave the battleground and sign the peace treaty." The judge responded, "Now that's progress talking." Skip succeeded in conveying his motivations to alter his substance-use habits and to reinvent himself without using treatment language. He used his own language to relate his acceptance of the addict identity as well as his motivations to change.

Clients in the court are encouraged to develop self-care practices. In the language of addiction recovery, much self-care is imagined in terms of coping with triggers. The thinking here is that the root of addiction lies in being triggered, in craving drug use. If the person can be taught how to deal with this craving, then she can learn how to stop herself from using drugs.

The government of British Columbia issues social assistance cheques to all recipients on the same day each month. In drug-using communities, this day, reputed to take on a carnivalesque air, is known as "welfare Wednesday." The day's reputation and effects are well known in the VDTC. The practitioners I interviewed indicated that, of all the days in the month, the days after welfare Wednesday see the highest rates of arrest, hospitalization, and failure to appear in court. In the court sessions preceding welfare Wednesday, there is a great deal of focus on devising plans to cope with triggers. Clients are asked to relate to the court their plans for the day and for the two or three days following. "Good" plans usually include vacating the downtown core by signing oneself into detox or going to stay with (non-drug using) family outside of the city. Attending the treatment centre and staying in close contact with a therapist or other support person are also viable strategies. These schemes are all intended to help court clients deal with the triggers of having money and being exposed to the elevated levels of drug use that characterize Vancouver's drug-using communities in the aftermath of the mass issuance of welfare cheques. It is instructive that clients are not forcibly locked away during this period or given directives by the court; rather, as part of the larger initiative to educate court clients in acceptable practices of self-care, clients are requested to develop their own plans, which are then reported to the court for approval.

Following Foucault's (1994) observation that self-care involves changing oneself, clients are also counselled to reinvent themselves as part of the bid to take better care. The assumption here is that the old self is dysfunctional and needs to be shed to allow for the blossoming of the new one. Rabinow (2003) describes the care of the self as a life-long battle of ethics. Thus, the transformations that take place through caring for oneself are not finite, and the care of the self does not happen in one particular moment (even if "bottoming out" stories are fundamental to the discourse of recovery in these courts) (Nolan 2001; and more broadly, Valverde 1998b). While the care of the self is meant to be about remaking oneself, this remaking is an extended project of renegotiation. Goffman (1961) shows this in his descriptions of the intake in the mental hospital. Mental patients lose their identity in many ways. They are stripped of personal possessions and made to wear uniforms; their contact with the outside world is severely limited, if allowed at all; their days are strictly ordered; and they lose personal autonomy. Their selves are mostly erased in order to be rebuilt to better fit with the "outside" world. After release, mental patients are equipped (Rabinow 2003) with technologies to help them maintain their new selves and also to help the new self evolve. Again, the ideal scenario is to recruit the mental patient as an active participant in his own recreation. As Goffman and Foucault indicate, the point is not to constitute the person as part of an aggregate; rather, these projects of self are very individualized and draw on particular norms regarding what is healthy, good, and acceptable. And they encourage the person to take direction of her own self-realization only within those norms.

The act of stripping and recreating the self is familiar to the DTC. When clients first come into the program, they are required to shed their old selves. In both the VDTC and the TDTC, clients are expected to let go of jobs, leave old (drug-using) friends, and free themselves of family responsibilities. This poses particular problems for the women in the court. By virtue of their drug-using and criminal activity, most of the women in the early stages of the court program have lost custody of their children.[14] The courts uphold this practice, suggesting that a woman in the early stages of addiction recovery cannot be distracted from her recovery by the task of mothering. Women who bemoan this practice in court, attempting too soon to position themselves to regain custody of their children, are routinely chastised by the judge, who reminds them that they must "take care of [themselves] first" before attempting to take care of their children. Women are told that, in the early stage of recovery, they need to let go of all their extant responsibilities so that they can focus completely on the hard work of becoming drug free.

While women must suspend motherhood in order to recover from addiction, all court clients are afforded some leeway in the process of shedding their old selves. This is particularly true of the VDTC, where, in a remarkably progressive move, the court recognizes that drug users are capable of forming important, supportive, and healthy relationships with other drug users in a drug-using community. This being the case, the VDTC does not actively encourage court clients to sever all ties with drug users if there are people to whom they are connected who provide a degree of support and nurturance in their lives. Still, it appears that, somewhere between the three- and six-month anniversary of a person's enrolment in either court, a significant change is meant to have taken place. Those who have not demonstrated a notable shift in their selfhoods by this point are routinely ejected from the courts. Those who have changed are carefully monitored so that the courts can raise red flags in the event they appear to be slipping back into their old ways. In so doing, the courts are able to remind clients of the lengthy project in which they are engaged – a project requiring constant vigilance and modification (Rose 2003) in order to guard against slips.

Invoking the old self is a common setup for a serious warning from the judge. For example, one client in the TDTC came before the judge to report that he had been using heroin almost constantly for the past two weeks. The judge responded, "Why are you letting yourself go like this? Why are you going back to the old you? I'm really disappointed." In both courts, clients are routinely cautioned against revealing or resembling their old selves. The old self of the criminal addict is an undesirable character. Unlike the new person invented through the DTC program, the old self lacks insight and self-knowledge and thus has no ability to take care of herself. She is also often unattractive, apathetic, and uninteresting. On the other hand, the new self displays all the markers of self-care. She is capable of resuming old roles, such as mothering and working, that were too much for her in the initial stages. She knows how to handle triggers, she has new friends, she looks better, she is in better health, and she feels better about who she is.

The newly invented, drug-free self is what is featured at DTC graduations, which are held roughly every three months. They are designed as celebrations for and of clients who have successfully completed the program, and they are often grand affairs. In Toronto, they are held in an oak-panelled courtroom (regular court is held in a considerably less grand, makeshift court void of any impressive trappings). Dignitaries (and funders) are invited, as are past DTC graduates. Usually two or three clients graduate at a time. Each is called individually before the judge for personally tailored acclamations from the court personnel. Usually the judge, both lawyers, the treatment liaison, and the individual's therapist will speak about the client's progress, achievements, and future goals. The client is also invited to address the court. The purpose of graduation is not only to celebrate individual successes but also to underscore to all the court clients (who must be in attendance) the benefits of getting clean and to give them a particular vision of what successful addiction recovery looks like.

Shelley's graduation from the VDTC is a good example not only of how graduations work to lock in a particular notion of the newly minted, self-aware and self-caring, drug-free subject but also how this subject is gendered:

> At Shelley's graduation from the VDTC, court officials make varying positive comments about her. The duty counsel notes that she is different both in demeanour and appearance from when he first met her. The treatment liaison comments that she has made a number of positive changes in her life, including finding a job and reconnecting with her children. He credits her as a role model to others in the program. When invited to speak she holds back tears as she tells the court about her life before treatment court. A long-time sex trade worker, she was routinely a victim of sexual and physical assaults. She begins to cry, saying that she does really feel like a new person and she is very grateful to be clean.

Shelley's graduation was all about her before and after selves. Before DTC involvement, her life was riddled with violence and volatility, and she was unable to care for her children. True to form, the unattractiveness of her life is reflected in her "appearance and demeanour." The "after" image of Shelley is a changed self, employable, maternal, attractive, and pleasant. These kinds of comments are reflective of those generally made in court when a woman graduates. Appearance and parenting are rarely addressed when men graduate. What makes this woman successful as a court graduate is her ability to remake herself into an appropriate, attractive, and motherly person. This vision of what makes a woman "uncriminal" is well documented as a gender norm (Boritch 1997; Bosworth 1999; Hannah-Moffat 2001; Smart 1995).

Beyond such gendering, the successful DTC client bears no resemblance to the person who first walked into the court. Most important, eyeing the pervasiveness of self-care in this discourse, he did this "himself." Much of the emphasis of graduation is placed on the client's tenacity with regard to personal recovery. For example, when Tim graduated from the VDTC, he thanked the court profusely for all the help and support it provided. To this, the judge responded, "It's you Tim. We provide the structure but you do the work, and now you have to get on with your life. And we believe you will keep working on it in your new life." Clients are applauded for sticking with it and are reminded of how hard they had to work, and must continue to work, for something *they* really wanted.

The DTC client can embody the notion of the care of the self. In embracing the addict identity, the court client works to know herself better as a drug user. This self-knowledge is her path to emancipation as the better she knows herself the more able she is to identify the things in her life that lead her to use drugs. The known trigger is more easily avoided. This process of self-knowing and avoidance becomes one of intended self-destruction and rebuilding. The DTC client abandons all the pieces of her old self that caused her to use drugs, replacing them with "healthy" features like non-drug using friends, geographic relocation, and self-help meetings.

The Probationer's Self

Learning how to care for oneself through the probation program is a much more passive process than the one utilized in the DTCs. The program is intended to function as an educational tool that encourages probationers to accept the truth about themselves and then to learn how to develop a personal ethic around that truth. Because the program is aimed at getting probationers to accept their addictions, it is largely educational. The initiative lacks much of the kind of therapeutic engagement characteristic of the DTC program. Probationers are meant to learn about substance abuse generally in order to better equip themselves to "choose" whether or not they want to be substance free. Once they have made this choice, probationers are directed to varying treatment options. The Change Is a Choice initiative is best captured in the program manual that guides POs delivering the program. The manual sets out techniques by which POs are meant to get probationers to realize the truth about themselves – and to act on that truth (thus moving through the stages of change) – without actually directly telling a probationer that he is an addict.

While the intent and content of this program are markedly different from those of the DTC, the Change Is a Choice initiative still aims at teaching probationers how to care for themselves. Much of this rests on the constitution of the addict identity. The program is separated into four sessions. The goals of the first session are "to provide general introductory information about drugs and alcohol and their effects; and to provide an opportunity for the offender to personalise this information" (Cox 2001, 34). While the session starts off with the disclaimer that POs are not assuming that any of the probationers have an addiction problem, the training manual directs the PO, as the third order of business in this first session, to discuss strategies for coping with triggers. The manual urges the presenting PO to "inform the group that the videos and/or discussions over the four sessions, while interesting and informative, may trigger urges or cravings in some members" (35). The manual directs probation officers to brainstorm with the group during the first session about different strategies for coping with triggers. Probationers who feel the urge to use drugs are encouraged to use positive self thoughts, to acknowledge that what they are experiencing is a craving, to consider the negative consequences of using, or simply to "think of a stop sign." The foregrounding of coping with triggers underscores POs' assumption that group members do have addiction issues, even as they bracket the discussion claiming the contrary.

In the first session, probationers watch a film entitled *A Matter of Balance*, which is about the ill effects of drug use. They then conduct a general discussion about how one might know whether one's use is "out of balance." The probationers are then asked to personally reflect on their own habits and to think about whether or not their use is balanced. In this session, probationers also provide handouts about addiction treatment programs.

The second session has the same goals as the first. Its focus is to facilitate the probationer's decision about whether or not he ought to change his habits. Again, the manual cautions POs against using words like "addiction," urging them, instead, to help the probationer decide for himself where he is. In order to do this, probationers are directed through a cost-benefit analysis of their drug use, which is designed to help them discern whether or not their use is "worth it." In this session, probationers are presented with examples of warning signs that their use is not worth it. Echoing the self-screen, probationers are taught that if they find themselves in conflict with the law, get into accidents, notice a drop in their grades, make it to work less frequently, forget things, or spend too much money on drugs then clearly their substance use is not "worth it" as these are "warning signs" of addiction.

The third session is meant to underscore the importance of practising coping skills for dealing with triggers, to provide techniques meant to equip probationers with long-term self-care strategies (Rabinow 2003). Probationers are taught about meditation and progressive muscle relaxation. They are also taught both about ways to seek treatment and about varying barriers to the treatment process (such as "denial").

Probationers are made to watch a video called *The Wall of Denial* in which addicts categorically deny their addictions while clearly exhibiting "warning signs" similar to those described in the second session. Spliced with the footage of addicts in denial is narration explaining why the individual is in denial and the negative effects of this state. One narration (Rabinow 2003, 59) states, "When we are living in denial our addictions impose behaviours and beliefs and feelings which makes the addiction itself grow in severity and strength."

The fourth and final session is a wrap-up, in which probationers are asked to fill out program evaluation forms, coping strategies are reviewed, and the PO gives the probationers additional information on treatment services available in the community. The fact that the program is designed to have probationers realize their addictions is underscored in the report on the program evaluations, which uses the number of probationers claiming addiction and seeking treatment after completing the program as a measure of program effectiveness. Despite this, the program manual repeatedly reminds POs that they are meant to facilitate self-realization on the part of the probationer rather than to simply tell him that he has an addiction problem. Thus, the probationer is placed at the centre of this intervention and is recruited as his own agent in his change process. That he is constantly reminded he is not being told he is an addict or that he has to change is tempered by the program's clear underlying message to the contrary. The entire program is about realizing oneself in the form of a particular identity. Just as the self-test is designed to embrace virtually anyone in the folds of the addict identity, so the entire Change Is a Choice program is designed to have probationers realize that identity. Probationers are meant to attend sessions in which, only moments after they are told that no one is calling them addicts, they are asked to talk about how people in the group ought to cope with cravings. They are required to engage in a cost-benefit analysis of their substance use in which many of the costs are also warning signs of an addiction. They are taught about denial and about how addiction works to create and support this state. Finally, in every session, they are given information about how to seek help for an addiction.

The Change Is a Choice program closely resembles Rose's (1998) model of top-down self care. Using Rose's parlance, the probationers are responsibilized to "invent themselves" but are placed in a situation in which there is only one possible self to be invented: the addict. Any other self-understanding or conclusion is simply a form of denial. The probationers are meant to care for themselves in this context by being led to a particular self-realization. Learning and starting to exercise coping strategies as well as seeking out additional treatment are long-term goals of this form of self-care.

In explorations of the kinds of interventions meant to be carried out on people in conflict with the law, the addict identity emerges as a readily discernable and accessible site of intervention. When both probationers and DTC clients are constituted under this identity, they are recruited into their own process of change, entreated to learn to accept the truth about themselves and then care for themselves as part of a broader governing initiative (Rabinow 2003; Rose 1998). This kind of top-down self-care is not, however, the only means by which probationers and DTC clients take care of themselves in these settings. At the same time as members of both groups are meant to engage in practices of self-care iterated as a strategy of governing, they also engage their own practices of self-government, which work both to help them navigate a situation in which they find themselves subjugated and to serve as a rejoinder to that subjugation.

Resistance

Both the DTC and the Ministry programs work through the addict identity to effect a governing regime. While the emphasis on self-realization, self-care, and self-change succeeds in creating a strategy of control that works "at a distance" (Rose 1996b), power is still exerted on the probationers and DTC clients to change them into governable subjects. To cure the offender is still to exercise power over her, to place her in a position of subjugation and act on her in such a way that she is more easily shaped into the desired subject. Thinking about attempts to cure the criminal drug addict in this way creates a skewed interpretation of the distribution of power in these sites. Thus far, it appears as though the dynamics of both the probation office and the DTC set up a zero-sum relation of power, with the probationers and the court clients on the zero end.

Throughout *Criminal Artefacts*, I have used Foucault's model of power as a reference point. In this model, power is not a zero-sum game. Power cannot be exclusively owned or monopolized as it exists in relationships. Because power is relational, everyone involved in a governing regime can exercise it, even those who are subjugated. Foucault (in Sawicki 1991, 25) states:

> I'm not positing a substance of power. I'm simply saying: as soon as there's a relation of power there's a possibility of resistance. We're never trapped by power: it's always possible to modify its hold in determined conditions and following a precise strategy.

Resistance is always possible in power relations. Echoing this point in studying the constitution and care of the self, Rose (1998) suggests that conflict between the individual in the making and the authority or regime doing the making is to be expected. Because the self is constantly being invented and reinvented as part of governing and self-care strategies, its iterations are bound to encounter contestation. Although Rose is hesitant on the use of the term, for my purposes, it is useful to think of the contestations in terms of resistance. Resistance, the self, and identity are closely linked. This point is easily made if we think of resistance through identity politics. Women participate in Take Back the Night marches every year as a means of asserting that, as women, we are not afforded the same degree of safety and security as are men. This is one kind of resistance Foucault imagines. Resistance through identity politics is often organized, strategic, and targeted.

Resistance can also happen outside of the (less than tidy) parameters of identity politics. It can be spontaneous, disorganized, non-strategic, and imprecise. DTC clients and probationers exhibit this kind of resistance. Both these groups work to subvert the power exerted over them and, while at times this kind of resistance might be read as political, I suggest that resistance, in these contexts at least, can also emerge as a kind of counter-practice of self-care, a subverted ethics of the self that does not necessarily have a political basis.

Bosworth's work on identity and resistance in women's prisons is helpful here. Invoking Foucault, Bosworth (1999, 130) notes that "resistance, like power, is everywhere." She argues that resistance proves to be a useful concept because

> it illuminates small-scale attempts to disrupt power relations, by drawing attention to a variety of minor acts and rebellions which may otherwise escape notice ... Appreciating these subordinate acts as forms of critique demonstrates that power relations inside may not be as fixed or as unchangeable as they appear.

Many of the small-scale acts of resistance Bosworth observes concern the kinds of contestations of selfhood Rose imagines. Because the addict identity is the primary location of criminal justice intervention, the primary target of the project of change, the contestation of that selfhood is an important means by which those caught up in the CJS work to carry out a subverted notion of self-care. It provides them with a way of supporting themselves as they move through the process of being criminally sanctioned and altered. Rose (1999) points to the multiple selves that become sites of intervention and controversy. If there are multiple selves, it follows that there must be multiple forms of self-care. Self-care is not only a technology of governing; it is also a technology of resisting. Even within the broad and troubled category of resistance, self-care is a many-headed beast. Probationers often work to take care of themselves by explicitly rejecting the identity placed on them, whereas the resistance of DTC clients is much more about particular practices than it is about broader identities.

Rejecting the Addict Identity: The Self on Probation

Probationers find themselves in a difficult position. Even if they do not believe themselves to be addicts, to outwardly deny this identity by refusing to participate in the program or by rejecting their PO's assessment of their addiction status means that they end up in denial. Being in denial, they could be found to be non-compliant with their probation and thus become subject to even greater interventions. To care for themselves in this situation, probationers affect acceptance of the addict identity. Like

Goffman's mental patients going along with the expectations of the hospital officials, probationers affect resignation to the CJS process. All but one of the men I interviewed talked about experiences within the CJS as something they simply had to "get through," regardless of their own personal feelings and opinions of their CJS involvement. One probationer stated:

Yeah, I don't care really ... I'm mandated to come here [to the program]. Once a month I do. I'm always on time and I'm prepared to do whatever I have to do even if I think it's unfair. It's mandatory. I mean, I know I'm not a druggie and I know I'm innocent but here I am, right? I've just got to sit tight until this is over.

Throughout the interview, this man repeatedly stated his strong belief that the CJS cannot rehabilitate people. He explained that he had found his whole experience in the CJS dehumanizing and that he could not imagine people who actually do have addiction problems getting better within this system. His comments showed the tension between subjugation and self-care. This man knew he was assigned the addict identity through his enrolment in the Ministry program. He also knew that to reject that identity would likely further increase the controls under which he was placed. Despite his stated rejection of the addict identity, he outwardly resigned himself to the process in the interest of hastening the end of his supervision.

Worked into the program design of Change Is a Choice is the anticipation of a resigned resistance on the part of probationers. An individual can fail in the program if he is designated as non-compliant. During the first program session, the facilitators explain that participation is expected from each person in the group and that failure to participate can be construed by the POs as non-compliance. One probationer explained:

My PO told me from the get go that I couldn't just sit there and do nothing. She said I didn't have to like being there but I did have to go and I did have to participate. So I made sure that I answered one question each class or made one comment and that was it. There you go, participation.

Like most of the other probationers, this man rejected the claim that he had an addiction issue, and he expressed a great deal of resentment at being made to participate in the program. When asked why he didn't just tell his PO he wasn't going to comply, he explained that he knew the consequences for non-compliance would be worse than feigning resignation. Affecting interest in the program by asking one question per session was, for this man, a way of preventing more extensive interventions. It was a technology of the self, a way of taking care.

Another man offered similar sentiments on his own and others' experiences in the program:

> They [the POs] are dying of effort at trying to get everyone into it – motivated. But when you got a bunch of guys who didn't know each other and they're all in there and they've all been charged or whatever. The vibe wasn't that great. They were just kind of sitting. Like there wasn't any anger ... There was only a few guys in there that were actually positive in trying to get ahead.

Again, resignation emerges as a key factor in how the men manage themselves in the program. What is most interesting about this man's comments is the centrality of motivation within the program. He was keenly aware that he and the others were supposed to be motivated through participation. Resignation, in this context, is an act of subversion. Some of the men I interviewed related their own attempts at engaging in more explicit forms of resistance at different stages through their involvement with the CJS: altercations with prison guards, defying judges, and swearing at POs are all example of this resistance. In all of these cases, the men felt that the aftermath of these actions was severe. One man talked of being made to stand, by himself, for two hours in a room because he had tried to read something a prison guard told him to sign without reading. Another described having his bail revoked because he swore in the presence of his PO.[15] Given the severity of response to those who engaged in such explicit actions, the technique of resignation makes sense. Resignation is neither compliance nor non-compliance. It is an acquiescence to the demands of another, without agreement or disagreement, and it allows both people to maintain internal opinions about what is being done and/or asked.

Just as the men I interviewed described the ways in which they navigated the probation program through affecting a level of participation, acceptance, and subjugation, all but one steadfastly resisted the addict identity and its accompanying regime.[16] As a response to the addict selfhood, probationers pointed to those aspects of their lives that did not fit with the story of addiction as told through the program. One man described the circumstances surrounding his arrest:

> I was drunk when it happened... I think they [the judge and the POs] took it the wrong way. It was my birthday, I was so wasted I was blacking out, and when I came to I was just at a different stage, I didn't know what I was doing. And the next day I thought it was all a joke. I felt kind of ruined. And then I was charged. The only way I found out what I did was when I had to read my disclosure.

He was arrested for assault causing bodily harm. He returned home on the night of his arrest to find people breaking into his house and got into a physical altercation with the intruders. In the interview, he repeated several times that he was not a drinker and hardly ever used drugs but had "overdone it" on this particular night. He felt quite strongly that he was mandated to attend a substance-use program because he was intoxicated at the time of the offence, not because he had any long-term or discernable substance-use problem.

Another of the interviewees told a similar story. This individual, who was charged with assault, claimed that he was not intoxicated at the time of the offence and that he was mandated to attend the program because he had told his PO that he occasionally drank, smoked marijuana, and used cocaine. Others also denied that they had substance-use problems and contrasted themselves with their own images of what constitutes a criminal addict. One man, for example, explained that he was "not like the other losers in the program," adding, "I have an education, I work, I own a home, I have no criminal record, just bad luck." Another man raised a similar sentiment: "I'm a health care worker. I work with substance abuse all the time and that's not me. If anyone knows if someone's an addict it would be me." These men saw themselves as the antithesis of the addict. Addicts, in their view, were unemployed, in need of care – in a word, losers. Juxtaposed to these "losers," these men saw themselves as professional and educated. Bad luck rather than substance abuse had led them to be convicted of a criminal offence.

While the probationers articulated resistance to the addict identity, none of them indicated that he acted out that resistance in front of a probation officer; instead, reflecting the technologies of self-care I describe above, they "went along" with program expectations even as they personally resisted the adoption of the selfhood that went with it. When I asked probationers about this, they said it was easier to go along than to resist as they knew that they would get little benefit out of actively working against the program and the probation officers. Ewick and Silbey (1998, 184) describe this kind of action as a form of "tactical resistance." In their study of people's everyday interactions with the law, they note that people who feel they do not have the authority to, or would not benefit from, directly resisting the law deploy sideways actions as forms of resistance. The probationers felt there was little to be gained from direct contestation. At the same time, however, they all knew the Ministry would receive a final copy of this research. Expressing their resistance to me in the relatively safe context of a confidential interview, the results of which would not be made available to the governing authorities until well after their warrants had expired, was a strategic action on the part of the probationers. These actions are also technologies of self. Overtly denying the addict identity only cements that identity (as they become addicts in denial). Active resistance displayed in the program or directed at the PO is likely to result in increased supervision conditions or possible charges of breach of probation, leading to incarceration. Telling me about their resistance to the addict identity allowed the probationer to navigate his own subjugation, while, at the same time, ensuring that his resistance was documented. The men who most vehemently resisted the probation regime also directed me to "write this down" and "make sure you print that" when they expressed their rejection of the program, the addict identity, and, more generally, their probation experiences.

Resistance and the DTC

Tactical resistance as a strategy of self-care is also apparent in the DTC. Because courtrooms are highly formalized spaces in which obvious acts of resistance typically meet with swift and certain consequences (Ewick and Silbey 1998), court clients engage in very subtle subversions. These acts rarely concern the addict identity specifically (as DTC clients generally accept that identity) but, rather, are micro-challenges to the court's attempts to guide the individual's technologies of self, which are designed to facilitate recovery.

For example, a woman was called before the judge, who questioned her about a missed urine screen. The woman explained that she was quite ill and could not make it to the treatment centre to give the sample. The judge asked why the woman failed to call the treatment centre to tell them about her illness, and she responded that she was "really ill and not thinking straight." The judge let her off with a warning that next time she would be sanctioned. The woman turned to the gallery and mimed wiping sweat off her brow, signalling to the other treatment court clients her relief at escaping punishment. In successfully avoiding a sanction, this woman had cared for herself by keeping herself out of jail and circumventing increased supervision. Artfully navigating punitive terrain is one form of self-care that is iterated through resistance. In other instances, clients engaged in this kind of subversion by avoiding punishment for producing a dirty urine test, missing treatment groups, or being found in areas marked on their bail restrictions.

Beyond navigating around sanctioning, court clients also resisted attempts to order their day-to-day lives. In the VDTC, housing and homelessness are consistent issues. Some homeless people prefer the relative freedom, privacy, and safety of living on the streets over temporary housing in shelters. Many homeless shelters have zero tolerance policies for alcohol and drug use, meaning that you cannot stay at the shelter if you are intoxicated. Shelters are also high crime areas, where it is difficult to securely store personal possessions. Shelters often have curfews and rules about when you can come and go. Religious teachings also keep people away. Placing court clients in homeless shelters is a common occasion for conflict in the VDTC. The following research notes illustrates this issue:

> Ty is before the judge. He asks for the judge to lift his curfew because he doesn't have a place to stay at the moment. He is sleeping on a friend's couch but may also decide to go back out to the street. The treatment liaison stands to tell the judge that shelter beds have been arranged for Ty on a number of occasions and each time Ty has failed to show up. When the judge asks Ty about this he says he will not stay in shelters no matter what. He says they are disgusting and filled with vermin and dirty people. The judge reprimands Ty, saying that he must comply with his bail conditions. She tells him that if he doesn't like shelters he needs to go and get welfare sorted out so that he can secure housing. She tells Ty to show up at the shelter tonight.

For Ty, resisting the shelter was an act of maintaining autonomy and certain living standards. He actively asserted his personal ethics about living conditions even though they directly conflicted with the court's vision of what was best for him.

Court clients use the addict identity not only as a means of taking care of themselves but also as a means of engaging in acts of resistance in the court. Ronald's case in the TDTC is a good example:

> Ronald is brought into court for intake. The judge is generally pleased with Ronald's file and is prepared to admit him pending approval of the housing plan. Ronald is planning on returning to his home and the judge wants to check with Ronald's wife to make sure that she is in agreement with Ronald returning. A treatment team member reports that she has been unable to contact Ronald's wife. The judge decides that Ronald's release will have to wait until the court is able to confirm his living arrangements. Ronald is angry with this and starts talking back to the judge. The judge motions to the bailiff to take Ronald. Ronald swears audibly as he is taken out of the courtroom. Two days later Ronald is called back. The Crown explains that based on his outburst during his previous court appearance Ronald has been deemed unfit for the court program. This makes Ronald very angry. He claims this decision is unfair, stating "I'm an addict too." He goes on to suggest that the DTC program is "bullshit" and the defence lawyer a "crack head." The bailiffs place Ronald in handcuffs and take him down to the holding cells.

Ronald claimed the addict identity as a means of resisting a DTC decision. His actions, although more extreme than those in the other DTC scenarios I describe, were still attempts to engage in a particular ethic of self. Ronald asserted the need for assistance in recovery as a rationale for why the court made the wrong decision in ejecting him.

In the DTC, the addict identity is not grounds for resistance, even if it can be used as a tool in a resistant act. Court clients accept their identities and work to maintain selfhood and to act out counter-strategies of caring for themselves through small-scale forms of resistance, such as contesting living arrangements or avoiding punishments. When the addict identity is evoked in the context of resisting a court action, it is as a means of claiming the legitimacy of the client's own version of self-care. In knowing herself, the client makes the case that she is able to care for herself even if that ethic is different from the one imagined by the DTC actors.

Court officials and probation officers are interested in educating court clients and probationers in particular self-care strategies as a means of rendering them governable, as an exercise of power. This, however, is not the only version of self-care that operates in these sites. The court clients and the probationers are also interested in caring for themselves. Indeed, they have been engaged in self-care practices all along. These practices, however, are markedly different from those imagined by CJS actors. The self-care practices of both the probationer and the court client are designed to lighten the amount of control exerted over them and to carve out space for alternate ethics of self. Going along with what is asked of them and engaging in tactical subversion of the CJS through techniques such as ensuring their rejections of the addict identity are all events that are recorded. Avoiding punishment and attempting to maintain a certain lifestyle are all strategies of self-care that tactically subvert the governing strategy. Self-care, then, is available as both a strategy of control and a strategy of resistance.

The Psychology of Governing: Planning for Resistance

The subversions discussed above are not unanticipated either by court personnel or by POs. Rather than act to counter acts of resistance, CJS actors call up psy rationalities as rejoinders to them. Rose (1998, 95) marks this use of psy:

> Psychological techniques have come to infuse, dominate or displace theological, moral, bodily, dietary, and other regimens for bringing the self to virtue or happiness... And if the experts on hand to guide us through the conduct of our lives are not all psychologists, they are nonetheless increasingly trained by psychologists, deploy a psychological hermeneutics, utilize psychological explanatory systems and recommend psychological measures of redress.

A psychological hermeneutics is mobilized as a means by which to diffuse attempts to resist being governed.

In the probation program, the probation officers, feeling that a job is well done when they know that a probationer has accepted the truth about himself, are not deterred by those who reject that truth. The logic of addiction recovery is foolproof in this regard. Men who reject the identity or resign themselves to the process are merely stuck in precontemplation. There is no telling, so the logic goes, how much of what they learned in the program will sink in or how technologies like coping strategies will re-emerge in the future. According to the program designer, getting a probationer through the door is a success in and of itself because, even if he isn't "ready to hear it" right away, at least he is exposed to important information about addiction and recovery. The probationer's bid to "get through," even if he disagrees with the program and the criminal addict identity imposed upon him, is anticipated by the POs. The program developer explains that the program is designed to speak specifically to the most reticent probationer. In fact, it is precisely because these men are not ready to admit to having a problem that they are in this program. Eventually, the probationers will reach a point where they are able to synthesize what they learned in the program and to apply it to their own lives, thus coming to the realization that they do, in fact, have substance-abuse problems. The purpose of the program is to "plant the seed" of addiction recovery.

The same premise holds true, according to the program designer,[17] with regard to any response a probationer has to the program. If the probationer appears resigned, that is "where he is at" and he will store the information until he is ready to use it. If the probationer can only see substance abuse as an issue for others and not for himself, that is the start of critical thinking about substance abuse, and he will eventually turn that gaze inwards. The program manual (Cox 2001) outlines four types of precontemplators and gives the PO specific strategies to deal with each type. POs are encouraged to provide "sensitive feedback" to reluctant probationers, choices to those who are hostile and rebellious, hope to those who are resigned, and empathy to those who try to rationalize themselves out of the criminal addict identity.

Similar notions of the criminal addict work to diffuse acts of resistance in the DTC. Failure to engage in the court program (not attending groups, missing urine screens, relapsing) is not an act of resistance in the eyes of the court team; rather, these actions are read as indicators of a slip back into the "old ways" (for someone who has been in the program for a while) or a "lack of motivation" (for someone who is new to the program). Repeated "slips" may result in sanctioning or even ejection from the program; however, again, these actions are not punitive responses to wilful acts of defiance but, rather, caring strategies with particular therapeutic purposes. In this sense, sanctions are not responses to resistance but answers to a therapeutic need on the part of the client. In the examples of court clients attempting to resist the court's assertions of power, the court responds by either accepting the clinical reasoning for the client's resistance (as with the woman who missed her urine screen) or by deploying its own therapeutic logic to countering the client's actions (as with the client's contesting his housing situation). Even in ejecting Roland from the program, the court read his actions as indicators that he was "not well suited" to DTC rather than as outward acts of defiance.

Conclusion

My purpose in this chapter is to show the different ways in which the criminal addict is constituted within a strategy of governing that favours the notion of addiction. The benefit of using data from both the DTCs and the Ministry program in my analysis is that this makes it possible to see similar trends emerging out of somewhat different sites. The result, I hope, is a disruption of the notion that addicts are somehow scientifically knowable beings; rather, the addict is a strategic, governable identity, the ascription of which mobilizes a range of governing strategies. These strategies rely on the individual's acceptance of the governable identity of the drug addict. For probationers loath to accept this identity, varying techniques are deployed to hasten that acceptance. Non-acceptance indicates a more serious problem on the part of the probationer (denial) rather than a failure of the governing initiative. Individuals embracing the addict identity, as evidenced by DTC clients, are schooled in responsible practices of self-care that direct them to ultimately remake themselves. Self-care in these settings is not, however, exclusively a technique of the CJS project of change. It is also a practice of resistance. Probationers and DTC clients maintain personal action and a sense of selfhood through deploying their own techniques of self-care. I hesitate to see these counter-practices of self as necessarily tactical or subversive (although some of them are). In many instances, such as Ty's struggle to be allowed to stay on the street, these counter self-care practices are merely about survival, maintaining a sense of personal dignity, or attempting to exercise a degree of autonomy. Reflecting the ongoing dialogue of power and also the generative capacities of those in conflict with the law, these acts of resistance are anticipated by the authorities who read them not as plays of resistance but, rather, as evidence of the deeper pathology of the individual, flagging the need for increased therapeutic interventions.

My project is not an ideological initiative seeking to ultimately identify the means by which one side might "win" and another "lose." I am not interested in measuring power through determining the successes or failures of those who engage it in attempts to subject and subvert each other as well as overarching governing schemes. I imagine that I would fail even at defining the sides. Instead, I am interested in charting the relations of power in this site and showing the different ways in which people can and do act both as governors and as subjects of rule. People use liberal governing strategies, like the care of the self, as a means of exerting their own power in a governing relation. Even those who are under more extreme forms of control (such as those who are in conflict with the law) are able to take up particular technologies, languages, and even the identities used to subjugate them as a means of subverting that governing relationship.

6
Conclusion

I have used a variety of theoretical/methodological tools to frame the criminal addict as a curiosity, a social artefact of our time. The network overlay results in a broad survey of the relationships and connections that surround and work on this person. Located within the network, the criminal addict is subject to a full range of interventions and influences, which themselves are subject to each other as well as to the addict. This approach reveals interconnections, thus serving the understanding that there is no one actor, object, knowledge, or governing mentality that stands outside the site. Through focusing on intersections of drugs, users, and the state, I make the case that the criminal addict is governed through a messy constellation of contingencies.

Working through these contingencies, my work is not directed towards tidying the disarray of treating the criminal addict. The absence of prescriptions in *Criminal Artefacts* is a reflection of the nature of my project. Foucault's work is often criticized for having an anaesthetic effect on the sites under study. Concerns are raised that, because he patently refuses to offer recommendations about the prison or mental health systems in his academic work (although he wore an activist hat in other contexts), his work is at best apolitical and at worst a loosely veiled attempt to undermine political struggles (cf. Naffine 1996). Foucault (1991b, 84) was mindful of such criticisms, and he offered a lucid response:

> [Practitioners] are not likely to find advice or instructions in my books that tell them "what is to be done." But my project is precisely to bring it about that they "no longer know what to do," so that the acts, gestures, discourses which up until then had seemed to go without saying become problematic, difficult, dangerous.

Foucault maintains that the purpose of his work is to destabilize assumptions, to undermine logics and established practices, and to force questions about otherwise unproblematized forms of rule. Because the work is meant to challenge normative ways of thinking, it is counter-intuitive to expect prescriptions about what might be "best" or "right."

Rounding out his own work, Latour (1993, 145) concludes: "I have done my job as a philosopher and constituent by gathering together the scattered themes of a comparative anthropology. Others will be able to convene the Parliament of Things." Latour aims to gather together and Foucault aims to disrupt. The two are not mutually exclusive goals as, in both, the aim is not to reinvent truth (or power or knowledge) but, rather, to offer a different way of thinking about what is. The effect (and this is Latour's caution) is not to deny the material but, rather, to disrupt the assumptions that surround it. Disruption is a notable and sufficient project in and of itself. As Latour suggests, the project then moves to other actors who take on different projects and, it is to be hoped, are informed by and able to build on this disruptive work. It is enough, then, to reveal the problems, the relations of power, and the networks of action through which the criminal addict is discovered and constituted. It would be presumptuous for an outsider to assume the authority to tell others how to go about their business. I offer different ways of thinking about that business by making certain observations about power dynamics – observations that challenge the mentalities of governance.

One of my main concerns is to challenge the rather fixed cultural, governmental, and clinical assumptions that the criminal addict is a natural truth, a fact of human existence. I am in no way interested in ignoring the material reality of drug addiction or crime. My point is to rupture the assumed connections that constitute the criminal addict. The criminal addict, like the homosexual, is made. This figure is a particular human kind (Hacking 1999) whose existence is both strategic and iconic. The criminal addict is born of political need, she is one of the vessels that carries the criminal justice project of change through waning welfarism and into waxing neoliberalism. And each time she is poured out onto a political landscape, she shifts to fit the contours of her surroundings. The criminal addict can be the welfare case of the 1960s, prostrate before her own diseases and compulsions, in need of holistic care and attention. She can also be the neoliberal subject of the 1990s, tripped up by her own irrational thought processes and at total liberty to choose to direct her recovery from addiction and thus pull herself out of her criminal lifestyle. Far from lying at the etiological root of crime, the criminal addict is the answer to an altogether different question: how to maintain a seemingly benevolent, change-oriented agenda of criminal justice within political climates within which broader, explicitly social projects have waning appeal.

Just as she is a tool in a political strategy, the criminal addict is also a cultural trope whose behaviour is marshalled by the drugs she uses. The user is the victim of the drug: she becomes what the drug can make of her. These generative capabilities, driven in part by the materialism of the clinical actions of these substances, are best known through their cultural representations. Criminogenic representations of drugs are over a century old and pervade North American culture. Against this cultural backdrop, the criminal addict emerges as an almost irresistible target for criminological intervention. After all, what better way to persuade the public (and perhaps, more important, funding bodies) of the need for greater and greater interplay between law and psy than to trot out the hapless, yet dangerous, criminal addict as the prime example of both the problem and the solution. The cultural writers I rely upon (Klein 1993; Marlow 1999; Szasz 1985) all attribute amazing powers to drugs not only as pharmacological agents but also as social actors. Marlow chooses heroin as a primary lens through which to view her life not because she feels it is the most important aspect of her autobiography but, rather, because of the huge social import placed on the substance. Similar points are made by Klein and Szasz and a growing number of scholars who are attempting to unpack the ubiquity of drugs in cultural narratives (Acker 2002; Campbell 2000; Peele 1999; Reeves and Campbell 1994).

These cultural understandings are also important because they exist in a culture within which attempts to cure the criminal addict are entrenched in the justice system. By and large, everyone who works in and around the CJS is exposed to these same cultural understandings. And, while I would not suggest that the lawyers, judges, therapists, and advocates (or, for that matter, the clients and probationers) who participated in this study are only informed by popular understandings of substances or that they absorb cultural representations uncritically, these actors have never, at any moment, stood outside a culture in which crack equals chaos, drugs fry your brain, and smoking a joint could make you a heroin addict. Court actors reflect particular understandings of drugs that exist "outside" of the courtroom (see Chapter 3). Of course, these people receive clinical training on drugs and drug use. But this training itself is born of a cultural context that already views certain drugs in certain ways. Clinical and scientific inquiry into drugs is itself a product, at least in part, of cultural understandings. The idea, for example, that a heroin user is "better off" and potentially "on the road to recovery" when he takes up a regime of methadone maintenance is a normalized and subjective assessment. Even the discovery of addiction as a result of using a particular substance (see Chapter 5) is itself discretionary. There is no addiction "cell," like a cancer cell, that proves the clinical existence of the disease; rather, addiction is discovered through a range of arbitrarily defined behavioural abnormalities, which, when ordered in a particular way, form the criminal addict. The criminal addict is, in this sense, a problem of order. The same characteristics, organized differently, can reveal vastly different results. The students in my honours class, despite being

revealed as such, are not criminal addicts in the same way as are the probationers. Their substance use practices are ordered differently, giving them
different cultural and clinical meanings.

I also show that attempts to govern the criminal addict are not driven by
any one source of power or knowledge. In particular, much of *Criminal Artefacts* reveals how this governing initiative relies on the harmonization of
different knowledges and disciplines. The decision to locate treatment programs focusing on particular addictive pathologies within prisons relied on
a reconceptualization, as forwarded in the Fauteaux (1956) and Ouimet
(1969) reports, not only of what legally sanctioned punishment was capable
of but also of what it was obliged to do. The discovery of the addict as a
particular kind of criminal identity marks a general reimagining of the purpose of justice and allows the criminological enterprise to absorb a whole
area of disciplinary expertise and a range of possible goals and purposes.
The addict reifies criminal justice alliances with psy professions – a move
that refreshes the project of change in the CJS.

The advent of the DTCs have the same effect on the court system as the
rise of the medical model had on the penal system in the 1960s. Like prisons (and, later, community corrections initiatives, including probation),
these courts now have a whole new range of disciplinary tools and
knowledges at their disposal. My study of the dynamics of the DTCs shows
exactly how these tools and knowledges are deployed to work on the criminal addict. The results, of course, are a series of translations that work effectively to create interdisciplinary courtrooms in which actors have at the
ready a wide range of interventionist tools. Organized as such, these legal
spaces take on a new, far more targeted purpose, in which their goals are no
longer the vaguely defined and impossibly measured aspirations of "justice" or "fairness" but, rather, the far more targeted and specific aspiration
of "curing the offender."

These translations support Latour's (1993) critique of modernity and be-
lie the claim that the rehabilitative project is dead. This reveals a distinct
lack of purity in the practices of punishment and cure. And, if these two
practices are neither pure nor easily extracted from one another, then it is
difficult to see how one can die and the other thrive (as the punitive turn
and new penology theorists suggest). It makes more sense to see how the
flow of knowledges and practices around these two supposed disciplines
changes over time. In so doing, it is possible to see that the project of change
endures because of the intersections and overlaps between legal and therapeutic initiatives. The lines between the two, even in the most seemingly
absolute legal space of the courtroom, are being formally blurred.

This trend is not exclusive to this particular site. In their day-to-day activities, broader criminal justice initiatives are also moving more and more
towards blending disciplines. The same courthouse that hosts the TDTC

also houses a mental health court and a family violence court, both of which function on the same interdisciplinary principles as do the DTCs. The trend is also visible internationally. DTCs now operate in thirteen countries. Penal systems in the United Kingdom, Australia, New Zealand, and the United States all offer drug treatment programming to prisoners and probationers.

Moves towards disciplinary intersectionality as a means of maintaining projects of change are not exclusive to criminal justice. In a previous paper (Moore 2000), I show how universities mobilize similar initiatives around students who break university rules while drinking. The growing Collaborative Family Law movement sees lawyers trained in counselling and dispute resolution skills in order to mediate relationship dissolutions. Social work and social service delivery are also increasingly intersectional as social service workers are expected to be trained in and able to carry out a wide range of tasks, which could include anything from performing a policing function vis-à-vis social assistance clients, to carrying out risk analyses, to executing psychological interventions, to conducting advocacy and client support (cf. Dzeigeilewski and Holliman 2001).

At the same time, we should not assume that this lack of purity is a new development. The history of punishment and addiction treatment in Ontario is not anomalistic; rather, it follows trajectories that are remarkably similar to those of other social service initiatives in the province, where interdisciplinary practices merge with projects of change directed towards other socially concerning behaviours. Struthers (1994), for example, details welfare programs that deploy logics and practices similar to those found in the penal systems. After the Second World War, there was a push to "rehabilitate" welfare recipients to get them off social assistance and make them contributing members of society. Social workers intervened with welfare recipients to motivate them to find and keep work; welfare staff were trained in intervention techniques such as psychotherapy to help recipients improve their lives.

These intersections are not limited to the crossovers of interdisciplinarity. My project is about mapping the governing relationships that exist between drugs, users, and the state. Selves, then, emerge as important generative actors in governing initiatives. Rose (1998, 1999) is clear about the importance of understanding the self within broader governing contexts. In so doing, he acknowledges the possibilities of resistance but concludes that the concept of resistance is itself over-simple and "flat" because the notion is predicated on a dominance model of power. Resistance works as an analytic concept in these sites because power, even though it is relational, contributes unmistakably to a project of dominance. The kinds of resistance available to court clients and probationers is not explicitly political. The DTC client who refuses to stay at a housing shelter is not rejecting the court's directions on political grounds; rather, his reasoning comes out of a particular sense of caring for himself. This self-care is not about identity politics but personal ethics. Thus, another way to think about resistance is as a personal, ethical practice, designed to meet individualized and particular needs rather than political ones.

People in conflict with the law find themselves under amplified degrees of control, which work largely through particular notions of and actions on the self. The discovery of the addict as a governable identity in the form of the probationer is a case in point. It stands to reason, then, that if interventions and forms of control are justified and carried out in the name of attending to troubled selfhoods, the subjected selves will work through self-practices as a means of managing. This is a reflection of wider trends in neoliberalism and locates the generative capabilities of people in conflict with the law in shifts towards individual responsibility. Perhaps what is reflected in the self-care practices of the probationers and DTC clients is a change in patterns and practices of resistance. If the responsible self is the neoliberal subject, then this same subject must work through selfhood in order to manage and potentially resist attempts to govern her.

Even if the actions of those caught up in governing regimes are not meant to be explicitly resistant, they still have generative effects on the regimes themselves. What is most remarkable about the initiatives I discuss is the way in which all self-action is routinized as simply another aspect of the troubled addict identity. Criminal justice on its own has only a narrow range of responses available to those who attempt to counter actions carried out against them. With the injection of psy discourses into criminal justice processes, it is possible to explain and respond to resistive acts through a wider range of technologies and discourses. Lying, acting out, relapsing, and denying addictions do not have to be read as outright attempts to resist criminal justice authority; rather, these behaviours translate into further indications of a particular pathology. Resistance serves as proof that the assignation of an addict identity is accurate and that the person so defined is in need of interventions.

Ultimately, *Criminal Artefacts* shows the complexity of governing relations. Governing actions are best understood through a variety of lenses that unveil the plurality of regimes of rule. In approaching the criminal addict from this perspective, I am contributing to an emergent field of criminological inquiry that is aligned with the critical project of challenging the assumptions and practices of mainstream, vocational, or managerial criminology while resisting the urge to apply a grand narrative to counter understandings of the nature of criminal justice. Thus, this work most closely aligns with the projects set out by a growing list of scholars, including Cole (2001), Doyle (2003), Hannah-Moffat (2001), Kramar (2005), O'Malley (2001), Pavlich (1999), Simon (1993), and Valverde (2003a, 2005). In terms of substantive areas, this group is wildly eclectic. It also varies considerably in terms of methodological and theoretical frames of reference. Still, there are similarities among these scholars that denote a departure from both the managerial and critical camps.

This approach to research is premised on the rejection of metanarratives of crime. Rather than starting with the assumption that there is a generalized story to tell about crime control, scholarship in this field tends to focus on the site-specific, allowing the practices, habits, knowledges, and discourses of particular regimes to emerge as the bases from which to learn more about crime control and to build critiques of the assumptions and practices upon which contemporary systems are constructed. So Cole (2001), for example, takes the fingerprint as an entry point to understanding the ways in which semiotics and technology intersect to form a particular strategy of governing. The purpose here is to extract criminological research from what Pavlich (1999) points to as the largely unreflexive nature of the critical criminology project. Pavlich suggests that, without this reflexivity, the project of critical criminology becomes one akin to a left-wing, emancipatory managerialism. The goal, instead of being to challenge foundational thinking about crime, is to make a better, more fair and humane crime control system. While this is hardly an objectionable goal, the concern is that it is too narrow. Building a more humane CJS means working within the extant framework. This being the case, it becomes very difficult to extract the humanization process from assumptions that, for example, drugs cause crime. There is, then, a political limit to this way of seeing. Working within the parameters of the system obscures its strangeness and protects its assumptions. Calls for greater therapeutic responses to those who use drugs and are in conflict with the law fall squarely within this way of thinking. The merging of psy and law appears hugely benevolent and humane, especially in the face of hyper-criminalization and punishment. But these responses still rest on massive assumptions – the same assumptions that serve to make up the system that humanization is trying to improve. Pushing for more treatment offers no challenge to the notion that drugs cause crime or, even more broadly, to criminalizing drugs, anticipating that the best response to drug use is treatment, or that somehow it is the state's responsibility to ensure that people stop using drugs.

The scholars whose work I align with are interested in looking upon criminal justice practices as a means of injecting foundational challenges to existing systems. My study of the criminal addict not only challenges assumptions about the management and cure of this individual as a viable target of criminological practice but also resonates with the overall strangeness of the criminological enterprise. In the face of the brutal inhumanity of some of the most salient contemporary criminal justice trends (racial profiling, mass incarceration, warehousing, unlawful confinement in the name of national security), the appeal of initiatives such as the ones I describe above is hard to argue against. Indeed, I have had these difficult arguments with activist friends who work on behalf of penal abolition, the amelioration of prison conditions, the fight against gendered and racial discrimination, and the alleviation of some of the more heavy-handed laws (especially around drugs). I am sympathetic to the claims that treatment has got to be better than prison and rarely hesitate to make political claims in political circles decrying the inhumanity of the current state of criminal justice. My impotence as an activist (and the reason I do not give great media interviews) is due to the fact that I hesitate to offer viable alternatives or prescriptions. To do this would, I fear, land me in exactly the trap that Pavlich notes, and from which this emerging group of criminological scholars is attempting to extricate itself. In assuming that one way of acting out criminal justice is better than another, one loses the potential for seeing criminal justice differently or exacting radical changes in the system (like eliminating it altogether). I am more interested in challenging the necessary rightness of the either/or dichotomy. My hope is that doing this will enable us to hit upon fresh ways of thinking about how we respond to crime, perhaps even to rethinking the notion of crime itself.

Notes

Chapter 1: Introduction

1 See Correctional Service Canada, http://www.csc-scc.gc.ca/text/prgrm/correctional/sub_e.shtml, accessed 9 January 2006.
2 The one exception here is Nolan's (2001) work, which theorizes drug courts as part of the rise of a therapeutic state. I refer back to this argument at points throughout the text.
3 "Psy" is the term Rose (1996a) uses to denote psychology, psychiatry, and social work.
4 Hannah-Moffat (2001) makes a similar observation about women's prisons in Canada.
5 For a thoughtful account of the history of Canada's drug schedule, see Carstairs (2005).
6 The treatment centre in the Vancouver court is run by a private contractor who would not grant permission for the therapists to be interviewed.

Chapter 2: Mentalities of Treatment

1 For a strong account of these shifts in the American parole system, see Simon (1993).
2 I use the term "neoliberalism" to refer to the broader socioeconomic trends that typify our present. Borrowing from Unger (1998), neoliberalism is understood as a style of governing that privileges macroeconomics and fiscal responsibility and follows an agenda of decentring the state, largely through privatization and responsibilizing the individual. With regard to criminal justice settings, neoliberalism often includes tailoring policies around notions of efficiency, responsibilizing the individual offender, and implementing such initiatives as privatizing penal and policing services (Ericson and Haggerty 1997).
3 The term "neoconservative" is employed to indicate approaches to governing that draw heavily on morality and (often) religion to guide practice. In criminal justice terms, neoconservativism often indicates regimes with mandatory minimum sentences, extended prison terms, and capital punishment.
4 This point is also made repeatedly in CSC's research publication *Forum on Correctional Research*, which focuses almost exclusively on research initiatives organized around rehabilitation.
5 Outside of the penal system, other treatment institutions were also being developed, including the Addiction Research Foundation and the Homewood Sanitorium (Carstairs 2005).
6 *Classification and Treatment: New Concepts in Correctional Custody*, 1970, RG 20-148-0-10.4. Minister's Advisory Counsel on the Treatment of the Offender (MACTO).
7 The Ouimet Commission (1969), which was mandated in part to explore why it was that none of Fauteaux's recommendations were applied to penal practice, reemphasized the need for a focus on rehabilitation and also called, as much as possible, for the movement of penal practice from the institution to the community.
8 Ministry of Correctional Services Act, 1976, RG 20-155-0-11, Probation and Parole Service Legislative References.

9 The rise of this kind of approach is also documented by Simon (1993) in the California parole system.

10 *Hansard Parliamentary Debates,* Legislature of Ontario, 7 April 1970, at 1207.

11 The Guelph Reformatory had one of the most notorious reputations during this period. Labelled a "bucket" by prisoners, it was the location of any number of human rights abuses and riots and one of the locations upon which the prison reform movement was built (Caron 1978; McMahon 1992).

12 While fairly innovative for its time, the assessment unit is a common feature of penal establishments in Canada. Usually a separate section of a larger prison, the assessment unit is the prisoner's first point of contact with the penal system. Typically, prisoners go through a period of assessment (anywhere from a few weeks to several months, depending on sentence length), in which they undergo a series of actuarial assessments intended to assess their risk levels and also their programming needs.

13 These facilities, largely led by ex-addicts, often offered spiritually based treatments and commanded the total surrender of the individual to the dictates of the program. They were heavily moralistic and often adopted the philosophy that you had to break the individual down in order to build her/him back up (cf. White 1998, 246).

14 Notes from the Superintendent, *Correctional Update* 12 (2), May 1984.

15 In the interest of protecting the anonymity of all interviewees, names, places, and dates have been changed or omitted.

16 *Ministry of Correctional Services Newsletter* 1, 5 (October 1973).

17 *Hansard Parliamentary Debates,* Legislature of Ontario, Standing Committee on Administration of Justice, 20 January 1987, J180.

18 Ibid., 15 March, 34th Parliament, 1st session, 1988, J79.

19 Ibid., 24 January 1989, J104.

20 The Ontario Safe Streets Act was introduced in 2000. It was intended to target "squeegee kids" and panhandlers, placing strict regulations on the nature of interactions permissible on public highways (for further discussion on the Safe Streets Act, see Hermer and Mosher [2002]).

21 For a more detailed description of these changes, see Moore and Hannah-Moffat (2002).

22 *Hansard Parliamentary Debates,* Legislature of Ontario, 20 November 2000, at 350.

23 See Ministry of Community Safety and Correctional Services, http://www.mpss.jus.gov. on.ca/english/corr_serv/adult_off/earned_rem.html, accessed 26 January 2006.

24 In order to avoid the constant use of phrases such as "the individual," "this person," "the interviewee," and so on, I use the female and male personal pronouns interchangeably whenever referring to anonymous informants.

25 Despite the fact that Beck (1970) has emerged as the paramount "father" of CBT, Ellis (1962) and Frankl (1973) are also typically cited as having significant generative roles in the movement.

26 Interview with Susan Cox, Toronto, July 2002.

27 *Hansard,* Standing Committee on the Administration of Justice, 20 January 1987, 33rd parl., 2nd sess, J181.

28 *Hansard,* Standing Committee on the Administration of Justice, 14 December 1987, J79.

29 For a critique of this orientation, see Kendall (2000).

30 For a much more comprehensive account of this model of punishment as well as critical commentary on its implications, see Andrews and Bonta (1998), Kendall (2000), Hannah-Moffat (1999), and Hannah-Moffat and Maurutto (2005).

31 *Hansard Parliamentary Debates,* Legislature of Ontario, 19 December 2000, 37th parl., 1st sess, at 49.

32 This rivalry was made apparent when the Harris Ontario government was first introducing its correctional renewal strategy. One of the main justifications for changing the system was to move away from the "club fed" approach – a critique that suggested that the federal system was too soft on prisoners.

33 See Correctional Service of Canada, http://www.csc-scc.gc.ca/text/prgrm/correctional/ sub_e.shtml, accessed 27 December 2005.

34   For a much more detailed discussion of these events, see Comack (1991) and Giffen, Endicott, and Lambert (1991).
35   "Compulsory Heroin Treatment in British Columbia," *Cannabis Culture Magazine*, Alain Boisert (April 1995): 7–8.
36   See BC Ministry of Public Safety and Solicitor General, http://www.pssg.gov.bc.ca/corrections/in-bc/details/overview.htm, accessed 26 January 2006.
37   When I completed the research for this project, Drug Treatment Courts were only in operation in Toronto and Vancouver. As this book goes to press, there are six courts operating, which now include Ottawa, Winnipeg, Edmonton, and Regina.
38   See Federal Bureau of Prisons, http://www.bop.gov, accessed 12 January 2006.
39   See California Department of Corrections and Rehabilitation, http://www.cya.ca.gov, accessed 12 January 2006.
40   See Department of Correctional Services: New York State, http://www.docs.state.ny.us, accessed 12 January 2006.

Chapter 3: The Personalities of Drugs

Parts of this chapter appeared previously in Dawn Moore, "Mapping Drugalities: The Generative Actions of Drugs, *International Journal of Drug Policy* 15: 419-26. It appears here with permission from Elsevier.

1   I am not suggesting that there is a definitive "now-and-then" line to be drawn between discourses of dangerousness and discourses of risk within drug narratives. On the contrary, these languages easily blend into each other. In particular, the trope of dangerousness is still taken up in contemporary accounts of drugs.
2   Concerns about China and India, especially from the Western perspective, centred on trafficking, whereas concerns within North American and European countries were far more oriented towards the pernicious effects of opium use.
3   Cocaine was criminalized in Canada in 1911 and marijuana in 1923.
4   The existence of the RCMP appeared shaky throughout this period as politicians and members of provincial and municipal policing services argued that their role as the keepers of order throughout colonization had become defunct. The control of the opium trade, especially with regard to large-scale international trade, served as a useful justification for the RCMP's continued existence and allowed them a platform on which to make claims for increased funding, access to resources, and extended powers of search and seizure (Giffen, Endicott, and Lambert 1991).
5   The call for maintenance doses was one of the earliest forms of harm reduction and a precursor to the current practice of offering methadone maintenance to long-standing heroin users. Morphine maintenance clinics existed in the United States from the 1910s onwards (White 1998).
6   *Sgt. Pepper's Lonely Hearts Club Band* (1967), Capitol Music, Lennon/McCartney.
7   *Surrealistic Pillow* (1967), RCS, Slick.
8   The album title is in and of itself significant as the term "hot rocks" refers to the burning pieces of hash that sometimes fall on the person who is trying to "cook" them.
9   *The Velvet Underground and Nico* (1967), Polydor.
10   The first American war on drugs was declared in the 1940s by Harry Anslinger. In the early 1970s, Richard Nixon declared a second war. Both of these initiatives were similar in that they targeted the supply side of the drug trade while doing little to affect the demand side.
11   The exception is specific policy recommendations made with regard to opiate users and concerns about needle sharing and HIV/AIDS.
12   The US anti-drug campaign was quick to make the link between drugs and terrorism. A series of advertisements, funded by the American Office of National Drug Control Policy, first aired during the Superbowl in January 2002. These advertisements all carried the message that individual drug use made a direct contribution to terrorist activities.
13   See Royal Canadian Mounted Police, http://www.rcmp-grc.gc.ca, accessed 9 June 2003.
14   From my DTC research journal.
15   It is important to note the programmatic difference between Toronto and Vancouver. The VDTC does not sanction people for using drugs in the court, regardless of whether or not

they are candid about their use; rather, repeated drug use, as indicated by dirty urine screens, is cause for the court to mandate that an individual attend residential detox or treatment. In Toronto, repeated drug use and/or lying about drug use can result in sanction or dismissal from the court program.

16   As I show in Chapter 5, often those mandated to participate in these programs explained that they were so mandated simply because they had indicated to the assessment officer that they had, in fact, used a particular substance. Whether or not this substance use was at all linked to their criminal activity was entirely beside the point.

17   Latour argues that, within a network, explicit interests constitute a certain rigidity, which forms a solid barrier to translation. He maintains that, through having clearly defined interests, actors within a network "know too much" and become too readily wedded to their specific interests. He offers five different remedies to this problem. For a further discussion of this, see Latour (1987, 113-19).

18   This bill, An Act to Amend the Contraventions Act and the Controlled Drugs and Substances Act (marijuana), was originally introduced into Parliament on 26 October 1999 as Bill C-266. Martin's second introduction occurred on 4 May 2001.

19   For a broader discussion of the rise of risk and harm languages in systems of regulation (particularly in the realm of criminal justice), see Beck (1992) and his critics, Ericson and Haggerty (1997), O'Malley (1999a), and so on. While there is a good deal of contentious debate surrounding attempts to accurately describe the nature of contemporary forms of rule, there is agreement among both social theorists and those engaged in policy work that the notion of risk has come to play a substantially productive role in the generation of law and policy.

20   In *R. v. Parker* (2000), 49 O.R. (3d) 481 (O.C.A.), Terrence Parker, an epileptic, successfully argued that marijuana was the only substance that alleviated his seizures and other complications associated with his epilepsy. The Ontario Court of Appeal ruled that denying Parker access to marijuana through the Controlled Drugs and Substances Act constituted cruel and unusual punishment and was therefore unlawful under Section 12 of the Charter of Rights and Freedoms.

21   *R. v. Parker* (2000) at 39.

22   As of October 2006, the new federal Conservative government is promising that it will not reintroduce legislation to decriminalize marijuana.

23   The writing of alcohol as a non-criminogenic substance is in and of itself very interesting given that, of all psychoactive substances, alcohol is the one most often linked to criminal, particularly violent criminal, behaviours (Pernanen et al. 2002).

24   For a more extensive discussion of the gateway argument, see Fergusson and Horwood (2000) and Kandel, Yamaguchi, and Chen (1992).

25   Interview, DTC therapist 1, Toronto, March 2003.

26   Ibid., DTC therapist 2, Toronto, March 2003.

27   Ibid., DTC therapist 3, Toronto, March 2003.

28   Ibid., DTC therapist 1, Toronto, March 2003.

29   In order to receive an honours designation, a participant must be free of all substances for at least three months.

30   Arguably, these panics endure in current discourses around opiates.

31   Opium is the resinous extract from the poppy plant. Heroin and codeine are both chemically modified products of the original opiate alkaloid (morphine). Methadone is a synthetic version of this same chemical.

32   Hepatitis C is a blood-born disease that can be transmitted through sharing needles.

33   The film *Trainspotting* is an adaptation of the book of the same title, written by Irvine Welsh (1996).

34   The legal actors include the judge, Crown counsel, and defence counsel.

35   Interview, DTC therapist 4, Toronto, April 2002.

36   Ibid., DTC therapist 1, Toronto, March 2002.

37   Ibid., DTC therapist 2, Toronto, March 2002.

38   "On the nod" is a colloquial phrase used to describe a somnolent state associated with long-term opiate use.

39   Crack is a derivative of powdered cocaine. It is often referred to as "free base" because the process by which crack is made involves freeing the chemical base of cocaine to produce a purer, smokable form of the substance. The criminalization of cocaine in the 1920s was linked to racist fears about people of colour and threats to the sanctity of white youth (Carstairs 2005; Giffen, Endicott, and Lambert 1991).
40   Films like *Less Than Zero* and *Forest Gump* link cocaine with personal demise.
41   "Run," in this context, means being given an unfair deal, akin to "getting the run around."
42   Interview, DTC therapist 5, Toronto, April 2005.

Chapter 4: Translating Justice and Therapy

1   I am setting this binary between legal and non-legal (clinical/therapeutic) knowledges for the purpose of clarifying my argument. These are conceptual categories. I do not imagine that there are definite boundaries encompassing these or any knowledges.
2   Criminal Justice Abstracts, online database, 7 February 2004.
3   In tort law, cases are decided based on fault. In order to measure fault, judges often use a test for standard of care. In other words, judges look to see whether there was some kind of assumed responsibility of care or precaution within the relationship in question and whether, if such a responsibility existed, it was breached.
4   Beyond the usual bail directions, TDC bail typically entails conditions such as geographic restrictions, alcohol abstention, and reporting to designated treatment facilities.
5   A recovery house is a place where users go to detox in a supportive environment.
6   Geographic restrictions are prominent in the VDTC because of the concentration of drug use in the Hastings and Main corridor. All court clients are banned from Oppenheimer Park, one of the "hubs" of the Vancouver drug trade. Most have area restrictions that include the entire corridor (typically bordered by Princess Street, Cordova Street, Pender Street, and Carrall Street). The area restrictions are put in place not only because this area has the highest concentration of drug use but also to facilitate each client's break with the lifestyle associated with the neighbourhood by physically removing her from it (although she must return there regularly as the DTC is located in the heart of the Hastings and Main corridor). These restrictions predictably prove problematic for the court clients, and many of them are arrested for breaching bail by being in this neighbourhood. I revisit the question of these area restrictions in Chapter 5.
7   *Winnipeg Child and Family Services (Northwest Area) v. G. (D.F.)* [1997] 3 SCR.
8   Interview, DTC judge, Toronto, June 2002; interview, two DTC judges, Vancouver, June 2005; interview, four DTC therapists, Toronto, September-November 2002.
9   Interview, Crown counsel, VDTC, June 2005.
10   Interview, coordinator, TDTC, January 2003.
11   Interview, Crown counsel, TDTC, January 2003.
12   Interview, DTC therapist, 3 March 2003.
13   See Department of Justice Canada, Drug Treatment Court Funding Program, http://www.canada.justice.gc.ca, accessed 12 March 2004.
14   See http://www.prevention.gc.ca, accessed 15 January 2004.
15   In *We Have Never Been Modern*, Latour (1993) argues that society never passed through a stage of modernity because there has never been a time in which the purity and truth of the modernist project actually existed.
16   Interview, duty counsel, DTCT, February 2003.
17   Ibid.
18   Ibid.
19   Interview, duty counsel, VDTC, June 2005.
20   See Board of Registration for Social Workers, September 2005, http://www.brsw.bc.ca/resources_links/pdfs/CodeOfEthics.pdf, and http://www.collegeofpsychologists.bc.ca/documents/Code%20of%20Conduct.pdf, 20 September 2005.
21   The Code of Ethics for the Ontario College of Social Workers also outlines advocacy as one of the mandates of social work practice. This advocacy is specifically meant to be directed in favour of the best interests of the client.
22   Interview, TDTC therapist, March 2003.

23 Ibid., April 2003.
24 Interview, VDTC head of treatment team, June 2005.
25 Interview, DTC therapist, 1 March 2003.
26 *Winnipeg Child and Family Services (Northwest Area) v. G. (D.F.)* [1997] 3 SCR.
27 For rich accounts of paternalism in the courts, see Backhouse (1991) and Chesney-Lind (1977).

Chapter 5: Caring for the Addicted Self

1 At the time this research was conducted, the Ministry program was only offered to men.
2 I use the term "moments" deliberately as a way of circumventing suggestions that these two groups might be placed on a continuum. To place these actors on a continuum is to confirm a certain truth to their drug use and criminality that many reject. The continuum also supports the notion that the drug/crime nexus is a slippery slope: smoking pot and shoplifting is a precursor to mainlining heroin and boosting cars. This argument is notably void of persuasive powers.
3 Foucault wrote almost exclusively about men.
4 In clinical argot, this process is aligned with the notion of matching described in Chapter 2.
5 I describe the one exception below. This scenario does not involve open debate but, rather, a Crown counsel's suggestion that an individual is unaware of her addiction issue.
6 In the context of the probation office, probationers are unknown both to themselves and their probation officers.
7 These assessments are markedly similar to those used in the federal system and in other Western penal jurisdictions (see Hannah-Moffat 2001). As such, these tools and assessment techniques are subject to the same concerns. In other words, just as we have seen elsewhere, the use of actuarial assessment tools is no guarantee of objectivity or unbiased results. These tools are no more able to account for subtle and not so subtle differences between people (such as gender, race, and social class) than are their counterparts.
8 For an excellent critical assessment of these practices, see Hannah-Moffat (1999); and Hannah-Moffat and Maurutto (2005).
9 In the interest of protecting the confidentiality of the men who participated in the research, I am not noting any identifying information about them.
10 It is important to note that many of the men I interviewed maintained that they had been wrongfully accused of the offences for which they were convicted. Six of the ten interviewees had filed appeals at the time of the interviews, based on their claims that they were innocent of the charges for which they were convicted.
11 For critical commentary on this, see Rose (1998).
12 The term "governable identities" is mine, not Goffman's. Goffman only refers to the identities of mental patients and other "inmates."
13 For a wonderful account of the pervasiveness of therapeutic discourses, see Nolan's (1998) *The Therapeutic State*.
14 For an excellent discussion of the impact of imprisonment on mothers and children, see Mauer and Chesney-Lind (2002).
15 In their extensive ethnography of people's experiences with the law, Ewick and Silbey (1998) offer a comprehensive account of these kinds of interactions.
16 This one emerged as an exceptional interview on many levels. The man was very confused throughout the interview, unable to remember which program we were talking about, his age, or how long it had been since he was arrested.
17 Interview with Susan Cox, Toronto, July 2002.

References

Acker, Caroline Jean. 2002. *Creating the American Junkie: Addiction Research in the Classic Era of Narcotic Control*. Baltimore: Johns Hopkins University Press.

Allen, Chris. 2005. "The Links between Heroin, Crack Cocaine and Crime: Where Does Street Crime Fit In?" *British Journal of Criminology* 45 (3): 355-72.

Anderson, John. 2001. "What to Do about 'Much Ado' about Drug Courts?" *International Journal of Drug Policy* 12: 469-75.

Andrews, D., and J. Bonta. 1998. *The Psychology of Criminal Conduct*. 2nd ed. Cincinnati: Anderson.

Andrews, D.A., I. Zinger, R.D. Hoge, J. Bonta, P. Gendreau, and F.T. Cullen. 1990. "Does Correctional Treatment Work? A Clinically Relevant and Informed Meta-Analysis." *Criminology* 28: 369-404.

Anslinger, Harry. 1961. *The Murderers: The Story of the Narcotic Gangs*. New York: Farrar, Strauss and Cudahy.

Archives of Ontario. 1968. Printer Materials: Rules, Regulations and Manuals. Series RG 20-155-0-10.

–. 1970a. Drug Abuse Conferences, Deputy Minister's Correspondence. Series RG 20-8-003.

–. 1970b. Minister's Advisory Council on the Treatment of the Offender: Classification and Treatment – New Concepts in Correctional Custody. Series RG 20-148-0-10.4.

–. 1972. Probation and Parole General. Series RG 20-0-0-19.7.

–. 1974. Series RG 20-8-0010.13. National Conference, Directors of Probation, 13-15 May 1974.

–. 1975. Hamilton Liquor Court Project. Series RG 20-8.

–. n.d. Alex G. Brown Memorial Clinic Information Booklet. Series RG 20-155-0-11.

Arrigo, Bruce. 2002. *Punishing the Mentally Ill: A Critical Analysis of Law and Psychiatry*. Albany: SUNY Press.

Backhouse, Constance. 1991. *Petticoats and Prejudice: Women and Law in 19th Century Canada*. Toronto: Women's Press.

Bauman, Zygmunt. 2000. "Social Issues of Law and Order." *British Journal of Criminology* 40 (2): 205-21.

Beck, Aaron. 1970. *Cognitive Therapy and Emotional Disorders*. New York: International Universities Press.

Beck, Aaron, and John Rush. 1988. "Cognitive Therapy." In *Comprehensive Textbook of Psychiatry*, 5th ed., ed. Harold I. Kaplan and Benjamin J. Sadock, 1541-49. Baltimore: Williams and Wilkins.

Beck, Urlich. 1992. *The Risk Society: Towards a New Modernity*. London: Sage.

Becker, Howard S. 1966. *The Outsiders: Studies in the Sociology of Deviance*. New York: Free Press.

Beiras, I. 2005. "State Form, Labour Market and Penal System: The New Punitive Rationality in Perspective." *Punishment and Society* 7 (2): 167-82.

Belenko, Steve. 1999. *Research on Drug Courts: A Critical Review*. New York: National Centre on Addiction and Substance Use.

Bentham, Jeremy. 1962 [1791]. *Panopticon* (London).

Bentley, Paul. 2000. "Canada's First Drug Treatment Court." *Criminal Reports* 31 (5): 257-74.

Berridge, Virginia, and Griffith Edwards. 1981. *Opium and the People: Opiate Use and Drug Control Policy in Nineteenth and Early Twentieth Century England*. London: Free Association Books.

Boldt, Richard. 2002. "The Adversary System and Attorney Role in the Drug Treatment Court Movement." In *Drug Courts in Theory and Practice*, ed. James Nolan, 48-51. Hawthorne: Aldine de Gruyter.

Boritch, Helen. 1997. *Female Crime and Criminal Justice in Canada*. Scarborough: Nelson.

Bosworth, Mary. 1999. *Engendering Resistance: Agency and Power in Women's Prisons*. London: Ahsgate.

Bourgeois, Philippe. 2003. *In Search of Respect: Selling Crack in El Barrio*. London: Cambridge University Press.

Boyd, Neil. 1984. "The Origins of Canadian Narcotics Legislation: The Process of Criminalization in Historical Context." *Dalhousie Law Journal* 8: 102-36.

Boyd, Susan. 2004. *From Witches to Crack Moms: Women, Drug Law and Policy*. Durham: Carolina Academic Press.

Burgess, Anthony. 1967. *A Clockwork Orange*. New York: Norton.

British Columbia. Department of Corrections. 1957-78. Annual Reports.

Burstow, Bonnie. 2005. "Feminist Antipsychiatry Praxis: Women and the Movement(s) – A Canadian Perspective." In *Women, Madness and the Law: A Feminist Reader*, ed. Wendy Chan, Dorothy E. Chunn, and Robert Menzies, 245-58. London: Glasshouse.

Callon, Michel. 1999. "Some Elements of a Sociology of Translation: Domestication of Scallops and the Fishermen of St. Brieuc Bay." In *The Science Studies Reader*, ed. Mario Biagioli, 67-83. New York: Routledge.

Campbell, Nancy. 2000. *Using Women: Gender, Drug Policy and Social Justice*. New York: Routledge.

Canada. 2000. *Canada's Drug Strategy*. Ottawa: Ministry of Health.

Caron, Roger. 1978. *Go Boy! The True Story of Life behind Bars*. Toronto: McGraw-Hill Ryerson.

Carrigan, Owen. 1991. *Crime and Punishment in Canada: A History*. Toronto: Oxford University Press.

Carstairs, Catherine. 1999. "Deporting 'Ah Sin' to Save the White Race: Moral Panic, Racialization and the Extension of Canadian Drug Laws in the 1920s." *Canadian Bulletin of Medical History* 16: 65-88.

–. 2005. *Jailed for Possession: Illegal Drug Use, Regulation and Power in Canada, 1920-1961*. Toronto: University of Toronto Press.

Castel, Robert. 1991. "From Dangerousness to Risk." In *The Foucault Effect: Essays on Governmentality*, ed. Graham Burchell, Colin Gordon, and Peter Miller, 281-98. Chicago: University of Chicago Press.

Chesney-Lind, Meda. 1977. "Judicial Paternalism and the Female Status Offender: Training Women to Know Their Place." *Crime and Delinquency* 23 (2): 121-30.

Chunn, Dorothy, and Bob Menzies. 1990. "Gender, Madness and Crime: The Reproduction of Patriarchal and Class Relations in a Court Clinic." *Journal of Human Justice* 1 (2): 33-54.

Coldren, James R. 2004. *Patuxent Institution: An American Experiment in Corrections*. New York: Peter Lang

Cole, Simon. 2001. *Suspect Identities: A History of Fingerprinting and Criminal Identification*. Cambridge: Harvard University Press.

College of Psychologists of Ontario. 2004. Toronto: The College of Psychologists in Ontario.

Comack, Elizabeth. 1991. "'We Will Get Some Good out of This Riot Yet': The Canadian State, Drug Legislation and Class Conflict." In *The Social Basis of Law: Critical Readings in the Sociology of Law*, ed. Elizabeth Comack and Stephen Brickey, 48-70. Halifax: Garamond.

–. 2000. "The Prisoning of Women: Meeting Women's Needs." In *An Ideal Prison? Critical Essays on Women's Imprisonment in Canada,* ed. Kelly Hannah-Moffat and Margaret Shaw, 117-27. Halifax: Fernwood.

Commission on Systemic Racism in the Ontario Criminal Justice System. 1995. *Report of the Commission on Systemic Racism in the Ontario Criminal Justice System.* Toronto: The Comission.

Courtwright, David. 2001. *Forces of Habit: Drugs and the Making of the Modern World.* Boston: Harvard University Press.

Cox, Susan. 2001. *Change Is a Choice: Substance Misuse Orientation Program Training Manual.* Toronto: Ontario Ministry Correctional Services.

Cruickshanks, Barbara. 1996. "Revolutions from Within: Self-Government and Self-Esteem." In *Foucault and Political Reason: Liberalism, Neo-Liberalism and Rationalities of Government,* ed. Andrew Barry, Thomas Osborne, and Nikolas Rose. Chicago: University of Chicago Press.

Culhane, Clare. 1991. *No Longer Barred from Prison: Social Injustice in Canada.* Montreal: Black Rose Books.

Cullen, Francis. 2005. "The 12 People Who Saved Rehabilitation: How the Science of Criminology Made a Difference." *Criminology* 43 (1): 1-42.

Cullen, F.T., and K.E. Gilbert. 1982. *Reaffirming Rehabilitation.* Cincinnati: Halstead.

Dean, Mitchell. 1999. *Governmentality: Power and Rule in Modern Society.* London: Sage.

Denton, Barbara, and Pat O'Malley. 2001. "Property Crime and Women Drug Dealers in Australia." *Journal of Drug Issues* 1 (2): 365-86.

DiClemente, Carlo, and James Prochaska. 1998. "Toward a Comprehensive, Transtheoretical Model of Change: Stages of Change and Addictive Behaviours." In *Applied Clinical Psychology,* ed. William Miller and Nick Heather, 3-24. New York: Plenum Press.

Dobash, Russell, R. Emerson Dobash, and Sue Gutteridge. 1986. *The Imprisonment of Women.* Oxford: Blackwell.

Dobson, Keith, ed. 2001. *Handbook of Cognitive Behavioral Therapies.* New York: Guilford Press.

Doherty, Diana, and John Ekstedt. 1991. *Conflict, Care and Control: The History of the British Columbia Corrections Branch, 1848-1988.* Burnaby: Simon Fraser Institute for Studies in Criminal Justice Policy.

Doyle, Aaron. 2003. *Arresting Images: Crime and Policing in Front of the Television Camera.* Toronto: University of Toronto Press.

Dzeigeilewski, Sophia, and Diane Holliman. 2001. "Managed Care and Social Work: Practice Implications in an Era of Change." *Journal of Sociology and Social Welfare* 28 (2): 125-39.

Ekstedt, John, and Curt Griffiths. 1988. *Corrections in Canada: Policy and Practice.* 2nd ed. Toronto: Butterworths.

Elias, Norbert. 1984. *The Civilizing Process.* Oxford: Blackwell.

Ellis, A. 1962. *Reason and Emotion in Psychotherapy.* New York: Lyle Stuart.

Erickson, Pat, Diane Riley, Yeut Cheung, and Patrick O'Hare. 1997. "Introduction: The Search for Harm Reduction." In *Harm Reduction: A New Direction for Drug Policies and Programs,* ed. Pat Erickson, Diane Riley, and Yuet Cheung, 3-11. Toronto: University of Toronto Press.

Erickson, Pat, and Reginald Smart. 1988. "The LeDain Commission Recommendations." In *Illicit Drugs in Canada: A Risky Business.* Pat Erickson and Judith Blackwell, 48-63. Toronto: Nelson.

Ericson, Richard, and Aaron Doyle. 2003. "Risk and Morality." In *Risk and Morality,* ed. Richard Ericson and Aaron Doyle, 1-10. Toronto: University of Toronto Press.

Ericson, Richard, and Kevin Haggerty. 1997. *Policing the Risk Society.* Toronto: University of Toronto Press.

Ewald, Francois. 1991. "Insurance and Risk." In *The Foucault Effect: Studies in Governmentality,* ed. Graham Burchell, Colin Gordon, and Peter Miller, 197-210. Chicago: University of Chicago Press.

Ewick, Patricia, and Susan Silbey. 1998. *The Common Place of Law: Stories from Everyday Life.* Chicago: University of Chicago Press.

Ewick, Patty, Robert Kagan, and Austin Sarat. 1999. *Legacies of Legal Realism: Social Science, Social Policy and the Law.* New York: Russell Sage Foundation.

Fauteaux, G. 1956. *Report of the Committee Appointed to Inquire into the Principles and Procedures Followed in the Remission Service of the Department of Justice of Canada.* Ottawa: Queen's Printer.

Feeley, Malcolm, and Jonathan Simon. 1992. "The New Penology: Notes on the Emerging Strategy of Corrections and Its Implications." *Criminology* 30: 449-74.

Fergusson, David, and John Horwood. 2000. "Does Cannabis Use Encourage Other Forms Of Illicit Drug Use?" *Addiction* 95 (4): 505-20.

Ferri, Enrico. 1967. *Criminal Sociology.* New York: Agathon.

Fisher, Benedikt, Julian Roberts, and Maritt Kirst. 2002. "Compulsory Drug Treatment in Canada: Historical Origins and Recent Developments." *European Addiction Research* 8: 61-68.

Fisher, Fenaughty, and Amy Paschane. 1997. "Hepatitis C Virus Infection among Alaskan Drug Users." *American Journal of Public Health* 87: 1722-24.

Foucault, Michel. 1965. *Madness and Civilization: A History of Insanity in the Age of Reason.* New York: Vintage.

–. 1977. *Discipline and Punish: The Birth of the Prison.* New York: Vintage Books.

–. 1978. *The History of Sexuality.* Vol. 1: *An Introduction.* New York: Vintage Books.

–. 1980. *Power/Knowledge: Selected Interviews and Other Writings, 1972-77.* Ed. Colin Gordon. New York: Pantheon.

–. 1991a. "Governmentality." In *The Foucault Effect: Essays on Governmentality,* ed. Graham Burchell, Colin Gordon, and Peter Miller, 87-104. Chicago: University of Chicago Press.

–. 1991b. "Questions of Method." In *The Foucault Effect: Essays on Governmentality,* ed. Graham Burchell, Colin Gordon, and Peter Miller, 73-86. Chicago: University of Chicago Press.

–. 1994. *Ethics, Subjectivity and Truth: The Essential Works of Michel Foucault, 1954-84.* Ed. Paul Rabinow. New York: The New Press.

–. 2001. *Fearless Speech.* Ed. Joseph Pearson. Los Angeles: Simiotext(e).

Frankl, J.D. 1973. *Persuasion and Healing: A Comparative Study of Psychotherapy.* Baltimore: Johns Hopkins University Press.

Garland, David. 1985. *Punishment and Welfare: A History of Penal Strategies.* Aldershot: Gower.

–. 1996. "The Limits of the Sovereign State: Strategies of Crime Control in Contemporary Society." *British Journal of Criminology* 36 (4): 173-214.

–. 2001. *The Culture of Control: Crime and Social Order in Contemporary Society.* Chicago: University of Chicago Press.

Garland, David, and Richard Sparks. 2000. "Criminology, Social Theory and Challenges of our Times." *British Journal of Criminology* 40 (2): 189-204.

Gendreau, P., and P. Goggin. 1996. "Principles of Effective Correctional Programming." *Forum on Corrections Research* 8 (3): 38-41.

Gendreau, P., and B. Ross. 1978. *Effective Correctional Treatment: Bibliotherapy for Cynics.* Ontario: Ministry for Correctional Services.

–. 1980. *Correctional Potency: Treatment and Deterrence on Trial.* Toronto: Ministry of Correctional Services.

Giddens, Anthony. 2000. *The Third Way and Its Critics.* Cambridge: Polity.

Giffen, P.J., Shirley Endicott, and Sylvia Lambert. 1991. *Panic and Indifference: The Politics of Canada's Drug Laws, a Study in the Sociology of Law.* Ottawa: Canadian Centre on Substance Abuse.

Goffman, Erving. 1959. *The Presentation of Self in Everyday Life.* New York: Doubleday.

–. 1961. *Asylums: Essays on the Social Situation of Mental Patients and Other Inmates.* New York: Garden City.

Goldkamp, John, Michael White, and Jennifer Robinson. 2001. "Context and Change: The Evolution of Pioneering Drug Courts in Portland and Las Vegas." *Law and Policy* 23 (2): 141-70.

Goldsmith, Margaret. 1939. *The Trail of Opium: The Eleventh Plague.* London: Robert Hale.

Gordon, Colin. 1991. "Governmental Rationality: An Introduction." In *The Foucault Effect: Studies in Governmentality,* ed. Graham Burchell, Colin Gordon, and Peter Miller, 1-52. Chicago: University of Chicago Press.

Graham-Mulhall, Sarah. 1926. *Opium: The Demon Flower.* New York: Arno Press.

Gubrium, Jaber, and James Holstein. 1999. "At the Border of Narrative and Ethnography." *Journal of Contemporary Ethnography* 28 (5): 561-73.

Hacking, Ian. 1999. *The Social Construction of What?* Cambridge: Harvard University Press.

–. 2004. "Between Michel Foucault and Erving Goffman: Between Discourse in the Abstract and Face-to-Face Interaction." *Economy and Society* 33 (3): 277-302.

Hannah-Moffat, Kelly. 1999. "Moral Agent or Actuarial Subject? Risk and Canadian Women's Imprisonment." *Theoretical Criminology* 3 (1): 74-91.

–. 2000. "Prisons that Empower: Neoliberal Governance and Canadian Women's Prisons." *British Journal of Criminology* 40 (3): 510-31.

–. 2001. *Punishment in Disguise: Penal Governance and Federal Women's Corrections.* Toronto: University of Toronto Press.

Hannah-Moffat, Kelly, and Paula Maurutto. 2005. "Assembling Risk and the Restructuring of Penal Control." *British Journal of Criminology* 46 (3): 438-54.

Harrison, Lana, Patricia Erickson, Edward Adlaf, and Charles Freeman. 2001. The Drugs-Violence Nexus among American and Canadian Youth." *Substance Use and Misuse* 36 (14): 2065-86.

Hathaway, Andrew, and Patricia Erickson. 2003. "Drug Reform Issues and Policy Debates: Harm Reduction Prospects for Cannabis in Canada." *Journal of Drug Issues* 33 (2): 465-95.

Hermer, Joe, and Janet Mosher, eds. 2002. *Disorderly People: Law and the Politics of Exclusion in Ontario.* Halifax: Fernwood.

Hoffman, Nicolas. 1984. "Cognitive Therapy: Introduction to the Subject." In *Foundations of Cognitive Therapy: Theoretical Methods and Practical Applications,* ed. Nicolas Hoffman, 173–209. New York: Plenum Press.

Hornblum, Allen. 1998. *Acres of Skin: Human Experiments at Holmsburg Prison.* New York: Routledge.

Hudson, Barbara. 1987. *Justice through Punishment: A Critique of the Justice Model of Corrections.* Basingstoke: St. Martin's Press.

Huxley, Aldous. 1954. *The Doors of Perception.* New York: Harper.

Incardi, James. 1981. *The Drugs-Crime Connection.* London: Sage.

Jasanoff, Sheila. 1995. *Science at the Bar: Law, Science and Technology in America.* Cambridge: Harvard University Press.

Jay, Mike. 1999. *Artificial Paradises.* New York: Penguin.

Jenkins, Phillip. 1999. *Synthetic Panics: The Symbolic Politics of Designer Drugs.* New York: New York Press.

Jensen, Eric, and Jurg Gerber. 1993. "State Efforts to Construct a Social Problem: The 1986 War on Drugs in Canada." *Canadian Journal of Sociology* 18 (4): 453-62.

Jorgess, Bernward. 1999. "Do Politics Have Artefacts?" *Social Studies of Science* 29 (2): 411-31.

Kandel, D., K. Yamaguchi, and K. Chen. 1992. "Stages of Progression in Drug Involvement from Adolescence to Adulthood: Further Evidence for the Gateway Theory." *Journal of Studies on Alcohol* 53: 447-57.

Keane, Helen. 2002. *What's Wrong with Addiction?* Victoria: Melbourne University Press.

Kemshall, Hazel. 2003. *Understanding Risk in Criminal Justice.* Philadelphia: Open University Press.

Kendall, Kathy. 2000. "Psy-ence Fiction: Governing Female Prisons through the Psychological Sciences." In *An Ideal Prison? Critical Essays on Women's Imprisonment in Canada,* ed. Kelly Hannah-Moffat and Margaret Shaw, 82-93. Halifax: Fernwood.

–. 2005. "Beyond Reason: Social Constructions of Mentally Disordered Female Offenders." In *Women, Madness and the Law: A Feminist Reader,* ed. Wendy Chan, E. Chunn, and Robert Menzies, 41-57. London: Glasshouse.

Kesey, Ken. 1969. *One Flew Over the Cuckoo's Nest.* New York: Viking Press.

Klein, Richard. 1993. *Cigarettes Are Sublime.* Durham: Duke University Press.

Kramar, Kirsten. 2005. *Unwilling Mothers, Unwanted Babies: Infanticide in Canada*. Vancouver: UBC Press.

Latour, Bruno. 1987. *Science in Action: How to Follow Scientists and Engineers through Society*. Cambridge: Harvard University Press.

–. 1993. *We Have Never Been Modern*. Trans. Catherine Porter. Cambridge: Harvard University Press.

Law, John, ed. 1999. *After Actor Network Theory*. Oxford: Blackwell.

Law Society of Upper Canada. 2000. *Rules for Professional Conduct*. Toronto.

Leary, Timothy. 1968. *The Politics of Ecstasy*. New York: Putnam.

LeDain, Honourable Justice Gerald, Chair. 1972. *Commission of Inquiry into the Nonmedical Use of Drugs*. Ottawa: Government of Canada.

Leiss, William, and Steve Hrudey. 2005. "On Proof and Probability: Introduction to 'Law and Risk.'" In *Law and Risk*, ed. Law Commission of Canada, 1-19. Vancouver: UBC Press.

Leukefeld, Carl. 2002. *Treatment of Drug Offenders: Policies and Issues*. New York: Springer.

Lightfoot, Lynn. *Choices: Offender Substance Abuse Program*. Ottawa: Correctional Service of Canada.

Lindesmith, Alfred. 1965. *The Addict and the Law*. Bloomington: Indiana University Press.

Logan, Enid. 2000. "The Wrong Race, Committing Crime, Doing Drugs, and Maladjusted for Motherhood: The Nation's Fury over 'Crack Babies.'" *Social Justice* 26 (1): 115-38.

Lutpon, Deborah. 1997. "Foucault and the Medicalization Critique." In *Foucault, Health and Medicine*, ed. Alan Petersen and Robin Bunton, 94-112. London: Routledge.

Mander, Christine. 1985. *Emily Murphy: Rebel – First Female Magistrate in the British Empire*. Toronto: Simon and Pierre.

Mannheim, Karl. 1970. "The Sociology of Knowledge. In *The Sociology of Knowledge: A Reader*, ed. J.E. Curtis and J.W. Petras, 107-29. New York: Praeger.

Marez, Curtis. 2004. *Drug Wars: The Political Economy of Narcotics*. Minneapolis: University of Minnesota Press.

Marlow, Ann. 1999. *How to Stop Time: Heroin from A-Z*. New York: Basic Books.

Martinson, Robert. 1974. "What Works? Questions and Answers about Prison Reform." *The Public Interest* 35: 204-18.

Matthews, Roger. 2005. "The Myth of Punitiveness." *Theoretical Criminology* 9 (2): 175-201.

Mauer, Marc. 1999. *Race to Incarcerate: Marc Mauer and the Sentencing Project*. New York: The New Press.

Mauer, Marc, and Meda Chesney-Lind. 2002. *Invisible Punishment: The Collateral Consequences of Mass Imprisonment*. New York: New York Press.

McGuire, James. 1995. *What Works: Reducing Reoffending – Guidelines for Research and Practice*. Chichester: John Wiley and Sons.

McGuire, James, and Philip Priestley. 1985. *Offending Behavior: Skills and Stratagems for Going Straight*. New York: St. Martin's Press.

McLean, Edward. 1992. *Law and Civilization: The Legal Thought of Roscoe Pound*. Lanham: University Press of America.

McLean, Edward, and Philip Priestley. 1985. *Offending Behavior: Skills and Stratagems for Going Straight*. New York: St. Martin's Press.

McMahon, Maeve. 1992. *The Persistent Prison? Rethinking Decarceration and Penal Reform*. Toronto: University of Toronto Press.

–. 1999. *Women on Guard: Discrimination and Harassment in Corrections*. Toronto: University of Toronto Press.

Miller, Toby. 1993. *The Well Tempered Self: Citizenship, Culture and the Postmodern Subject*. Baltimore: Johns Hopkins University Press.

Mitchell, Chet. 1990. *The Drug Solution: Regulating Drugs According to Principles of Efficiency, Justice and Democracy*. Ottawa: Carleton University Press.

Moore, Dawn, and Kelly Hannah-Moffat. 2002. "Correctional Renewal without the Frills: The Politics of Get Tough Punishment in Ontario." In *Disorderly People: Law and the Politics of Exclusion in Ontario*, ed. J. Hermer and J. Mosher, 102-13. Halifax: Fernwood Publishing.

–. 2005. "The Liberal Veil: Revisiting Canadian Penality." In *The New Punitiveness: Trends, Theories, Practices,* ed. John Pratt, David Brown, Mark Brown, Simon Hallsworth, and Wayne Morrison, 214-35. Devon: Wilan.

Moore, Dawn, and Kevin Haggerty. 2001. "Bring It on Home: Home Drug Testing and the Relocation of the War on Drugs." *Social and Legal Studies* 10 (3): 377-95.

Moore, Dawn, and Mariana Valverde. 2000. "Maidens at Risk: Date Rape Drugs and the Formation of Hybrid Risk Knowledges." *Economy and Society* 29 (4): 514-31.

Morgan, H. Wayne. 1981. *Drugs in America*. Syracuse: Syracuse University Press.

Morris, Norval. 1995. "The Contemporary Prison, 1965-Present." In *The Oxford History of the Prison: The Practice of Punishment in Western Society,* ed. Norval Morris and David Rothman, 202-31. Oxford: Oxford University Press.

Mosher, Clayton. 1998. *Discrimination and Denial: System Racism in Ontario's Legal and Criminal Justice Systems, 1892-1961*. Toronto: University of Toronto Press.

Mugford, Jane. 1987. *Court Support and Advisory Services*. Sydney: Australian Institute of Criminology.

Murphy, Emily. 1922. *The Black Candle*. Toronto: Thomas Allen.

Murphy, Sheila, and Marsha Rosenbaum. 1999. *Pregnant Women on Drugs: Combating Stereotypes and Stigma*. New Brunswick: Rutgers University Press.

Musto, David. 1973. *The American Disease: Origins of Narcotic Control*. New Haven: Yale University Press.

–. 2002. *One Hundred Years of Herion*. London: Auburn House.

Nolan, James. 1998. *The Therapeutic State*. New York: NYU Press.

–. 2001. *Reinventing Justice: The American Drug Treatment Court Movement*. Princeton: Princeton University Press.

Nadelmann, Ethan. 1993. *Cops across Borders: The Internationalization of US Criminal Law Enforcement*. University Park: Penn State Press.

Naffine, Ngaire. 1996. *Feminism and Criminology*. Philadelphia: Temple University Press.

Oliver, Peter. 1985. *Unlikely Tory: The Life and Politics of Alan Grossman*. 1st ed. Toronto: Lester and Orpen Dennys.

O'Malley, Pat. 1996. "Risk and Responsibility." In *Foucault and Political Reason: Liberalism, Neo-Liberalism and Rationalities of Government,* ed. Andrew Barry, Thomas Osborne, and Nickolas Rose, 189-207. Chicago: University of Chicago Press.

–. 1999a. "Consuming Risks: Harm Minimization and the Government of 'Drug Users.'" In *Governable Places: Readings on Governmentality and Crime Control,* ed. Russell Smandych. Aldershot: Ashgate.

–. 1999b. "Volatile and Contradictory Punishments." In *Theoretical Criminology* 3 (2): 252-75.

–. 2001. "Geneaology, Systemisation and Resistance in 'Advanced Liberalism.'" In *Rethinking Law, Society and Governance: Foucault's Bequest,* ed. Gary Wickham and George Pavlich, 13-25. Portland: Hart.

O'Malley, Pat, and Mariana Valverde. 2004. "Pleasure, Freedom and Drugs: The Uses of 'Pleasure' in Liberal Governance of Drug and Alcohol Consumption." *Sociology* 38 (1): 25-42.

Ontario College of Social Workers and Social Service Workers. *Code of Ethics 2000*. Toronto: Ontario College of Social Workers and Social Service Workers.

Ontario Ministry of Correctional Services. 1983. *Maximum Impact Counselling*. Pamphlet.

–. 1988. *Corrections in Ontario: Institutional Program*. Pamphlet.

–. 2000. *Probation and Parole Service Delivery Model*. Toronto: Ontario Ministry of Correctional Services.

Orbis. 2003. *Evaluation of the Vancouver Drug Treatment Court*. 3rd ed. Vancouver: Orbis.

Ouimet, R. 1969. *Report of the Canadian Committee on Corrections: Toward Unity – Criminal Justice and Corrections*. Ottawa: Information Canada.

Pasquino, Pasquale. 1991. "Criminology: The Birth of a Special Knowledge." In *The Foucault Effect: Studies in Governmentality,* ed. Graham Burchell, Collin Gordon, and Peter Miller, 235-50. Chicago: University of Chicago Press.

Pavlich, George. 1999. "Criticism and Criminology: In Search of Legitimacy. *Theoretical Criminology* 3 (1): 29-51.

Peele, Stanton. 1989. *Diseasing of America: How We Allowed Recovery Zealots and the Treatment Industry to Convince Us We Are Out of Control*. San Francisco: Josey-Bass.

Perlin, Michael. 1996. "The Jurisprudence of the Insanity Defense." In *Law in a Therapeutic Key: Developments in Therapeutic Jurisprudence*, ed. David Wexler and Bruce Winnick, 108. Durham: Carolina Academic Press.

Pernanen, Kai, Maria-Marthe Cousineau, Serge Brochu, and Fu Sun. 2002. *Proportions of Crimes Associated with Alcohol and Other Drugs in Canada*. Ottawa: Canadian Center for Substance Abuse.

Petchesky, Rosalind. 1990. *Abortion and Woman's Choice: The State, Sexuality, and Reproductive Freedom*. Boston: Northeastern University Press.

Pound, Roscoe. 1914. "Law and Liberty." In *Lectures on the Harvard Classics, Political Science. V. Law and Liberty*, ed. William Nelson et al. In *The Harvard Classics*, ed. Charles Eliot. New York: P.F. Collier and Son.

–. 1921. *The Spirit of the Common Law*. Boston: Marshall Jones.

Pratt, John, David Brown, Mark Brown, Simon Hallsworth, and Wayne Morrison, eds. 2005. *The New Punitiveness: Trends, Theories, Perspectives*. Devon: Willan.

Prochaska, James. 1999. "Stages of Change Approach to Treating Addictions with Special Focus on DWI Offenders." In *Research to Results: Effective Community Corrections*, ed. Patricia Harris, 191-214. Lanaham: American Correctional Association.

Prochaska, James, W. Velicer, Carlo DiClemente, and J. Fava. 1988. "Measuring Processes of Change: Applications to the Cessation of Smoking." In *Journal of Consulting and Clinical Psychology* 56: 520-28.

Proctor, Dorothy, and F. Rosen. 1994. *Chamaeleon: The Lives of Dorothy Proctor from Street Criminal to International Special Agent*. Far Hills: New Horizon Press.

Rabinow, Paul. 2003. *Anthropos Today: Reflections on Modern Equipment*. Princeton: Princeton University Press.

Rafter, N. 2004. "The Unrepentant Horse-Slasher: Moral Insanity and the Origins of Criminological Thought." *Criminology* 42 (4): 979-1008.

Reeves, Jimmie, and Lynn Campbell. 1994. *Cracked Coverage: The Anti-Cocaine Crusade and the Reagan Legacy*. Durham: Duke Press.

Reinarman, Craig, and H. Levine. 1997. *Crack in America: Demon Drugs and Social Justice*. Berkeley: University of California Press.

Roach, Kent. 2000. *Criminal Law*. Toronto: Irwin Law.

Rose, Nikolas. 1996a. "The Death of the 'Social'? Refiguring the Territory of Government." *Economy and Society* 26 (4): 327-46.

–. 1996b. "Governing 'Advanced' Liberal Democracies." In *Foucault and Political Reason: Liberalism, Neoliberalism and Rationalities of Government*, ed. Andrew Barry, Thomas Osborne, and Nickolas Rose, 327-56. Chicago: University of Chicago Press.

–. 1998. *Inventing Our Selves: Psychology, Power and Personhood*. Cambridge: Cambridge University Press.

–. 1999. *Powers of Freedom: Reframing Political Thought*. Cambridge: Cambridge University Press.

–. 2003. "The Neurochemical Self and Its Anomalies." In *Risk and Morality*, ed. Ericson and Doyle, 407-37. Toronto: University of Toronto Press.

Rothman, David. 1980. *Conscience and Convenience: The Asylum and Its Alternatives in Progressive America*. Boston: Little Brown.

Sawicki, Jana. 1991. *Disciplining Foucault: Feminism, Power and the Body*. New York: Routledge.

Senate Special Committee on Illegal Drugs. 2002. *Final Report*. Ottawa: Senate of Canada.

Senate Special Committee on Non-Medical Use of Drugs. 2001. *Final Report*. Ottawa: Government of Canada.

Sheptycki, James. 2000. "The Drug War: Learning from the Paradigm Example of Transnational Policing." In *Issues in Transnational Policing*, ed. James Sheptycki, 15-40. London: Routledge.

Shiff, Alison, and David Wexler. 1996. "Teen Court: A Therapeutic Jurisprudence Perspective." In *Law in a Therapeutic Key: Developments in Therapeutic Jurisprudence*, ed. David Wexler and Bruce Winnick, 342. Durham: Carolina Academic Press.

Shuman, Daniel. 1996. "Therapeutic Jurisprudence and Tort Law: A Limited Subjective Standard of Care." In *Law in a Therapeutic Key: Developments in Therapeutic Jurisprudence,* ed. David Wexler and Bruce Winnick, 42-60. Durham: Carolina Academic Press.

Sim, Joe. 1990. *Medical Power in Prisons: The Prison Medical Service in England, 1774-1989.* Philadelphia: Open University Press.

Simmons, Harvey. 1982. *From Asylum to Welfare.* Downsview: National Institute on Mental Retardation.

Simon, Jonathan. 1993. *Poor Discipline: Parole and the Social Control of the Underclass, 1890-1990.* Chicago: University of Chicago Press.

Singh, Amardeep. 2002. "We Are Not the Enemy: Hate Crimes against Arabs, Muslims, and Those Perceived to be Arab or Muslim after September 11." In *New York: Human Rights Watch,* 40-56.

Sloman, Larry 'Ratso.' 1979. *Reefer Madness: A History of Marijuana.* New York: St. Martin's Griffin.

Smart, Carol. 1995. *Law, Crime and Sexuality: Essays in Feminism.* London: Sage.

Struthers, James. 1994. *The Limits of Affluence: Welfare in Ontario 1920-1970.* Toronto: University of Toronto Press.

Szasz, Thomas. 1985. *Ceremonial Chemistry: The Ritual Persecution of Drugs, Addicts and Pushers.* Rev. ed. Holmes Beach: Learning Publications.

Tomlins, Christopher. 2000. "Framing the Field of Law's Disciplinary Encounters: A Historical Narrative." *Law and Society Review* 34 (4): 911-72.

Unger, Roberto. 1998. *Democracy Realized: The Progressive Alternative.* New York: Verso.

Valverde, Mariana. 1991. *The Age of Light, Soap and Water: Moral Reform in English Canada 1885-1925.* Toronto: McClelland and Stewart.

–. 1995. "Building Anti-Delinquent Communities: Morality, Gender and Generation in the City." In *A Diversity of Women: Ontario 1945-1980,* ed. Joy Parr, 221-54. Toronto: University of Toronto Press.

–. 1998a. *Diseases of the Will: Alcohol and the Dilemmas of Freedom.* Cambridge: Cambridge University Press.

–. 1998b. "Governing Out of Habit." *Studies in Law, Politics and Society* 18: 217-42.

–. 2003a. *Law's Dream of a Common Knowledge.* Princeton: Princeton University Press.

–. 2003b. "Targeted Governance and the Problem of Desire." In *Risk and Morality,* ed. Richard Ericson and Aaron Doyle, 115-43. Toronto: University of Toronto Press.

–. 2005. "Authorizing the Production of Urban Moral Order: Appellate Courts and Their Knowledge Games." *Law and Society Review* 39 (2): 419-55.

Valverde, Mariana, Ron Levi, and Dawn Moore. 2005. "Legal Knowledges of Risk." In *Law and Risk,* ed. Law Commission of Canada, 50-73. Vancouver: UBC Press.

Vantour, Jim. 1991. *Our Story: Organizational Renewal in Federal Corrections.* Ottawa: Canadian Corrections Service.

Wacquant, Loic. 2001. "Deadly Symbiosis: When Ghetto and Prison Meet and Mesh." *Punishment and Society* 3 (1): 95-134.

–. 2005. "The Great Penal Leap Backward: Incarceration in America from Nixon to Clinton." In *The New Punitiveness: Trends, Theories, Practices,* ed. J. Pratt, D. Brown, and B. Brown. Devon: Wilan.

Waldorf, Dan, and Craig Reinarman. 1975. "Addicts: Everything but Human Beings." *Urban Life* 4 (1): 30-53.

Webster, Chris. 1990. "Compulsory Treatment in Narcotic Addiction." In *Clinical Criminology: Theory, Research and Practice,* ed. Hilton, Margaret Jackson and Christopher Webster, 63-87. Toronto: Scholars Press.

Welsh, Irvine. 1996. *Trainspotting.* London: Minerva.

Wexler, David, and Bruce Winnick. 1996. "Introduction." In *Law in a Therapeutic Key: Developments in Therapeutic Jurisprudence,* ed. David Wexler and Bruce Winnick, 112-32. Durham: Carolina Academic Press.

White, William. 1998. *Slaying the Dragon: The History of Addiction Treatment and Recovery in America.* Bloomington: Chestnut Health Systems.

Williams, Terry. 1993. *Crackhouse: Notes from the End of the Line*. New York: Penguin.

Winner, Langdon. 1980. "Do Artefacts Have Politics?" *Daedalus* 109 (1): 121-36.

Winnick, Bruce. 1996. "The Psycho-Therapist Patient Privilege: Therapeutic Jurisprudence in View." In *Law in a Therapeutic Key: Developments in Therapeutic Jurisprudence*, ed. David Wexler and Bruce Winnick, 212-30. Durham: Carolina Academic Press.

Woolgar, Steve, and Geoff Cooper. 1999. "Do Artefacts Have Ambivalence? Moses' Bridges, Winner's Bridges and other Urban Legends in S&TS." *Social Studies of Science* 29 (3): 433-49.

Young, Alan. 2003. *Justice Defiled: Perverts, Potheads, Serial Killers and Lawyers*. Toronto: Key Porter.

Index

LAW AND
SOCIETY

Lori G. Beaman, *Defining Harm: Religious Freedom and the Limits of the Law* (2007)

Stephen Tierney (ed.), *Multiculturalism and the Canadian Constitution* (2007)

Julie Macfarlane, *The New Lawyer: How Settlement Is Transforming the Practice of Law* (2007)

Kimberley White, *Negotiating Responsibility: Law, Murder, and States of Mind* (2007)

Dawn Moore, *Criminal Artefacts: Governing Drugs and Users* (2007)

Hamar Foster, Heather Raven, and Jeremy Webber (eds.), *Let Right Be Done: Aboriginal Title, the Calder Case, and the Future of Indigenous Rights* (2007)

Dorothy E. Chunn, Susan B. Boyd, and Hester Lessard (eds.), *Reaction and Resistance: Feminism, Law, and Social Change* (2007)

Margot Young, Susan B. Boyd, Gwen Brodsky, and Shelagh Day (eds.), *Poverty: Rights, Social Citizenship, and Legal Activism* (2007)

Rosanna L. Langer, *Defining Rights and Wrongs: Bureaucracy, Human Rights, and Public Accountability* (2007)

C.L. Ostberg and Matthew E. Wetstein, *Attitudinal Decision Making in the Supreme Court of Canada* (2007)

Chris Clarkson, *Domestic Reforms: Political Visions and Family Regulation in British Columbia, 1862-1940* (2007)

Jean McKenzie Leiper, *Bar Codes: Women in the Legal Profession* (2006)

Gerald Baier, *Courts and Federalism: Judicial Doctrine in the United States, Australia, and Canada* (2006)

Avigail Eisenberg (ed.), *Diversity and Equality: The Changing Framework of Freedom in Canada* (2006)

Randy K. Lippert, *Sanctuary, Sovereignty, Sacrifice: Canadian Sanctuary Incidents, Power, and Law* (2005)

James B. Kelly, *Governing with the Charter: Legislative and Judicial Activism and Framers' Intent* (2005)

Dianne Pothier and Richard Devlin (eds.), *Critical Disability Theory: Essays in Philosophy, Politics, Policy, and Law* (2005)

Susan G. Drummond, *Mapping Marriage Law in Spanish Gitano Communities* (2005)

Louis A. Knafla and Jonathan Swainger (eds.), *Laws and Societies in the Canadian Prairie West, 1670-1940* (2005)

Ikechi Mgbeoji, *Global Biopiracy: Patents, Plants, and Indigenous Knowledge* (2005)

Florian Sauvageau, David Schneiderman, and David Taras, with Ruth Klinkhammer and Pierre Trudel, *The Last Word: Media Coverage of the Supreme Court of Canada* (2005)

Gerald Kernerman, *Multicultural Nationalism: Civilizing Difference, Constituting Community* (2005)

Pamela A. Jordan, *Defending Rights in Russia: Lawyers, the State, and Legal Reform in the Post-Soviet Era* (2005)

Anna Pratt, *Securing Borders: Detention and Deportation in Canada* (2005)

Kirsten Johnson Kramar, *Unwilling Mothers, Unwanted Babies: Infanticide in Canada* (2005)

W.A. Bogart, *Good Government? Good Citizens? Courts, Politics, and Markets in a Changing Canada* (2005)

Catherine Dauvergne, *Humanitarianism, Identity, and Nation: Migration Laws in Canada and Australia* (2005)

Michael Lee Ross, *First Nations Sacred Sites in Canada's Courts* (2005)

Andrew Woolford, *Between Justice and Certainty: Treaty Making in British Columbia* (2005)

John McLaren, Andrew Buck, and Nancy Wright (eds.), *Despotic Dominion: Property Rights in British Settler Societies* (2004)

Georges Campeau, *From UI to EI: Waging War on the Welfare State* (2004)

Alvin J. Esau, *The Courts and the Colonies: The Litigation of Hutterite Church Disputes* (2004)

Christopher N. Kendall, *Gay Male Pornography: An Issue of Sex Discrimination* (2004)

Roy B. Flemming, *Tournament of Appeals: Granting Judicial Review in Canada* (2004)

Constance Backhouse and Nancy L. Backhouse, *The Heiress vs the Establishment: Mrs. Campbell's Campaign for Legal Justice* (2004)

Christopher P. Manfredi, *Feminist Activism in the Supreme Court: Legal Mobilization and the Women's Legal Education and Action Fund* (2004)

Annalise Acorn, *Compulsory Compassion: A Critique of Restorative Justice* (2004)

Jonathan Swainger and Constance Backhouse (eds.), *People and Place: Historical Influences on Legal Culture* (2003)

Jim Phillips and Rosemary Gartner, *Murdering Holiness: The Trials of Franz Creffield and George Mitchell* (2003)

David R. Boyd, *Unnatural Law: Rethinking Canadian Environmental Law and Policy* (2003)

Ikechi Mgbeoji, *Collective Insecurity: The Liberian Crisis, Unilateralism, and Global Order* (2003)

Rebecca Johnson, *Taxing Choices: The Intersection of Class, Gender, Parenthood, and the Law* (2002)

John McLaren, Robert Menzies, and Dorothy E. Chunn (eds.), *Regulating Lives: Historical Essays on the State, Society, the Individual, and the Law* (2002)

Joan Brockman, *Gender in the Legal Profession: Fitting or Breaking the Mould* (2001)

Printed and bound in Canada by Friesens

Set in Stone by Artegraphica Design Co. Ltd.

Copy editor: Joanne Richardson

Proofreader and indexer: Dianne Tiefensee